DAILY GRACE
FOR WOMEN

DEVOTIONAL REFLECTIONS TO NOURISH YOUR SOUL

Daily Grace for Women – Devotional Reflections to Nourish Your Soul
Copyright © 2022 by Honor Books
ISBN: 979-8-88898-021-7 - *Paperback*
ISBN: 979-8-88898-022-4 - *Hardcover*
ISBN: 979-8-88898-023-1 - *Ebook*

Design by Faille Schmitz. Manuscript written by Molly Detweiler, Susan Duke, Shanna D. Gregor, Susan Titus Osborn, Barbara J. Scott, Donna Shepherd, and Marnie Wooding. Editing and project management by Betsy Williams in association with Snapdragon Editorial Group, Inc.

THERE IS NOTHING BUT GOD'S
GRACE. WE WALK UPON IT; WE
BREATHE IT; WE LIVE AND DIE BY
IT; IT MAKES THE NAILS AND
AXLES OF THE UNIVERSE.

ROBERT LOUIS STEVENSON

Dear Reader:

Daily Grace for Women: Devotional Reflections to Nourish Your Soul has been written and compiled with much love and care. As you read through these pages in the days, weeks, and months ahead, it is our prayer that the revelation of the riches of God's grace will abound in your heart and mind.

We've designed this book with you in mind, combining the wonderful truth of God's Word with devotional readings relevant to everyday life. A variety of writers were chosen—people from divergent backgrounds and seasons of life—to give each daily reading a fresh, unique perspective. And a "grace principle" has been included so you will have a bit of God's grace to carry with you throughout your day. For the weekend entries, we've taken from the works of classic and well-known writers and added a prayer to help you take hold of these remarkable insights and principles.

We pray that God will bless you as you read, fill your heart with grace and peace, and draw you closer to the God who gave His all to meet your every need.

The Publisher

OUR HERO

[God] has rescued us . . . and he has brought us into the
Kingdom of his dear Son. God has purchased our freedom.
COLOSSIANS 1:13-14 NLT

"Once upon a time . . ." Those words signal the beginning of a story filled with adventure and romance, where great battles are fought and where good always wins, tales that have been retold for centuries. While the details may change with each new generation, the basic plot remains: transformation. Cinderella the servant girl becomes Cinderella the queen; a kiss makes a prince out of a frog; a beauty tames a beast with true love. Inside us all is a longing for these stories to be our story—we want to be transformed.

GRACE FOR TODAY

JESUS IS OUR REAL-LIFE HERO, AND BY HIS GRACE, HE TRANSFORMS THOSE WHO FOLLOW HIM.

Another beautiful story has been told throughout the ages. It begins, like many fairy tales do, with a poor but loving family. They go through many harrowing adventures, facing long journeys and evil kings. The firstborn Son grows up to be a great hero although in the beginning, not even His closest friends realize it. The young man does great deeds for good and inspires many to follow Him in His quest to rescue people from bondage. And one day, the young hero gives up His own life, as the ultimate expression of love. But unlike any other story, our hero's tale doesn't end here. In the greatest act of heroism ever, this brave man defeats death itself and is resurrected to lead His people to freedom and eternal life!

Did you know that you are a part of this hero's story? You are the reason this brave hero faced dangers, battles, and finally death. For this is the true tale of the Prince of Peace, Jesus Christ. And if you will take His hand and give Him your life, not only will He transform you, but you will be assured of the ultimate—and very real—"happily ever after."

ACTION OF LOVE

Love one another deeply, from the heart.
1 PETER 1:22 NIV

The 1979 Nobel Peace Prize Laureate had this to say, "Every time you smile at someone, it is an action of love, a gift to that person, a beautiful thing." If anybody can fully understand the power of compassion, that would be Mother Teresa—she was that Laureate. In 1950 she was given permission to start her own order, The Order of the Missionaries of Charity. She and her Sisters of Charity loved and cared for people the world had rejected—the poor of Calcutta.

She said, "If you can't feed a hundred people, then feed just one." This tiny woman's philosophy of mercy created missions all around the world. Her frank manner and direct words impacted presidents and inspired a generation. She challenged each and every one of us to care more deeply. "If you judge people, you have no time to love them."

Mother Teresa's fame came not in how much she did for people but rather how deeply she cared about them. She said, "It is not how much we do, but how much love we put in the doing. It is not how much we give, but how much love we put in the giving." Her message was simple—love each other. God created us to love, and that message will live on. He will continue to remind us through the lives of many people. She followed the footsteps of Jesus in a most humble yet remarkable way.

GRACE FOR TODAY

ONE ACT OF KINDNESS, ONE ACT OF CARING, MAY CHANGE A PERSON'S LIFE. IT COULD HE YOURS.

9

ENCOURAGING ONE ANOTHER

Speak encouraging words to one another. Build up hope so you'll
all be together in this, no one left out, no one left behind. I know
you're already doing this; just keep on doing it.
1 THESSALONIANS 5:11 MSG

In the spring, geese instinctively fly in a V-shaped formation when they travel north. The flock all work together in unison. As each bird flaps its wings, it reduces the wind resistance on the bird behind it. Thus, each goose cuts an easier path for the one following it. This allows the geese to cover a greater distance than if each bird flew on its own. Some fly as far north as the Arctic Circle, and some as far south as Mexico. Amazingly, they can soar as high as twenty-nine thousand feet!

GRACE FOR TODAY

GOD NEVER INTENDED FOR US TO "GO IT ALONE" ON OUR JOURNEY THROUGH LIFE. HE DESIGNED US TO BE CARRIERS OF HIS GRACE TO ENCOURAGE ONE ANOTHER.

Interestingly, when the lead goose becomes weary, it drops back in the formation and allows another goose to fly point. The geese at the back of the formation honk to encourage those in front of them to keep going. The geese stay in their perfect V- shaped formation, and not one goose is left behind.

Just as God prepares geese for their migration, He also takes care of His people as they journey through life here on earth. He never intended for us to "go it alone." Through His grace we find comfort and strength, and He often uses others to love and encourage us. Since He cannot be seen, often His light shines best through people—through their caring, their listening, and their understanding.

Try coming alongside and "honking" to encourage someone who is feeling the force of turbulence in her life. And when you feel the harsh wind on your face and are weary from experiencing downdrafts, drop back in formation for a while to receive encouragement from God. Call on a friend, so you can gain the strength to keep going.

THE PERFECT GENTLEMAN

Let the rivers clap their hands, let the mountains sing
together for joy.
PSALM 98:8 NASB

Most of us lead nearly frantic lifestyles in this busy world. We hit the floor running to do all we have to do, to get the kids to school on time, to get ourselves to work, or to make an early appointment. Hectic mornings turn to days, days turn to weeks, and weeks become months of a life squeezed tight by the busyness we call life.

The old adage, "The squeaky wheel gets the grease," still speaks volumes to us. The child that cries the loudest usually gets the first response. The hottest item on our to-do list takes priority for the day. With all the voices pulling at us, sometimes God's gentle, grace-filled voice gets lost in the crowd. Patiently, He waits to be included in our lives.

GRACE FOR TODAY

GOD IS A GENTLEMAN—HIS PRESENCE IS ABLE TO REVEAL WHAT OUR LIFE WAS MEANT TO BE.

When we slow down and take a breath, we can discover the life He created for us to enjoy. The waves of the ocean laugh all the way to the shore, racing to touch the earth, only to tickle it and run away again. White, fluffy clouds sway to the whisper of God's song, changing shape and form to the beat of His music. Even the soil, rich with the goodness of God, compels life and growth in everything it touches.

It is the simple things like these that help us focus on what matters most—time with the Father. He is the perfect gentleman, waiting to be acknowledged when we finish our list or decide to set it aside. Take time to enjoy the simple pleasure of His presence today.

11

THE LIGHTS OF GRACE

[Jesus said,] "You're here to be light, bringing out the God-colors in the world."
MATTHEW 5:14 MSG

The strange phenomenon of the Northern Lights is incredible to behold. They are rare unless you live in certain parts of the world, but once you've seen them, you never forget their beauty. The Northern Lights are caused by solar flares reacting with the Earth's atmosphere. The result of this interaction is beautiful, dancing colors that can range from soft blues and greens to vibrant reds and pinks. They are truly awe-inspiring!

GRACE FOR TODAY

THE COLORS OF GRACE PAINT OUR VIEW OF LIFE AND ITS EVENTS WITH HOPE.

God's grace has that same awe-inspiring effect. It can elude us unless we look for it and seek it. The experience of grace is hard to describe, but it is always unforgettable. When flares of hardship and trouble touch our lives, God's grace reacts, leaving our memories colored with the assurances of His loving care.

The softer colors are the small, daily graces like the gentle blush of pink when a friend encourages you with a much-needed compliment. A lovely flash of green colors your heart when God reveals a new truth to you from His Word and your trust in His grace grows.

Then there are days of vibrant color! These are the days when you are overwhelmed to realize that Christ would have died for you alone—and the red of His saving blood comes to mind. A dancing parade of royal purple floods your soul when you finally find freedom from a hurt that has plagued you for years. The light of God's grace fills our lives with incredible hope during these times.

Take some time today to remember the lights of grace that have colored your life. Remember, too, that this beauty is too wonderful to keep all to yourself. Take the hand of another and help them see the dancing lights of God's grace—the colors are meant to be shared.

Training Your Soul to Be Thankful

By Shelly Esser

First Thessalonians 5:18 NIV tells us, that we are to "give thanks in all circumstances, for this is God's will for you in Christ Jesus." This includes giving thanks for how God has made us. God has something wonderful in mind for each of us that no one else can do quite as well. So we need to put our false perceptions aside and ask ourselves, "What is the best way — given my gifts and abilities — to fulfill the calling God has given to me?" When I focus on these things, my heart is freed from the feeling of needing to be like someone else. God didn't make us all alike, anyway. If we're not careful, looking at how others do it can eventually crush us, leading us to be more discontent and ungrateful. It can also prevent us from doing things the way God wants to do them.

Next time you're tempted to compare yourself to someone else, remember that God wants to use you in the place of His calling, a place that only you can fill in His garden of life. Then you will be able to shine contentedly.[1]

HEAVENLY FATHER,

Forgive me for comparing myself to others and for trying to be someone I am not. By Your grace, you give each of us unique gifts and talents, and I do You a disservice when I covet what you've given others. You hold the master plan, and I ask You to help me to fulfill the part You've assigned to me. Help me to develop my abilities to the utmost for Your glory.

AMEN

There are different kinds of gifts, but the same Spirit. There are different kinds of service, but the same Lord. There are different kinds of wording, but the same God words all of them in all men.
1 CORINTHIANS 12:4-6 NIV

THE BATTLE OF LIFE AND DEATH

"Death has been swallowed up in victory." . . . [God] gives us
the victory through our Lord Jesus Christ.
1 CORINTHIANS 15:54,57 NIV

How many times, in an effort to bring comfort, have we said these words: "Death is just a natural part of life," or something similar? Deep down, though, we know that this sentence rings hollow to the grieving person—and even to us when we say it. If death is so natural, why does it always bring such sorrow? Why do we feel that dying is somehow unfair?

Perhaps it is because we weren't designed for death. We were created for life; and deep in our souls, we fight against its end. The good news is that we aren't alone in our battle—God is on our side.

Death, at least as it is now, was not a part of God's original creation. It came into the world through the disobedience of Adam and Eve. And though we brought death upon ourselves by turning our backs on God, He did not abandon us. Jesus, God in human flesh, conquered death and gave us new life—eternal life.

So, as the poet Dylan Thomas wrote, we "do not go gentle into that good night. Rage, rage against the dying of the light." As we face death in this difficult world, we will grieve. But we can also stand strong in the battle, with the Author of Life as our leader. Because of His grace, death will not be the final victor!

GRACE FOR TODAY

JESUS, GOD IN HUMAN FLESH, CONQUERED DEATH AND
GAVE US NEW LIFE—ETERNAL LIFE.

GRACE IN THE GARDEN

You should not be like cowering, fearful slaves. You should
behave instead like God's very own children, adopted into
his family—calling him "Father, dear Father."
ROMANS 8:15 NLT

Think for a moment about the Garden of Eden. Wouldn't you like to live in a place of such incredible beauty—with flowing waters, lush forests, and the perfect atmosphere? Adam and Eve did not fear the animals or anything else on Earth. What must it have been like to walk with lions and tigers, yet have no concern of being gobbled up?

GRACE FOR TODAY

BY GOD'S GRACE, OUR EVERY SIN HAS BEEN FORGIVEN AND TAKEN AWAY.

After Adam and Eve chose to sin, they became fearful and tried to hide from God among the trees in the Garden. They attempted to cover up their sin with fig-leaf fashion, but manmade garments could not cover their shame. They knew instinctively the trust and fellowship they had shared with God had been shattered. Yet God wanted to restore their relationship. He sought them, and Adam had to confess, "I heard you in the garden, and I was afraid because I was naked; so I hid" (Genesis 3:10 NIV).

God reached out to Adam and Eve by clothing them with the world's first leather garments. Although the Bible does not go into detail, these garments suggest an animal had to be sacrificed and symbolized a coming sacrifice, perfect and complete. Only God can atone for our sins.

Jesus is that sacrifice for us. He is the Lamb of God, who not only covers our sin but also takes our sin away. Aren't you thankful that when you sin, you do not have to cower in fear? You have only to ask the Lord for forgiveness, and He is faithful and just to forgive your sins.

GOD READS YOUR MAIL

[Jesus said,] "I no longer call you servants, because a
servant does not know his master's business. Instead, I
have called you friends."
JOHN 15:15 NIV

Sometimes it seems like people have the inside scoop on what's happening in your life. It's as though they overheard a conversation or read your mail. As you experience many of life's ups and downs, it's comforting to have a friend who knows and understands what you're going through—whether it's a difficult situation or a reason to celebrate.

GRACE FOR TODAY

GOD IS A FRIEND WHO CAN "READ YOUR MAIL" AND ACCEPTS YOU JUST AS YOU ARE.

On those days when you feel like you've given 150 percent and have nothing to show for your effort, recognize that nobody knows you like your heavenly Father. You are constantly in His thoughts and on His mind. He knows your strengths as well as your weaknesses. He understands what makes you unique because He created you.

God celebrates everything that makes you different—unique from anyone else. Whether you look different, perceive life differently, or just have different life experiences from those you know and love—God loves everything that sets you apart and considers it special. There are people you can touch for Him because of your own ups and downs. The very celebrations in your own life may have started as challenges that caused you to grow stronger in Him.

When life seems to be more than you can handle, you are never isolated from His compassion or removed from His touch. Likewise, when your dreams come true, He's there to celebrate with you. He knows the desires of your heart, proving Him to be your most faithful friend.

JUST AS YOU ARE

Now I take limitations in stride, and with good cheer, these
limitations that cut me down to size . . . I just let Christ take
over! And so the weaker I get, the stronger I become.
2 CORINTHIANS 12:10 MSG

God will often use your greatest weaknesses as the foundation for His plans for you. Charlotte Elliott was born in England on March 18, 1798, and was struck by illness in her early thirties. She became an invalid struggling against pain, constant weakness, and bouts of depression. One day she poured all her feelings into a song that she hoped would inspire others. She published it anonymously in a newspaper.

GRACE FOR TODAY

GOD'S GRACE IS MOST EVIDENT WHEN HE TURNS AROUND OUR BIGGEST WEAKNESSES AND CAUSES OUR MOST EFFECTIVE MINISTRY TO FLOW OUT OF THEM.

Just as I am, without one plea,
But that Thy blood was shed for me,
And that Thou bidd'st me come to Thee,
O lamb of God, I come! I come!

Her own doctor later handed her this anonymous hymn in the hopes it might encourage her. She was stunned to discover that her simple hymn had stirred a nation and had been distributed throughout England. Through her struggles, she had found her own unique way to serve God. In her lifetime Charlotte Elliot wrote many more hymns, but a century later, "Just as I Am" would be sung by thousands, perhaps millions, worldwide as one of the favorite hymns in Billy Graham's crusades.

Contrary to popular culture, you don't have to reinvent yourself to find your purpose in life. Nor do you have to pull yourself out of personal struggles before God will reveal His plans for you. God will meet you just as you are, in all your strengths and weaknesses.

TRUE CONFIDENCE

The LORD will be your confidence.
PROVERBS 3:26 NRSV

Take a close look at any bookstore or checkout display rack, and you'll find a wealth of self-help books and motivational articles. Reportedly, the sales of these books and magazines rank number one above all other books on the market. Can you guess who the target market for this massive onslaught of self-improvement materials might be? Women like you and me who naturally want to look and be their personal best.

Our quest to make the most out of what God has given us is commendable, but many of these books and articles send mixed messages about confidence. Their primary themes suggest that if we lose enough weight, wear the hippest hairstyle, and maybe even have a little plastic surgery, we will exhibit an acceptable image in society and gain more confidence.

GRACE FOR TODAY

GOD'S PLAN FOR YOU PROVIDES ALL THE GRACE YOU NEED TO WALK AND GROW IN HIS CONFIDENCE.

It's a worthy endeavor to maintain a good physical image, but regardless of what lengths to which we are willing to go on our self-improvement journey, our truest confidence and self-worth will never be found in the mirror or in the eyes of marketing media.

God says that you are a woman of worth—fearfully and wonderfully made! His Word also declares that there is a false security in self-confidence. Proverbs 31:30 TLB confirms: "Charm can be deceptive and beauty doesn't last, but a woman who fears and reverences God shall be greatly praised."

You were born searching for significance. When you accepted God's love, your search ended. Certainly, God wants us to challenge ourselves physically, mentally, and spiritually. But the Bible warns that confidence in our own strengths, beauty, or righteousness is foolish.

Thank God today for giving you true confidence, peace, and assurance that you are valuable and precious to Him. Knowing who you are in Christ and who He is in you gives you all the confidence you'll ever need to be your personal best—and His.

HOW'S YOUR RESUME?

By Cheryl M. Smith

Only God knows in full all that He hopes for us to accomplish. The reality is that we may be doing better than we think! Success is being found faithful in doing the jobs we've been given.

God will judge us not only on our performance, but also by the motives of our hearts. This is a great anchor of hope and joy to me. This means that when our best intentions go awry, when our greatest plans fall flat, and when our critics are at our heels, God knows the motives of our hearts and will judge intentions as well as performance. In love He surrounds us in a mighty embrace and says, "It's all right. I know you meant things to turn out differently. Your heart is right, and that's the root of faithfulness. Well done, good and faithful servant."

Are you facing a tough assignment? Perhaps you are thinking about abandoning a difficult marriage, job, or relationship. Let me encourage you to hang in there. Faithfulness may not always bring results we can see and measure, but it is the yardstick by which God measures all believers. What is your faithfulness? It is staying until your job is done, no matter what others think. It is staying until your cry can become one with Christ's: "It is finished!" That's success![2]

DEAR GOD,

Sometimes things are so hard that I want to throw in the towel. But that would not please You. I choose to hang in there—with the help of Your grace—and ask You to cover my shortcomings and failures with Your mercy. Thank You for seeing my heart and for helping me bring this task to completion. I ask for Your blessing upon it.

AMEN

The faithful will abound with blessings.
PROVERBS 28:20 NRSV

GOD'S DESIRES WITHIN YOU

Take delight in the LORD, and he will give you the desires
of your heart.
PSALM 37:4 NRSV

Wouldn't it be nice if God were a genie in a magic lamp, our own personal concierge — on call 24/7? Well, if that's the kind of relationship we want with God, were going to be very disappointed in the end. While it is true that God is always there for us and wants to bless us, the relationship He has designed runs far deeper and is much more meaningful.

Remember King David of the Bible — a man after God's heart? He was a man of great success and often catastrophic failure. Despite his many human failings, however, David remained faithful to God all his life. This ancient psalmist actually tells us that God will give us our heart's desires. However, David knew that our wants would first be shaped by time we had spent with God. As we delight in Him, what we want becomes more and more what He wants for us. That's a fundamental change in perspective.

GRACE FOR TODAY

AS WE AVAIL OURSELVES TO HIM, GOD, IN HIS GRACE, WILL CREATE HIS DESIRES WITHIN US.

You find yourself living in partnership with your heavenly Father, seeking His direction. His grace will create in you the kind of person who wants what He wants. Living in tandem with God results in your trusting Him to lead you to right desires and having faith that He'll fulfill them. It might be that your dreams will change. But you will be glad they did. And you may find your new dreams are bigger than you imagined possible.

Delighting in God or having a good relationship with Him means achieving a lifelong open dialogue with Him. It has everything to do with spending time with Him — waiting on Him. Most importantly, it is learning to love what He loves, which leads to your being transformed into a woman after God's heart.

AMAZING GRACE

God is able to make all grace abound toward you.
2 CORINTHIANS 9:8 NKJV

God's grace is often showcased best in the midst of our toughest trials. When we've made the worst mistakes, when we've exhausted all of our own strength, and when all hope disappears from the shores of our pain and heartache, God shows up.

No matter what sins have marked our past, grace is the eraser that wipes the slate clean. In the realm of God's all-powerful grace, we find His forgiveness. When storms come to invade and destroy our lives, God sends His anchor of grace for our safekeeping. In our weakest moments, grace becomes our life preserver. Through the heaviest fog of grief, grace becomes a lighthouse that beckons us onward.

GRACE FOR TODAY

GRACE IS LOVE PERSONIFIED—GIVEN FREELY WITH NO STRINGS ATTACHED.

Do you ever wonder where you'd be without God's grace? You may feel you've done nothing to deserve it. If you had, then it wouldn't be such a gift—and it wouldn't be grace. Grace is love personified–given freely with no strings attached.

God's gift of grace comes wrapped in unconditional, unmerited favor. There are no works or requirements necessary for you to receive this precious gift—no point system that qualifies you as a worthy recipient. God's grace resounds with this simple truth: there is nothing you can do to make God love you more than He already loves you right now. What's more, He can never love you any less either. He said, "I have loved you with an everlasting love; I have drawn you with loving-kindness" (Jeremiah 31:3 NIV).

That's why God's grace is so amazing.

21

SYMBOLS OF GRACE

By taking a long and thoughtful look at what God has created, people have always been able to see what their eyes as such can't see: eternal power, for instance, and the mystery of his divine being.
ROMANS 1:20 MSG

Remember all those assignments from English class when the teacher asked you to describe the symbolism in various works of literature? According to the teacher, pretty much everything in any story you read had some kind of symbolic meaning. The horse wasn't just a horse — it was a symbol of freedom. The rocking chair wasn't just a piece of furniture — it was a symbol of old age. Learning to discern the symbolism beyond the surface of things is a big part of studying literature.

GRACE FOR TODAY

————————

SYMBOLS OF GOD'S LOVE AND GRACE ARE WRITTEN INTO THE WORLD ALL AROUND US.

Symbolism isn't confined to the realm of books alone, though. God has placed meaningful symbols of His grace in the world around us so that we might understand His great love for us. Just think of all the simple, everyday things that point to the truths of the Bible. The caterpillar that turns into a butterfly is the perfect symbol of the transformation we receive when we accept Christ. The simple trust a child has for her mother is a wonderful picture of the relationship God wants with us. Throughout the Bible, God uses symbols of sheep, grapes, farmers, birds, flowers, and a myriad of other everyday things to reveal His nature to us.

When we realize what the God of the universe has done just to help us know Him, can we do anything but love Him in return? He has written a story of love and grace in symbols and signs all around us so that we won't miss out. So read His story and do a little English class symbol-searching. You'll find symbols of God's unfathomable love and grace everywhere you look.

Travel Plans

The law of their God is in their hearts; their steps do not slip.
PSALM 37:31 NRSV

Raising children offers a taste of both obedience and disobedience. As good parents, we've traveled the road before our children and have had experiences that they lack. It is natural to want to spare them the pain of learning things the hard way, but they often insist on doing it their own way. They hunger for independence.

Like parents desire to have obedient children, God desires for us to be willing and obedient to Him. As we grow and develop in our relationship with Him, we sometimes step out on our own and find ourselves ahead of Him—without direction.

We can become so excited about our plans and pursuits that we leave God in the dust. When we get to our destination, we are surprised to find we've missed something significant by making our own way. Then, like a stop sign, we recognize we're off course, only to discover a yield sign pointing to the road of grace and mercy. His love surrounds us and brings us back to our place in Him.

> ## Grace for Today
>
> GOD'S WAY IS THE HIGH WAY. LIVING BY HIS GRACE AND WISDOM, WE CAN TRAVEL THAT ROAD AND EXPERIENCE TRUE SUCCESS.

His way is the right way. He is the ultimate parent with our very best interest at heart. He loves us more than parents can love their own children—which, if we are parents, seems difficult to comprehend.

Through obedience to His will, His Word, and His ways, we can find His dreams and desires for our lives. If we follow His example and allow Him to lead us, we will ultimately travel the higher road and experience true success.

OVERFLOWING GRACE

We have different gifts, according to the grace given us.
ROMANS 12:6 NIV

When we hear the word "grace," most of us think of salvation. While grace is behind God's plan to rescue our souls, its power doesn't stop there. The Bible speaks often of the grace given us in the form of spiritual gifts, talents, abilities, and opportunities for service.

First Corinthians tells us that the grace of Jesus enriches our speech and knowledge as well as providing us with all the spiritual gifts we need to serve Him. Second Corinthians shows us how grace allows us to excel in faith, sincerity, love, and generosity. God loves to pour out His grace to equip us for a full life: "God is able to make all grace abound to you, so that in all things at all times, having all that you need, you will abound in every good work" (2 Corinthians 9:8 NIV).

When you use your gift of teaching to help a child learn his memory verse — that's grace. When you open your home to others and make them feel comfortable and loved — that's grace. And when your neighbor confides in you about her mother's serious illness and you comfort her with your prayers — that's also grace.

The grace of God floods our hearts when we accept the gift of Jesus. Then it overflows as we reach out to others.

What a loving Father we have! His grace saves us. His grace fills us to overflowing. Then His grace teaches and equips us to pour out that same grace to all those around us.

GRACE FOR TODAY

GOD LOVES TO POUR OUT HIS GRACE TO EQUIP US FOR A
FULL LIFE OF JOY AND SERVICE.

GOD OUR CREATOR

By Evelyn Christenson

One of the favorite things we do during our vacation in Michigan, in August, is to lie on the beach at midnight and watch the fantastic display of shooting stars. The summer our Kurt was seven, I read an article in the Reader's Digest about a father who got his seven-year-old boy up in the middle of the night to see the shooting stars because, he reasoned, there were some things more important than sleep. So, when the exhibition was at its peak, we decided it was time for Kurt to join the rest of the family on the beach. The excitement and the "ohs" and "ahs" mounted with each display of God's celestial fireworks.

But the real excitement came the next morning when, as a family, we read at the breakfast table Psalm 33 KJV, and especially the fifth to ninth verses: ". . . the earth is full of the goodness of the Lord. By the word of the Lord were the heavens made; and all the host of them by the breath of his mouth . . . Let all the inhabitants of the world stand in awe of him, for he spake, and it was done." I found myself excited not only over an astronomical wonder, but changed into a mother awed at God's timing and selection of our daily reading — overawed that He wanted to tell us that He only had to speak and all this was done![3]

FATHER GOD,

You are awesome, and it thrills me to see Your grace at work in nature! The earth truly is full of Your goodness, a testament to the miracle of who You are. You are wonderful and greatly to be praised! I love You, Lord.

AMEN

Let them praise the name of the LORD, for his name alone is exalted; his splendor is above the earth and the heavens.
PSALM 148:13 NIV

GOD'S MESSENGERS

[The Lord said to Moses,] "I am sending an angel ahead of you, who will protect you as you travel. He will lead you to the place I have prepared."
EXODUS 23:20 NCV

What do you picture in your mind when you think of angels? Perhaps you have a collection of ceramic angels, or you have angel ornaments to hang on your Christmas tree or grace its top. Pictures of angels abound, mostly portraying celestial beings with blond hair, white robes, fluffy wings, and halos around their heads. Yet, this isn't the way they are described in the Bible.

GRACE FOR TODAY

*Sleep, my child, and peace attend thee
All through the night.
Guardian angels
God will send thee
All through the night.*

SIR HAROLD BOULTON

There are many biblical examples where the first words spoken by an angel were, "Do not be afraid." They were unsettling or fearsome in appearance. In Matthew 1:20 Joseph was told not to be afraid to take Mary as his wife. In Luke 1:13 Zechariah was told not to be afraid, that his prayers had been heard, and that his wife would bear him a son to be named John. In Luke 2:10-11 NCV an angel told shepherds, "Do not be afraid! I am bringing you good news that will be a great joy to all the people. Today your Savior was born in the town of David. He is Christ, the Lord!" In each instance, the angels brought a message from God to someone on earth.

A couple of questions arise: Do angels still bring messages to people on earth? Do they still take care of individuals today as they did in biblical times? Many people think they do, and stories abound of those who testify of personal encounters with angels.

Perhaps you have experienced an occasion where you sensed that a guardian angel protected you from harm. Take a moment to thank God for His omnipresence and His concern for your welfare.

26

ARE YOU BUGGED?

Take the helmet of salvation, and the sword of the Spirit,
which is the word of God.
EPHESIANS 6:17 KJV

The first of two e-mails arrived in Gloria's mailbox. "I got bit by something. Fever. Chills. Please pray." Gloria's friend Alyce was highly allergic to bee stings, which justified her concern. Friends encouraged her to visit the doctor.

If you have a "spiritual bite," when problems beset you and you're ailing, then what? Flow do you seek spiritual healing? Alyce called her doctor. Shouldn't that be our first response—to call upon the Great Physician, Jesus? Unlike an earthly doctor, our Physician never makes a mistake. His diagnosis is always right. His cure certain.

GRACE FOR TODAY

IN THE MIDST OF SORROW, FAITH DRAWS THE STING OUT OF EVERY TROUBLE, AND TAKES OUT THE BITTERNESS FROM EVERY AFFLICTION.

ROBERT CECIL

In fact, God has already written a prescription for you—the Bible. Proverbs 4:22 tells us that it is life to us and health to all our flesh. You could say that God's Word is soul medicine!

The Lord will also speak through wise counsel—perhaps from a mentor, a pastor, or a friend. A wise friend will help you examine your own life and point you to Jesus. Find like-minded people who will have your best interest at heart in a local congregation. In the Body of Christ, we find strength, a spirit of unity, and an atmosphere conducive to spiritual healing.

It's wonderful to have the family of God, and it's marvelous if you are blessed with an earthly family who serves God. Call on them too. When you feel under spiritual attack, you have a sure line of defense—God, His Word, His messengers, and His family.

A CALL FROM GOD

The Lord said, "I knew you before I formed you in your mother's womb. Before you were born I set you apart and appointed you as my spokesman to the world."
JEREMIAH 1:5 NLT

Are you thinking about a "safe" career for your future? One that gets you an upscale house, a nice car, and a calico cat in the yard? Well, God may think you are selling yourself short. He may have other plans that are more adventurous than you would ever imagine for yourself.

That is what happened to Jeremiah. God came to him when he was young and told him to start telling his entire country—including the king and his nobles—that they needed to change. Jeremiah was the quiet, sensitive type who didn't really go all out for in-your-face-confrontations, and he told God so.

GRACE FOR TODAY

GOD WILL NOT TAKE YOU WHERE HIS GRACE WILL NOT SUSTAIN YOU.

God's response? "I made you just for this job." Sometimes God has so much confidence in what He can do through you that it can scare you! But Jeremiah found that God was faithful to give him the courage to face down kings, nobles, armies, and Jeremiah's greatest opponent—discouragement. God gave Jeremiah the grace to do the job before he even left his mother's womb. Then He provided Jeremiah with the grace to fulfill that plan and protect him on a day-by-day basis—sometimes just in the nick of time. Jeremiah found God faithful and accomplished more in his lifetime than he would have ever done pursuing his own plan.

What about you? Are you playing it too safe with your life? Have you hidden away your abilities in order to stay within your comfort zone? Are you not quite sure that God's grace will be enough to sustain you as you go where He wants you to go? If so, consider the life of Jeremiah and talk to God about it. His grace will never let you down.

Silver for a Soul

We also glory in tribulations, knowing that tribulation produces perseverance; and perseverance, character; and character, hope.

ROMANS 5:3-4 NKJV

One of the most poignant portrayals of God's grace can be seen in Victor Hugo's novel *Les Miserables*. A kind priest takes in a recently released convict named Jean Valjean. In the middle of the night, Jean rewards the priest for his kindness by stealing all his fine silver flatware and disappearing into the darkness.

Early the next morning, the thief is caught; and the authorities drag him back to the priest's home so that charges can be filed. It is here that we see grace exhibited in a way that no one—not the police, and certainly not Jean Valjean—would have expected:

GRACE FOR TODAY

GOD SAYS: "OF COURSE, I WILL FORGIVE YOU. NOW YOU WILL BECOME MY VERY OWN CHILD."

"Ah! here you are!" [the priest] exclaimed, looking at Jean Valjean. "I am glad to see you . . . I gave you the candlesticks too, which are of silver like the rest . . . Why did you not carry them away with your forks and spoons?"

We are no different from Jean Valjean. We have all turned our backs on the goodness and love of God (Romans 3:23). But God did something that no one expected; "God proves his love for us in that while we still were sinners Christ died for us" (Romans 5:8 NRSV).

When we go before God, guilty and asking for mercy, He says, "I am glad to see you! Of course, I will forgive you. Now you will become My very own child, and I will send My Spirit to live within you."

After Jean Valjean is released, the priest speaks one last word to him—the same word that our hearts hear from Jesus: "You no longer belong to evil, but to good. It is your soul that I buy from you; . . . and I give it to God."

TO UNDERSTAND GOD'S HEART

"Let him who boasts boast about this: that he understands and knows me, that I am the LORD, who exercises kindness, justice and righteousness on earth, for in these I delight," declares the LORD.
JEREMIAH 9:24 NIV

The epitaph on the grave of George Washington Carver reads, "He could have added fortune to fame; but caring for neither, he found happiness and honor in being helpful to the world." Born a slave in Mississippi, Carver earned his high school diploma after the Civil War. He was the first African American to join the faculty at Iowa State College of Agriculture and Mechanics. He became one of the world's top agricultural chemists; and his groundbreaking work led to the invention of over three hundred plant products, from plastics to shaving cream.

GRACE FOR TODAY

KNOWING GOD IS A GRACE HE GIVES US THAT CHANGES HOW WE VIEW OUR WORK AND OURSELVES IN THE WORLD.

Amazingly, Carver freely gave away his research stating, "God gave them to me. How can I sell them to someone else?" He was offered enormous salaries to work with such legends as Thomas Edison and Henry Ford, but he turned them down. Carver is quoted as saying, "If I took the money, I might forget my people." He prayed each morning and credited his relationship with God as the source of his success.

Carver was a humble man who felt an enormous responsibility to work for the betterment of mankind. He received the Roosevelt medal in 1939 for his outstanding work in science and was made a member of the Royal Society of Arts in London. He is an amazing example for us to follow, a man who never abused or squandered the gifts God gave him, a man who understood God's heart. His faith, life, and work are reminders that knowing God affects how we handle our talents and opportunities.

REAL WOMEN, REAL BEAUTY

By Ingrid Lawrenz, MSW

God made us like the flowers of the field in all their beauty and glory, each one unique in color, shape, and design. Jesus said in Matthew 6:28-30 NIV, "See how the lilies of the field grow. They do not labor or spin. Yet I tell you that not even Solomon in all his splendor was dressed like one of these. If that is how God clothes the grass of the field, which is here today and tomorrow is thrown into the fire, will he not much more clothe you?" Our bodies are the uniforms in which we enter and exit this world. Each one is beautiful, each one is different.

Think about the women you've considered beautiful—the ones who have touched your heart and soul. Are they beautiful to you because they could be supermodels or because their character shines through in real beauty? Like it or not, you are a model to your daughters and your sisters in Christ. Half of all nine-year-old girls diet; 90 percent of high school girls do so regularly. Excessive attempts at beauty on your part can threaten other women. A real woman of internal beauty becomes a draw, a mentor, and a comfort to those around her. She exudes beauty. When God created the first real woman, Eve, (who knows what size she wore!) He said she was very good!

All of us need to see ourselves and others with Christ's eyes.[4]

HEAVENLY FATHER,

it's easy to be overly concerned with my appearance since beauty is so highly esteemed in our society, but I know that You are more concerned with my heart. Help me keep a pure heart that always puts You first. I want any beauty I possess to be a reflection of Your grace shining through me.

AMEN

It is not fancy hair, gold jewelry, or fine clothes that should make you beautiful. No, your beauty should come from within you— the beauty of a gentle and quiet spirit that will never be destroyed and is very precious to God.
1 PETER 3:3-4 NCV

WAITING IS AN ACTION

Wait for the LORD; be strong and let your heart take
courage; yes, wait for the LORD.
PSALM 27:14 NASB

In our fast-paced society, there is huge social pressure to be on the move and constantly proactive about our lives. Truly, busyness has become the sign of success. We are a generation of high-speed Internet, microwave ovens, and satellite technology. Waiting for anything has become intolerable. Waiting is what people do when they've hit the wall or run out of options.

GRACE FOR TODAY

GOD'S GRACE ENABLES US TO WAIT UPON HIM. AND IN HIS PRESENCE, HE WILL OPEN TO US A TREASURE TROVE OF WONDERFUL GIFTS—ALL FREELY GIVEN BY THAT SAME AMAZING GRACE.

Even though the speed of most things we do has increased, waiting takes the same amount of time as it always has. But the one thing we have to remember is that God's timing is always perfect, and He knows when we're ready to tackle those monumental events in our lives.

God's people in the Bible have a long history of waiting. Remember Moses? Sure, but how busy can sheepherders be? Even kings were expected to wait upon God because waiting wasn't inaction—it was action. It was an action designed to honor God. Waiting for God's direction was the most important and most dynamic thing they could do. And it is still the most important and most dynamic thing you can do today.

When you wait upon God, amazing things happen. Saul waited in Damascus and received revelation from God, which he preached to the Gentiles and even to kings. The disciples waited in Jerusalem and were given the priceless gift of the Holy Spirit.

Sometimes stopping the frantic pace of your life and waiting for God's direction can be the most important and active step you can take. What will waiting bring? You'll just have to wait and see.

DISCOVERING THE REAL YOU

O Israel, the LORD who created you says: "Do not be afraid,
for I have ransomed you. I have called you by name; you
are mine."
ISAIAH 43:1 NLT

Do you ever get caught up in obsessing about what others think of you? Do you feel you have to act one way in public and save the real you for when you're at home or with your family?

Authenticity is probably one of the healthiest attributes anyone can have. Yet, as women, we often fall into the trap of finding a role model that we can't possibly follow. Perhaps it's someone who always seems to be organized or exemplifies what we think a godly woman should be like.

GRACE FOR TODAY

BECAUSE THE CREATOR OF THE UNIVERSE DESIGNED US AS UNIQUE WORKS OF ART, WE CAN AFFORD TO BE AUTHENTIC.

We must exercise caution in trying to be like someone else, or we may lose our own God-given identity. For all you know, that person may be a version of someone else she is trying to copy.

God made you as you are for a purpose: the you with the funny little quirks that set you apart and define you, the you who may not always have it all together, and the you with your uniquely distinct personality. If you feel like you've lost sight of your authenticity, take some time to get to know yourself and what you're all about.

Who are you after you kick off your high heels or change into your pajamas? What evokes your deepest emotions? What is your heart's desire and deepest passion? What dreams do you dare dream when no one is looking? Who are you in the first light of morning?

There is real freedom in celebrating the uniqueness God created in you. Authenticity makes you more accessible to people, helps you develop true character, and radiates God's grace. Rest assured, the Master Designer makes no mistakes. You are His masterpiece, created for a purpose that only you can fulfill.

PHOEBE AND GIDEON

How many are your works, O Lord! In wisdom you made
them all; the earth is full of your creatures.
PSALM 104:24 NIV

Phoebe is a middle-aged lady who has lived most of her life in the same house. She's a little chubby, but still very attractive. She can be grumpy and distant with those who don't understand her, but with her closest loved ones she is gentle, sweet, and loving.

Gideon is a young guy in the prime of his life. He's tall, blond, and handsome. He loves the outdoors, and running and hiking are two of his favorite pastimes. He loves people and is quick to offer friendship to anyone he meets.

GRACE FOR TODAY

OUR LOVING
CREATOR DESIGNED
EVERYTHING, EVEN
ANIMALS, AS
EVIDENCE OF HIS
ABUNDANT GRACE.

What do these two very different personalities have in common? Well, first of all they are both the four-footed friends of the same family. Phoebe is a six-year-old Maine coon cat, and Gideon is a three-year-old yellow Labrador mix. And while they may not show too much grace to each other, they are evidence of God's grace to the family that loves them.

Phoebe is independent and reserved, like any good cat; but she is also quick to offer a soft touch and a happy purr to ease her person's loneliness or sorrow. Gideon has a puppy smile and a happily wagging tail ready for everyone, but he is especially loving and gentle with children. He has been known to bring a smile out of a child's tears more than once.

Perhaps they are just animals—doing what they do because of instinct and not because of love. But a loving Creator designed those instincts for His good purposes. And when a fluffy kitten or a warm puppy curls up beside you, without a care for what you look like or how accomplished you are, you sense something greater at work. You sense God's grace—grace so abundant that it overflows to us even from chubby cats and wet-nosed canines.

ONLY TEMPORARY

Momentary troubles are achieving for us an eternal glory that far outweighs them all. So we fix our eyes not on what is seen, but on what is unseen. For what is seen is temporary, but what is unseen is eternal.
2 CORINTHIANS 4:17-18 NIV

The apostle Paul was a man who seemed to find trouble wherever he went. In thirty years of preaching throughout the ancient world, he experienced an endless array of murderous plots against him. Many people didn't like what he preached. They tried to stone him in Iconium and partially succeeded in Lystra. He was driven out of countless towns and imprisoned in others.

But despite many hardships, Paul understood something very profound. Our present troubles are only momentary and small in the light of eternity in Heaven. Paul had a clear perspective on his earthly struggles—seeing them as a means to get closer to his Savior. "I know what it is to have little, and I know what it is to have plenty. In any and all circumstances I have learned the secret of being well-fed and of going hungry, of having plenty and of being in need. I can do all things through him who strengthens me," (Philippians 4:12-13 NRSV).

Embracing Paul's attitude doesn't change the fact of hardships. But it does help you gain a better perspective on them. God isn't here to make your troubles go away . . . He's here to help you through them. And Paul's life tells you that He will.

GRACE FOR TODAY

GOD HASN'T ABANDONED YOU TO FACE YOUR STRUGGLES ALONE. HE WILL GIVE YOU THE STRENGTH THAT YOU NEED TO OVERCOME ANY HARDSHIP.

Only for a Moment

You have turned for me my mourning into dancing; You
have put off my sackcloth and clothed me with gladness.
PSALM 30:11 NKJV

Grace for Today

WHEN THERE ARE
NO WORDS TO
SOFTEN THE PAIN
OF LOSS, GOD
COMFORTS US
WITH THE
THOUGHT OF OUR
FUTURE WITH HIM
AND OUR LOVED
ONES.

The loss of a loved one is hard to take, even when we know the person is with God. The realization that he or she is no longer with us on the earth can be overwhelming emotionally — sometimes to the point that we forget to live our own lives.

Our sorrow is not for our loved ones — but for us, and the pain we feel is because we can no longer enjoy their presence. We miss the exchange of conversation, their touch, and the way they made us feel when we were with them. We suffer because we are separated from them.

Imagine the pain God experienced when sin separated Him from His most prized creation — Adam, the first man, and every generation born into the world after him. God could no longer walk and talk with Adam and Eve in the garden. He could no longer touch them and freely enjoy them as a part of His life.

God's desire to have a relationship with us compelled Him to give His greatest gift — the life, death, and resurrection of His Son Jesus so that He could once again enjoy fellowship with us.

Just as God rejoices when we are reunited with Him through the gift of eternal life, we, too, have the hope of seeing again those we love. What's more, we will even touch the face of God.

Our time on earth is only a moment compared to eternity. It's something we struggle to comprehend because it's so vast. But we can look forward to the future because of what we've gained — eternity with God and all those who share our love for Him.

GOD: IN PROPORTION TO OUR NEEDS

By Evelyn Christenson

When we lose the security and help of human companionship, the gain we experience is that fantastic proportion in which God gives of himself to us. It was in a hospital that I first learned this concept. Hospitalization produces a particular kind of aloneness—the loss of security of all familiar human companionship. Absent, too, are all the familiar sounds, smells, and sights of our usual surroundings.

The night before surgery brings a very special kind of aloneness. I was just 34 when I entered a hospital for my first surgery. A lump in each breast foreshadowed an almost certain verdict of cancer. I had an overwhelming need—and God knew it.

After my husband and all the hospital personnel had left me, an amazing thing happened. It was not just that I was opening myself up to Him more, but I could suddenly sense God actually filling that stark, white room with himself. As I lay on that bed, I was acutely aware of His presence permeating the room right up to the corners of the ceiling. He was there—all that I needed of Him. More of Him than I could ever remember experiencing before. God understood the magnitude of my need and came accordingly.

As I reflect on this, I realize that this principle had been in operation without my recognizing it all of my Christian life—God coming in proportion to my need.[5]

DEAR GOD,

Great is my need, but even greater are You! You know my situation more intimately than I know it myself, and I ask You to intervene on my behalf and give me the grace I need to endure. Thank You for being my ever-present help in this time of need. I put my trust in You.

AMEN

Praise be to the God and Father of our Lord Jesus Christ, the Father of compassion and the God of all comfort.
2 CORINTHIANS 1:3 NIV

A CHILD'S SMILE

From the lips of children and infants you have ordained praise.
PSALM 8:2 NIV

The young woman sat, rather impatiently, at the stoplight. She was in the middle of another busy day, and she was anxious to get to her destination. She drummed her fingers on the steering wheel and craned her neck to see if the light was about to change. Her to-do list scrolled through her head, reminding her of how much awaited her that day. How long is this light, anyway?

GRACE FOR TODAY

EXPECT TO BE SURPRISED BY GOD'S GRACE.

Just then two women began crossing the street in front of her car. They were talking hurriedly together and seemed to be just as impatient as the young woman felt. But then, just a few steps behind the preoccupied women, came a little girl of about eight years old. She had lovely dark hair and large, expressive eyes. In contrast to the women she followed, this little one was silently taking in everything around her, from the line of waiting cars she walked by to the gray fall sky above her. And then, her big brown eyes found those of the young woman sitting in her car at the light.

For a moment they both just stared. Then, like the warm sun breaking through the clouds, the little girl smiled, warm and joyful. In spite of herself, the busy young woman smiled too. She smiled a real smile, inspired by the contagious beauty of this lone child.

The light turned green. Only a few moments had passed. But for the young woman everything was different. She drove away to face her busy day, but she left much of her anxiety there at that crossroads. Her day had been touched, and changed, by God's unexpected grace delivered through the gaze of a child.

BIRDS AND BLESSING

The Lord Jesus himself said, "It is more blessed to give
than to receive."
ACTS 20:35 NIV

Did you know that hummingbirds must feed approximately every ten minutes all day long? They can consume two-thirds of their body weight in a single day. It's no wonder they seem so greedy as they flutter around the feeders filled with nectar.

Every Sunday, two types of people walk through the church doors. The first group comes for a blessing. Like the little birds dipping their beaks into the sweet nectar of the Spirit, they chirp, "I came to be blessed." They flutter about, hungry only for a blessing.

The people in the second group arrive ready to be a blessing. They walk through the door of the church with the questions, "What would the Lord have me do today? How can I help?"

And isn't it funny how the Lord works? The people in the second group desire to be a blessing, and because they follow the leading of the Lord, they are blessed.

There are times when everyone becomes part of the first group. Perhaps we've endured a trial or feel we have nothing to give. The Psalmist wrote, "Have mercy on me, O God, have mercy on me, for in you my soul takes refuge. I will take refuge in the shadow of your wings until the disaster has passed" (Psalm 57:1 NIV).

But if we find ourselves being greedy most of the time, perhaps it is time we leave the nest and become more mature Christians. Do you desire to be a giver — someone who strives to bless others and work for the Lord?

GRACE FOR TODAY

GOD'S GRACE AT WORK IN BELIEVERS MOTIVATES THEM TO SEEK WAYS TO BLESS OTHERS.

CHILDREN

We will not hide them from their children; we will tell the
next generation the praiseworthy deeds of the LORD, his
power, and the wonders he has done.
PSALM 78:4 NIV

Jesus said, "Let the little children come to me, and do not hinder them, for the kingdom of heaven belongs to such as these" (Matthew 19:14 NIV). Our children will be the keepers of God's wisdom for the next generation. Understanding this, God encourages us to bring them up in His love and truth. But, it isn't just our children that are special and need to know the love of God. There are children all around the world who need our love and support to be that next generation of amazing people of God.

GRACE FOR TODAY

GOD HAS GIVEN YOU
THE GIFT OF
PROSPERITY, A GIFT
TO SHARE.

Dean R. Hirsch, President and Chief Executive of World Vision International said, "I cannot countenance a world that would allow the needless suffering of children. My mission and the mission of World Vision is to ensure that no child suffers or dies for lack of food, clean water, shelter, or protection from the ravages of war."

There are many outstanding organizations whose mandate is to assist children around the world, but they need your support to fulfill their commission. We are a global village, and we are the keepers of all our children. The children we help today will shape the future for all of us tomorrow. What kind of future do you envision for your family? Help make that same vision a reality for someone else. We can help bring life and hope to families enduring war, famine, exploitation, and profound poverty. Pray about ways to help a child in need. Then do it—it is as simple and as uncomplicated as that.

No Greater Love

The greatest of these is love.
1 CORINTHIANS 13:13 NLT

It's been called a phenomenon, a mysterious and splendid thing. It's as invisible as the air we breathe, yet equally essential. Poets have tried to describe it. Philosophers have sought to understand it. Songwriters have mined from their hearts the emotional treasure it evokes. But the mystery and miracle of love remains indescribable. What an amazing gift God has given us—not only to observe, but also to miraculously experience! His Word proclaims it to be greater than hope or faith.

> ## Grace for Today
>
> GOD'S LOVE FOR YOU IS A CONSTANT FIRE BY WHICH YOUR HEART WILL ALWAYS BE WARMED.

Long before St. Valentine was adopted as the patron saint of lovers, God's love was the foundation of true love. Because of the romantic symbols we use to celebrate Valentine's Day, we forget that St. Valentine actually lost his life because of his love for God. Beyond the glamour of roses and chocolate that help us celebrate the world's view of romantic love, we find a man who gave his all for the love of his Savior.

Love is the deepest and most fulfilling gift God has ever given us. That gift transcends outward symbols and trivial attempts to explain it. Without His love, we wouldn't experience God's mercy, His salvation, or His joy. Once received, the deep, abiding love of Christ in our hearts will overflow into every aspect of our lives. Real love, the kind of love that sacrificed all for you and me, came in human form to unite our hearts to God's.

Do you desire to love more and experience more love in your life? God's Word encourages, "If we love one another, God abides in us, and His love is perfected in us" (1 John 4:12 NASB).

Celebrate the sacred bliss of true love. Wrap yourself and others in this extraordinary gift that was hand delivered from Heaven by the Author and Creator of love.

OVERCOMING OBSTACLES

Everyone born of God overcomes the world. This is the
victory that has overcome the world, even our faith.
1 JOHN 5:4 NIV

The Warner sisters lost much of their fortune in the depression of 1837 when their father lost his law practice and was no longer able to work. They sold their beautiful home in New York City and moved to their summer home on Constitution Island, opposite West Point Academy. As their financial problems increased, Anna and Susan prayed about ways they could earn a living—a difficult task for two women residing in a fairly remote area in the 1800s.

One day Anna said, "Susan, you are a wonderful storyteller. I bet you could write a novel."

It wasn't considered proper for a female to write fiction, but Susan wanted to write under a female pseudonym, so she decided to use her deceased grandmother's name, Elizabeth Wetherell. The resulting novel titled *The Wide, Wide World*, became the first book by an American author to sell one million copies. Only *Uncle Tom's Cabin* eventually sold more copies during the mid-nineteenth century. Unfortunately, because of her dire financial needs, Susan sold her copyright outright.

Undaunted, Susan and Anna went on to write many more novels. One of the books was titled *See and Say*. Although Susan composed most of the words, Anna included a poem she had written to comfort a dying child. Her poem, now a well-known song, has taught more children about Christ over the years than any other. It is titled "Jesus Loves Me."

The main characters in the Warner sisters' books overcame adverse circumstances in their day-to-day living by learning to trust God and accept His gift of grace, just as the Warner sisters did in their own lives. Follow their example. You can do it too!

GRACE FOR TODAY

HOW CALMLY MAY WE COMMIT OURSELVES TO THE HANDS OF HIM WHO BEARS UP THE WORLD.

JEAN PAUL RICHTER

MISPLACED EXPECTATIONS

By Evelyn Christenson

Perhaps the reason so many are seeking alternative human companionship is because they have never found an adequate source to fulfill their needs. They may be expecting more than God intended from a human being. Should we expect anyone to be able to meet all of our needs at all times?

I have found that not being understood, not having my needs fulfilled, involves a very difficult kind of loneliness, a sense of being forsaken. But in this loss I have found an overwhelming gain.

When a parent, a friend, a roommate, or a spouse cannot or will not meet my needs, it is really an advantage. For this has always driven me to the One who not only understands but cares. To the One who is always there to meet my needs. I have learned that a fantastic relationship with the Lord develops only in this kind of loneliness. What a privilege! The loss produces a gain that no human companionship could ever match—fellowship with the Lord, who always understands. And bids us come to Him![6]

HEAVENLY FATHER,

Thank You for Your promise to never to leave me nor forsake me. You know and understand the loneliness in my heart–the yearning in my soul–and I look to You to fill me with Yourself. I want to know You more intimately, Father, than I know any other person. Wrap me in Your arms, and hold me close to Your heart. In You and by Your grace, I am complete.

AMEN

[Jesus said,] "Look! Here I stand at the door and knock.
If you hear me calling and open the door, I will come in, and we will share a meal as friends."
REVELATION 3:20 NLT

GOD'S TRADEMARK

Where morning dawns and evening fades you call forth songs of joy . . . The grasslands of the desert overflow; the hills are clothed with gladness. The meadows are covered with flocks and the valleys are mantled with grain; they shout for joy and sing.
PSALM 65:8,12-13 NIV

Henry Ward Beecher wrote that beauty is "God's trademark in creation." Everywhere we look we can see the mark of God's grace on our world. Consider the incredible diversity of our planet. From towering snow-capped mountains to the wonders of the ocean's depths, from the lush rainforests to the stark loveliness of the desert, our world is full of amazing beauty. Beyond all this there are the mysteries that surround our world — billions of stars; massive, colorful planets; and swirling and sparkling galaxies. Unfathomably beautiful wonders fill every part of this vast universe.

GRACE FOR TODAY

LIKE A MAN IN LOVE, THE CREATOR OF THE UNIVERSE SURROUNDS US WITH THE BEAUTIFUL GIFTS OF HIS GRACE AND LOVE.

So often, though, we don't take the time to really see the trademark of God all around us. We are blinded by our own worries and struggles. All the while, God is painting sunsets above us and sprinkling flowers at our feet! He's caressing us with raindrops and spreading a soft carpet of grass before us. Like a man in love, the Creator of the universe surrounds us with gifts of His grace and love — longing for our love and attention in return. Shouldn't gifts like this get our attention and inspire our praise?

Take some time today to see the evidence of God's grace in your corner of the world. Look at the trees swaying in the breeze. Marvel at the colors of the sky. Listen to a bird's song. Beauty is all around if you will have eyes to see. It is pointing you to the Master Artist whose greatest masterpiece is you — and whose deepest desire is to embrace you with His grace.

BECAUSE IT'S RIGHT

Teach believers with your life: by word, by demeanor, by
love, by faith, by integrity.
1 TIMOTHY 4:12 MSG

Have you ever dinged someone's car in the grocery store parking lot and driven off with the thought that they'd never know you did it? Have you ever taken a secret recipe that a friend confidentially shared with you and passed it off as your own? Have you lied, just a little, to make your story sound more exciting or to make your child appear more ideal?

Integrity is not the norm in today's society. People are surprised when a wallet is returned with the money still inside. They are shocked to find a note on their windshield with a name and insurance information when their car has been damaged. The heart of integrity is doing what's right even when you think no one is looking or no one will know. God knows. He sees your actions and the intent of your heart.

Your heart is like a well-lit cathedral before God. There is nothing hidden. He sees it all. A life of integrity is clean and pure with nothing to hide. It is a sign that grace is at work, empowering the individual to do the right thing.

Integrity may not be a virtue that most of the world esteems today, but the House of God applauds you. Even if your name is not well-known on the earth, it rings in the heavens as someone who chooses to do what's right—because it's right.

It's a better life, a higher road. And God can make you courageous enough to walk it.

GRACE FOR TODAY

INTEGRITY LIGHTS THE LIVES OF THOSE WHO CHOOSE IT. IT IS A SIGN THAT GRACE IS AT WORK, EMPOWERING THEM TO DO WHAT IS RIGHT.

45

ARE WE SURE ABOUT THIS?

Why do you see the speck in your neighbor's eye, but do
not notice the log in your own eye?
MATTHEW 7:3 NRSV

Gilbert Keith Chesterton once wrote, "The Bible tells us to love our neighbors and also to love our enemies; probably because they are generally the same people." For many of us that does pose a bit of a conflict. We can't pick our family and certainly in most cases not our neighbors. So? Flow do we love our obnoxious neighbor? Before we start compiling a list of the annoying things our neighbors do—STOP. Ever consider we might be driving them crazy as well? Are there things that we do that might be less than stellar?

GRACE FOR TODAY

LOVING THOSE WHO ARE HOSTILE IS A GRACE ONLY GOD CAN GIVE US.

Taking the other person's viewpoint is often the start to seeing a conflict in a new light. Putting ourselves in the other person's shoes can lead to understanding. Understanding can lead to compassion. Compassion can lead to action. Action in an amazing chain of attitude adjustments can lead to reconciliation. Is there anything we can rectify, reconcile, or simply change to pave the way to renewed neighbor relations? To begin a thawing of the cold war?

Sometimes the hardest thing in the world is to walk next door and make a new start. But in the end that moment of humility can lead to friendship or at the very least fresh understanding. Peacemaking is a reflection of Christ's grace operating within us. Remember, loving our neighbor is the second greatest commandment—no matter how hard it is. And the ability to do so is one of the greatest graces God gives to His own.

GRACE COMES THROUGH

I have set the LORD always before me. Because he is at my
right hand, I will not be shaken. Therefore my heart is glad
and my tongue rejoices; my body also will rest secure.
PSALM 16:8-9 NIV

*I don't think I could survive if that happened
to me.* How many times have you thought
this when you hear of tragedy or loss? We've
all witnessed people whose lives have been
torn apart by terrible circumstances. A
mother loses her tiny baby; a husband faces
an uncertain future as his wife battles cancer;
a family's dreams are dashed when their
business fails. We watch them, we mourn
with them, and in our hearts we fear that if
the same were to happen to us, we would
fall apart.

GRACE FOR TODAY

WE MUST LEAN ON
OUR LORD FOR WHAT
WE NEED EACH DAY,
EACH HOUR, EACH
MOMENT, TRUSTING
THAT HIS GRACE WILL
SEE US THROUGH.

Yet, over and over, people are faced
with their worst fears come true—and they survive. In fact, some
actually thrive and end up better, stronger, and more joyful than before.
That grieving mother becomes an inspiration to other women going
through loss. The husband and wife come to know a greater and deeper
love than they've ever known because of the struggle they endured
together. The family finds the joy and power in teamwork and gets a
new business up and running—together.

This is the miracle of God's grace. He gives us what we need to face
each day and each situation. We can't save it up like some rainy-day
fund. We must lean on our Lord for what we need each day, each hour,
each moment, trusting that His grace will come through. When we do,
we find the strength to make it—even through the darkest times, the
times we feared would destroy us.

So the next time you wonder, *Could I survive that?* remember: Trust
in God's grace. He will always come through when you need Him the
most.

THE SMALLEST DETAILS

Jesus answered him, " I hose who love me will keep my
word, and my Father will love them, and we will come to
them and make our home with them."
JOHN 14:23 NRSV

GRACE FOR TODAY

SOMEBODY LOVES US,
TOO—GOD HIMSELF.
WE HAVE BEEN
CREATED TO LOVE
AND TO BE LOVED.

MOTHER TERESA

Evangelist Joe Gatuslao had this to say, "If God had a refrigerator, your picture would be on it." Really? We often find it hard to believe that God's love for us is daily, constant, and wonderfully obsessive. And no, obsessive is not too strong a word. In fact, His love is fanatical.

God's love is beautifully depicted in three of Jesus' parables: the story of the lost sheep, the lost coin, and of course the prodigal son. What better illustration than a father searching the horizon; wishing and waiting for his son to return home. "But while he was still a long way off, his father saw him and was filled with compassion for him; he ran to his son, threw his arms around him and kissed him" (Luke 15:20 NIV). This father knew his son so well that he could recognize his walk or slightest gesture from a distance.

That's our Heavenly Father—He knows and cherishes the smallest details about us. Jesus wants us to understand how patient, forgiving, passionate, and very personal his Father's love is. However, there is something skeptical in us that resists the idea of such a loving God. We can imagine a God who sees only our flaws and sins, but not one who loves His creation, flaws and all. Yet that creation is us. And He does. We are truly precious in His sight.

48

RIPS AND HOLES

By Evelyn Christenson

In all families there are times when a few individuals or even all family members squabble and have misunderstandings, ripping holes in the under-girding fabric which has been woven by prayer. Some holes are easily patched and hardly affect the strength of the network at all; in some cases squabbles rip huge gaps in the prayer fabric, causing a serious disruption in the flow of family prayers or even a ceasing of praying altogether.

It is the threads of prayer that can mend the snags and gaping holes in family relationships. During the Depression of the 1930s, I used to watch my mother darn socks. She would take one strand of darning thread and painstakingly weave it back and forth until what had been a hole was stronger than the original sock. That is how prayer mends a family's rips and holes.

It is with just one or perhaps a few family members taking their threads of prayer and patiently, often painstakingly, weaving to mend the family fabric. Sometimes the weaving accomplishes its purpose quickly, but sometimes it takes faithful weaving for years before the rift is mended. Much mending prayer is done in weeping and even agonizing of spirit. But, stitch by stitch, God takes His holy hand and pulls those threads of prayer into place, supernaturally mending those hurtful holes.[7]

DEAR GOD,

You know the wounds that have been inflicted within our family that are threatening to pull us apart. Help us resist the urge to seek revenge; and instead, enable us to forgive and extend Your grace to one another. With Your skillful hands, knit our hearts together once again. Help us to love the way that You do–unconditionally and without reservation. Help us to put our differences behind us and to begin away.

AMEN

Don't repay evil for evil. Don't snap back at those who say unkind things about you. Instead, pray for God's help for them, for we are to be kind to others, and God will bless us for it.
1 PETER 3:9 TLB

NEVER ALONE

I am continually with you; you hold my right hand.
PSALM 73:25 NRSV

Loneliness is something we have all felt at one time or another. Sometimes we can feel completely lonely in a room full of friends. Circumstances can make us feel alone, like being single, divorced, or bereaved. And sometimes we are alone because we simply experience that deep emptiness inside. The strain comes when we allow loneliness to color our lives and dictate how we interact with others. If we're not careful, loneliness can become a lifestyle and not just a temporary feeling.

GRACE FOR TODAY

GOD'S PROVISION FOR LONELINESS IS ENJOYING INTIMATE FELLOWSHIP WITH HIM AND OTHER CHRISTIANS.

Loneliness mustn't always be viewed in a negative light, however. It can be a catalyst that pushes us outwards beyond ourselves to experience new things, people, and change.

Taking your feelings of loneliness to God in prayer is the first step—He is your constant companion, advisor, and friend. Ask God to help open doors of opportunity that will free you from loneliness. Dr. Neil T. Anderson wrote, "Aloneness can lead to loneliness. God's preventative for loneliness is intimacy—meaningful, open, sharing relationships with one another. In Christ we have the capacity for the fulfilling sense of belonging which comes from intimate fellowship with God and with other believers." God can give you the courage to ask for help.

Loneliness is such an internal struggle that one antidote is to completely serve others—get out of yourself. Find ways to get more involved at church or in the community. Mission trips are a great way to meet new friends and help others. Taking classes or exploring new hobbies are other ways to beat loneliness. Even though you may feel alone, you're never alone. God is with you and wants to help you remove the burden of depression and isolation from your life. But you have to give Him permission.

THE FATHER'S GRACE

The grace of God has been revealed, bringing salvation to
all people.
TITUS 2:11 NET

Have you ever been amazed to see people who are clearly not following God's ways yet are receiving His blessings? Doesn't it seem as if those who love God and follow Him closely should get a bigger share of "the good life"? Life can seem terribly unfair.

Let's look at this issue in a different light:

John has two daughters. The oldest, Sarah, is responsible, helpful, and kind. She eagerly listens to her father and obeys him quickly. She's not perfect, but she has a close relationship with her dad and finds joy in pleasing him.

> **GRACE FOR TODAY**
>
> OUR FATHER'S GRACE EXTENDS TO ALL HIS CHILDREN.

Sarah's younger sister, Mary, is quite the opposite. Mary is impulsive and stubborn. She struggles with authority and often rebels against her father's guidance, in spite of his obvious deep love for her.

Sarah and Mary are very different girls who react to their father in very different ways. But they are both John's children. He loves them equally, but he has to relate to them each according to their unique personalities. Sarah enjoys the freedom and security that comes from a close relationship and obedience. She has privileges and an intimacy with her father that Mary does not share. But Mary may actually get more attention and more special kindness from her father because she needs to be brought back into a close relationship with him.

It is similar with our heavenly Father. His grace extends to all of His children. Those who have accepted it enjoy special privileges, joy, and freedom. Those who rebel, though, need His touch in a different way. In fact, His goodness can lead them to repentance. (See Romans 2:4.)

On the surface it may seem that the defiant "children" are getting special treatment. But God loves them as much as He loves those who follow Him closely. He is extending His grace to those lost children in a language they will understand. He longs for all of His children to know the depth of His great love.

LASTING TREASURE

[Jesus said,] "Where your treasure is, there your heart will be also."
LUKE 12:34 NRSV

GRACE FOR TODAY

GOD SHOWERS HIS LOVE AND GRACE UPON PEOPLE, NOT THINGS.

We love pizza, fast cars, our best friend's hair color, and fashion nails. We love the spa, furniture, football games, and the sweater we bought at the mall. Our comments suggest that we have placed our affections on material things. Most of us would say that we don't truly love those things, but rather we like them. If so, then we should say what we mean. Possessions are for our pleasure. Things are here to serve us—to make life more enjoyable.

Love, however, is vital to relationships, not to be confused with personal preferences concerning material things. We are to love people instead of things. We are to develop relationships with people—not the material world. Relationships with people hold eternal value. They are the only treasures we can take with us and keep for all of eternity.

Jesus said the greatest commandment is to love the Lord your God with all of your heart, mind, and soul; and the second, to love your neighbor as much as you love yourself. (See Matthew 22:37-39.) Love is bestowing upon others what you have of God's character and nature. You demonstrate His love and grace through your actions and behavior. That means you prefer others, putting their needs and desires before your own.

Invest your time and energy in strong relationships with those whom God brings into your life by showing them His love and grace. Let them see a clear picture of the One you serve by reflecting Him in everything you do.

A right perspective on what you like and what you love will yield treasures to last a lifetime—an eternal lifetime!

DUST AND DISCIPLINE

These commands and this teaching are a lamp to light the way ahead of you. The correction of discipline is the way to life.
PROVERBS 6:23 NLT

A 1945 gospel song by Johnny and Walter Bailes has a stanza that says, "Dust on the Bible, dust on the Holy Word, the words of all the prophets and the sayings of our Lord."

How many people have treadmills, stationary bicycles, and several other fitness machines collecting dust in their basements or garages? You buy a new machine with good intentions, but buying the equipment alone doesn't help you become more physically fit. A vacuum cleaner with all the latest attachments might be an efficient machine, but it won't clean a house by itself.

Do you have a Bible sitting in your house collecting dust? In the same way

GRACE FOR TODAY

GOD'S WORD IS FILLED WITH HIS GRACE, FOR EVERYONE WHO WILL TAKE THE TIME TO PARTAKE IN IT.

that buying health food and letting it rot won't make you healthy, having a Bible won't feed your spirit if you don't read it.

Keeping a clean house or a fit, healthy body takes discipline. Likewise, it takes discipline to study the Word of God. The apostle Paul wrote to Timothy, "Be diligent to present yourself approved to God, a worker who does not need to be ashamed, rightly dividing the word of truth" (2 Timothy 2:15 NKJV). The Amplified Bible explains the last phrase as meaning that we rightly handle and skillfully teach the Word of Truth. How can we teach something we don't know?

God gave us the Bible to reveal himself to us and to guide our lives by showing us the difference between right and wrong. A mind studying the Word of God and meditating on the goodness of God can have perfect peace. Trust grows in the knowledge and wisdom of God's Holy Word.

Let's dust off our Bibles and study the Word of God.

FULFILLING GOD'S VISION FOR YOUR LIFE

The vision is yet for an appointed time; hut at the end it will speak, and it will not lie. Though it tarries, wait for it; because it will surely come.
HABAKKUK 2:3 NKJV

Inside the deepest part of your heart, is there an unfulfilled vision you've almost given up on? Perhaps it is buried beneath the everyday complexities of life and responsibilities. You may have talked yourself into believing it was just a silly idea that can never happen.

God-given visions take time. Much like a diamond in the rough, visions go through mining, cleaning, filtering, and a cutting process. Visions are mined and tested in our hearts, held up to the light of God's will, filtered to fit His plan for our lives, and then carefully cut and placed into a setting of time that will reflect God's glory.

GRACE FOR TODAY

GOD-GIVEN VISIONS TAKE TIME, BUT IF YOU WILL WAIT FOR IT, IT WILL SURELY COME.

From Genesis to Revelation, the Bible is full of reminders that even if a vision dies, God has a resurrection plan. Moses must have questioned his vision when he was rejected by his people and then forced to flee into the desert for forty years. Joseph's dream about his brothers bowing down to him must have seemed ridiculous after they sold him into slavery.

Timing is a key element in God's plan and vision for your life. Don't give up on the seed He planted in your heart. Waiting times are used to conform our perspectives to God's perspective.

Proverbs 16:3 AMP says, "Roll your works upon the Lord [commit and trust them wholly to Him; He will cause your thoughts to become agreeable to His will, and] so shall your plans be established and succeed." Isn't it wonderful knowing that God never gives up the visions He has planned for our lives, even when we think they will never come to pass? Rest in God's timing. Trust Him to direct you and guide you onward in your destiny.

(HEART-MAIDEN

By Jill Briscoe

Mary calls God her Savior. Even though Gabriel assures her that God's favor rests upon her, Mary is called to be not the source of grace but the object of it.

We can all imagine what sort of woman she must have been to be called to become the earthly mother of the Christ, but Mary's deep humility and own sweet testimony confirm the fact of her human need. Only imperfect people need a Savior. Only divinity is perfect.

The very best people need a Savior, because the very best people are sinners. It is as hard for some "good" people to believe that as it is for many to believe that Mary was a sinner. Yet there are good sinners! Does that sound like a contradiction? Good sinners sometimes find it difficult to see their need of God because they are almost good enough without Him! Yet a truly good person is ever conscious of his or her shortcomings. And that's exactly what the Bible teaches. We all "fall short of the glory of God" (Romans 3:23 NIV). "There is none who does good" (and in case one of us thinks that is an exception, the Bible adds) "no, not one" (Psalm 14:3 NKJV). Good people concentrate not so much on asking God to forgive them for the things they have done that they shouldn't have done, but rather on asking forgiveness for the things they haven't done that they ought to have done. A truly good person knows that all imperfection is sin.

How do good people know these things? I'm glad you asked! They come to know them by reading His Word. "Be it unto me according to thy word" (Luke 1:38 KJV), Mary said to Gabriel. Mary, after all, was not only a handmaiden, she was a heart-maiden too. She was a woman of the Word.[8]

GOD,

I am nothing without Your grace. Please fill me today, so my life will glorify You.

AMEN

[Mary said,] "My heart rejoices in God my Savior."
LUKE 1:47 NCV

Superman

The Word became flesh and made his dwelling among us.
We have seen his glory, the glory of the One and Only, who
came from the Father, full of grace and truth.
JOHN 1:14 NIV

"Faster than a speeding bullet, able to leap tall buildings in a single bound—it's a JL bird, it's a plane. No—it's Superman!" Born from the imaginations of two Midwestern teenagers in the 1930s, the "Man of Steel" has captivated people worldwide for decades. From comic book hero to television and film star, this superhero with a heart of gold never seems to lose his appeal. What is it about Superman that gives his story such staying power?

GRACE FOR
TODAY

OUR HEARTS
RESONATE TO GOD'S
STORY OF GRACE.

Perhaps Superman's commitment to "truth, justice, and the American way" resonates with people. Maybe he fulfills our dreams of rising above our everyday challenges to follow a higher calling—figuratively and literally. Or, could it be that Superman speaks to an even deeper longing in all of our hearts? Maybe his story whispers a truth that we are all desperate to hear.

Superman came to earth from the heavens as a baby—sent by his father. He was adopted by rural, working-class parents and raised in a small town. As a young man he left his humble home to use his power for fighting evil and saving lives in the city, and finally in the world. Does this sound at all familiar to you?

Jesus came to earth as a baby, sent by His Father. His adoptive parents were simple, rural folks. As a young man, He left His small town to use His power for good. But Jesus' story continues beyond where the legend of Superman ends. Jesus sacrificed His very life to save all of humanity and then defeated death as well.

So maybe Superman's story has been inspiring people for so many years because it follows the eternal pattern of the story of grace. The Man of Steel is a parable that points us to the Man of Sorrows—the ultimate Hero.

TIME-OUT

Anyone who enters God's rest also rests from his own
work, just as God did from his.
HEBREWS 4:10 NIV

We can by the nature of our biological rhythms have days of frenetic energy. Our roles at work and home can create days of fanatical stress. Combining these elements can create a berserk woman running around barking orders and doing the job of ten Amazonian females.

GRACE FOR TODAY

GOD'S GRACE INCLUDES THE FREEDOM BOUGHT BY CHRIST TO REST AND JUST BE.

Take time to rethink, reprioritize, and remember this: Wonder Woman is a myth and lives only in comic books—not at your house. Erma Bombeck wisely wrote, "My theory on housework is, if the item doesn't multiply, smell, catch on fire, or block the refrigerator door, let it be. No one cares. Why should you?"

You see, many of us are living a feminine guilt mythology—where we can do it all and still have the energy to exercise. But sometimes we allow resentment to build up because we feel burned out and used. In the Bible is a woman named Martha who was seething because she was doing all the work, and her sister Mary was sitting around listening to their guest— a man named Jesus.

When she complained, Jesus said, "Martha, Martha, you are worried and upset about many things, but only one thing is needed. Mary has chosen what is better, and it will not be taken away from her" (Luke 10: 41-42 NIV). Mary took a time-out, and Jesus approved.

Sometimes we just have to stop, laugh, and recite, "God created me— and I'm human." There's a reason God rested on the seventh day. And He wants you to give yourself a break and take a well-deserved time-out when you need it.

Maybe that means taking a walk through fallen autumn leaves, relaxing in a bubble bath, or playing a board game with the kids instead of doing housework. How about a romantic date with your husband? Maybe it just means ordering pizza on Friday nights. You decide what it is that gives you rest, and God will applaud you.

57

THE IMAGE

We look at this Son and see the God who cannot be seen.
We look at this Son and see God's original purpose in
everything created.
COLOSSIANS 1:15 MSG

When a legal document was drawn up in ancient Greece — such as a receipt or an IOU — it always included a description of the chief characteristics and distinguishing marks of the two parties involved. This helped in future identification. The Greek word for such a description is eikon, which is the same word Paul used to describe Christ as "the image of the invisible God."

Paul wrote Colossians to combat a growing heresy in the early Church called Gnosticism. The Gnostics believed that all matter was evil and only spirit was good. Therefore, they concluded that God could not become man, nor could He be the agent of creation.

Yet Scripture shows us that Jesus was born in the flesh. Because Christ is God, He is the image of the invisible God. Jesus came to earth and lived as a man, and in this way God provided an image of himself for us since He is invisible. We have an *eikon* to use as a guide by which to lead our lives.

We were made in God's image; and through His gift of grace we are saved by having faith in Him. Christ dwells in our hearts because of the Holy Spirit who lives within our innermost being.

Ephesians 5:1 challenges us to "be imitators" of God. Just as we become like the people we spend time with, we can spend time with God in prayer and Bible study to become like Him. Not only will we develop characteristics that please God, but we will become a mirror image of His grace — an *eikon* for others.

A Satisfied Life

Godliness with contentment is great gain.
1 TIMOTHY 6:6 NKJV

Perhaps you think a bigger house, a nicer car, a better job, and a bigger bank account would make you happy. If only your children were smarter, taller, more respectful, and helpful around the house, then you could have the perfect life. If your husband would lose thirty pounds, if you could get a face—lift and a tummy tuck, then you'd experience that "happily ever after."

God gave you the ability to plan, dream, set goals, and achieve them; but He wants you to get there His way—by the road of contentment. We were created to enjoy Him and each other on our way to the next level. Life is a journey, and getting there is most of the fun.

As we grow, we find out about ourselves—what we like, don't like, and where we can improve. We discover more about our relationship with God—who He is to us and for us, as well as who we are in Him. Our development extends to our relationships with others—how we impact their lives and how they influence us.

Don't wish your life away, hoping for tomorrow. God's grace is sufficient for today. Your best life is the one you are living now. You were created to live in the present with a contented heart. Make the most of every moment by looking for the positive in every situation. Be happy where you are on the way to where you're going. That is living the good life.

Grace for Today

GOD'S GRACE IS SUFFICIENT FOR TODAY, ENABLING US TO ENJOY THE JOURNEY TO OUR DESTINY.

GRACE GIVEN, GRACE RECEIVED

Those who live to please the Spirit will harvest everlasting life from the Spirit. So don't get tired of doing what is good. Don't get discouraged and give up, for we will reap a harvest of blessing at the appropriate time.
GALATIANS 6:8-9 NLT

Years ago, a movie called *Mr. Holland's Opus* was released. It was the story of a high school music teacher who put his heart into teaching his students, instilling in them more than just the knowledge of the notes to play, but also a true passion for music. All the while, he faces struggles with the deafness of his only child and his own unfulfilled dreams of composing and conducting his own symphony. Yet, through it all, he continues to love music and his students and to bring these two loves together.

GRACE FOR TODAY

WHEN WE SPEND OUR LIVES EXTENDING GRACE, GOD INSURES THAT IT COMES BACK TO US IN WONDERFUL, UNEXPECTED WAYS.

The movie follows Mr. Holland through many years of teaching. And then, after he has inspired hundreds of students, the school's music budget is cut completely, and Mr. Holland is forced to retire. But his story doesn't end there. As a tribute to his incredible dedication to teaching, Mr. Holland's students, both current and past, surprise him with a rousing send-off—a full auditorium; a standing ovation; and as the ultimate sign of respect, an orchestra of former students to play his as yet unperformed symphony. There wasn't a dry eye in the place once the last note was played, and a triumphant Mr. Holland took a bow.

Mr. Holland's Opus is a story of sowing and reaping—of grace given and grace received. When we spend our lives extending grace to others, we find it coming back to us in wonderful, unexpected ways. And even if we never experience a roomful of people giving us a standing ovation, we can be assured that it will all be worth it when we stand before the throne of grace and hear our Father say, "Well done, my good and faithful servant."

GOD THE HEALER

By Jill Briscoe

God is the healer of bodies, souls, spirits, characters, and relationships, Satan can mend inanimate matter but he cannot bring peace to minds or mend sick marriages or cast out demons, for after all, how can Satan cast out Satan? "So who qualifies for healing?" you may ask. "Those who have enough faith? Those who are good enough? Does it depend on me or on Him? Is He choosy? Does He draw our names out of a hat? Is it just potluck?"

First of all, all who come to God for soul healing, asking in faith to be saved, will receive it. He is "not willing that any should perish but that all should come to repentance" (2 Peter 3:9 NKJV, emphasis added). As we read in 1 John 5:11-12 NKJV, "And this is the testimony: that God has given us eternal life, and this life is in His Son. He who has the Son has life; he who does not have the Son of God does not have life." Some who ask for temporary bodily healing will receive it too. But not all who ask will. All of us will enjoy a final healing of the body in heaven. We shall receive, according to 1 Corinthians 15:34-35, a brand new body which will never feel pain or experience decay![9]

HEAVENLY FATHER,

Thank You for Your Word regarding healing. I ask You to heal my spirit, soul, body, character, and any of my relationships that are wounded. I need the blessing of Your grace to mend and make me whole so that I am complete in you.

AMEN

He was wounded for our transgressions, He was bruised for our iniquities; The chastisement for our peace was upon Him, And by His stripes we are healed.
ISAIAH 53:5 NKJV

WHAT DOES YOUR STYLE SAY ABOUT YOU?

Charm is deceitful, and beauty is vain, but a woman who fears the LORD is to be praised. Give her a share in the fruit of her hands, and let her works praise her in the city gates.
PROVERBS 31:30-31 NRSV

Imagine, if you will, the first female president of the United States stepping up to the podium in a half shirt, low riders, and a glittering stud in her navel. It may work for rock stars, but it would look ridiculous and seriously inappropriate for a president.

Fashion is an incredibly powerful medium. It's one of the ways we as individuals express ourselves. What we wear tells the world something about who we are. It tells the world whom we admire and what we care about. What is your fashion saying about you? What do you want it to say?

GRACE FOR TODAY

GOD DESIGNS EACH WOMAN TO BE BEAUTIFUL IN HER OWN UNIQUE WAY. HIS GRACE SHINING THROUGH ENHANCES THAT BEAUTY.

The media and the world we live in encourage women to flaunt their sexuality. Actually, that's nothing new. Men have been captivated by women since before Samson fell for Delilah. But for a woman to dress provocatively, she sells herself far too short of her actual worth. Sure, God designed women to be beautiful, but outer beauty should be a reflection of what is within. God made you a smart, caring, and pretty amazing human being. If you'll let Him, He can make that shine first.

Revealing sexuality is easy. Getting the professional respect you want at school or work is a lot harder to achieve. You want those brilliant, God-inspired ideas to be what people remember about you. And that's why the first Ms., Mrs., or Miss President won't be dressing like a rock star. She will be dressed like a serious world leader.

So what are your clothes telling people about you? You certainly don't have to dress in a power suit, but whatever you wear, you should dress for respect and to reflect God's grace within you. After all, you are an ambassador of the King.

MORE LIKE HIM

> [God] comforts us in all our troubles so that we can
> comfort others. When others are troubled, we will be able
> to give them the same comfort God has given us.
> 1 CORINTHIANS 1:4 NLT

One night a young girl was lying in bed, reflecting on her life. She had been a Christian for only two years, but she realized that her relationship with God was not what she wanted it to be. She prayed, "Lord, if You are really there, do something that will change me and turn me around."

Shortly after praying that prayer, Joni Eareckson dove into the murky waters of the Chesapeake Bay near her home. Her head struck something hard and unyielding, which caused a strange, electric buzzing sensation. Yet, she felt no pain. She tried to break free, but nothing happened. Joni's sister, Kathy, had witnessed the dive, and she pulled Joni to the surface, saving her life. However, this accident on July 30, 1967, left Joni a quadriplegic.

GRACE FOR TODAY

GOD ... DOES NOT COMFORT US TO MAKE US COMFORTABLE, BUT TO MAKE US COMFORTERS.

JOHN HENRY JOWETT

Joni thought back to what she had prayed shortly before the accident and realized that God was using the mishap to strengthen her, fill her with grace, and make her more like Him. Now she saw that her responsibility was to comfort those who had suffered the same kind of trials she had encountered. Friends and family members had provided hope for her during her difficult recovery, and now she would do the same.

And this Joni Earekson Tada has done. Through her ministry, Joni and Friends, she is dedicated to extending love and the grace of God to people affected by disabilities.

If you have gone through a difficult period in your life or overcome an obstacle, you, too, can provide comfort to those who are hurting. Through your experiences, you, too, can become more like Him.

ALL OF YOU

> May God himself, the God who makes everything holy and whole,
> make you holy and whole, put you together—spirit, soul, and
> body—and keep you fit for the coming of our Master, Jesus
> Christ.
> 1 THESSALONIANS 5:23 MSG

Eggs, bacon, and toast for breakfast; salad for lunch; a casserole for dinner. You have your groceries purchased and meals planned for the week. You are careful about your family's health and take steps to see that they eat the right kinds of foods.

It is just as important to take time to evaluate your spiritual and emotional wellbeing. Do you feed your spirit and soul a balanced diet of God's Word and time with Him? Just as your stomach craves food when it's hungry, your spirit and soul require nourishment. They need a big taste of God's goodness and a refreshing drink of His presence. They need God's grace.

You are a three-part being. Your spirit is the real you. You live in a body and experience life through your thoughts, intentions, and feelings. Take time to see that every area of your life gets the nourishment it needs to grow so that you can live a balanced life. Just as you set an appointment to get your hair done, run errands, and return phone calls, make it a point to set aside some time to study the Bible and examine God's truth. Purposefully make plans to get alone with Him each day to talk to Him about life and hear what He has to say.

God has some great recipes for all three parts of your life that He'd like to share with you one-on-one. Allow His grace to season your whole being—spirit, soul, and body.

GRACE FOR TODAY

GOD'S GRACE IS FOR YOUR WHOLE BEING—SPIRIT, SOUL, AND BODY.

GREAT GRACE FOR GREAT NEEDS

We always give thanks to God for all of you and mention you in our prayers, constantly remembering before our God and Father your work of faith and labor of love and steadfastness of hope in our Lord Jesus Christ.
1 THESSALONIANS 1:2-3 NRSV

She was barely thirty and the mother of six when her husband left. Young Martha would lay awake many a night wondering how she would raise her children alone.

Yet, in spite of it all, she didn't lose hope. Her husband had abandoned her—but her God had not. As she faced another sleepless night, she leaned hard on the grace of her Lord.

GRACE FOR TODAY

WE CAN ALWAYS COUNT ON THE POWER OF GOD'S GRACE.

Slowly the years passed. Through God's grace, she persevered through the hard and lonely days. In spite of it all, Martha faithfully shepherded her growing children to church every Sunday. She watched as her three boys and three girls grew into young adulthood. She lifted each one to God constantly, pleading for His grace to cover them all.

When her youngest son was only nineteen, he was drafted and sent to Vietnam. Her heart broke. But through the fear, Martha did what she had always done. She trusted God's grace. At the end of his yearlong tour, her son came home unharmed physically—but deeply scarred emotionally. Nightmares plagued him and alcohol became his way of silencing them. Many a night she would lay awake until she heard the squeal of tires announcing that her son was home. She would breathe a prayer of thanks and in the same breath plead with God to cover her boy with His grace.

Martha's trust in the grace of her God was not misplaced. Over time, her young son was transformed by God's grace—he became a strong, godly man. And when the faithful arms of the Lord embraced Martha and took her home, all who knew her spoke of her unwavering trust in the saving power of God's grace. He never failed Martha. He will never fail you.

THE DOOR TO THE MIND

Keep your minds on whatever is true, pure, right, holy,
friendly, and proper. Don't ever stop thinking about what
is truly worthwhile and worthy of praise.
PHILIPPIANS 4:8 CEV

GRACE FOR TODAY

GRACE-FILLED
THOUGHTS ARE
EVIDENCE OF A
GRACE-FILLED LIFE.

During a visit, Marilyn's granddaughter ran to the kitchen. "I'm hungry. Do you have anything to eat?" She turned to the refrigerator, flung the door open, and gasped. "Granny, your refrigerator looks like the ones on television."

Marilyn laughed. The inside appeared immaculate, filled with fresh vegetables, fruit, and juices. Marilyn knew her granddaughter was used to seeing boxes with leftovers from fast-food restaurants and sodas with the occasional splatter of sticky juice in the bottom. Marilyn patted her granddaughter's head and explained, "Since Granny's been on a fixed income, I only buy foods that keep me healthy."

What if someone needed spiritual food from you? What if you need to draw on your spiritual resources for your own hunger. When you rummaged through your mind, what would you find? A collection of useless trivia, memories of the latest television show, or possibly a fantasy inspired by a movie—the junk food of the mind? Or would you find food for the soul that came from the time you spent reading the Word and talking to God?

Jesus has told us the truth will set us free. God's Word is there for you to build a healthy spirit and to make you a channel of God's truth to set others free through your ministry. Spend time with Him, and watch what wonderful inner changes occur from His truth stored inside your heart.

Jesus in Outer Space

By Evelyn Christenson

Back in 1957, I was scheduled to speak at a women's meeting but could not get a message I felt God wanted me to bring them; every idea I had seemed inadequate. In desperation I arose early on the morning of the day I was to bring the message and sought out my old green "prayer" chair. Prayer and searching God's Word produced nothing. Finally, in exasperation, I laid aside my Bible and picked up the newspaper. The headlines stunned me. Russia had sent Sputnik I into outer space! The frenzied race to conquer outer space was on. (How foolish that word "conquer" sounds now.) President Eisenhower, astonished that the Russians had projectors and propellants which could cast that 184-pound object into outer space, gave a message of comfort and encouragement to the American people on the front page of the newspaper.

But almost immediately the Holy Spirit recalled a portion of Scripture that I had hidden deep in my heart when I had taught the book of Colossians to my Sunday school class: "For by Him [Jesus] were all things created that are in heaven and that are on earth, visible and invisible, whether thrones or dominions or principalities or powers. All things were created through Him and for Him. And He is before all things, and in Him all things consist" (Colossians 1:16-17 NKJV).

I had my message! Jesus made outer space! He put the stars and planets, the sun and the moon in place! Jesus holds them all together! He makes them run on course according to His will! We are not to fear some nation that can make a little piece of hardware circle our planet. But we are to put our trust in the One who created all of that outer space, the One by whom it all consists — Jesus![10]

GOD,

If You can control the universe, You can manage my life. By You grace, guide me in the path that pleases You.

AMEN

[The Son] holds everything together with his powerful word.
HEBREWS 1:3 NCV

No Payment Due

How much more will the blood of Christ, who through the
eternal Spirit offered himself without blemish to God, purify our
conscience from dead works to worship the living God!
HEBREWS 9:14 NRSV

Just like a computer, your mind keeps records or files of your past. Perhaps you keep documentation on many of the things you've done wrong, even after you have asked God for His gracious gift of forgiveness.

Jesus freely gave His life so that you could switch places with Him. He took your sin so that you could boldly appear before the throne of God's grace white as snow. He exchanged His freedom for your captivity. He gave you a get-out-of-hell-free card. These are all a result of His grace, His unmerited favor. All you have to do is receive.

Even if you know you've accepted His gifts, thoughts of the past can press in on you and make you feel that you should pay for everything you've ever done wrong. But the truth is, your debt has already been paid in full. The slate is clean, and you have a fresh, new start.

It's time to delete those old files. Purge them with the Word of God. Create new folders and fill them full of God's perspective and truth about your life. You are what the Bible says you are. You are His creation—a new creature in Christ. You have a new life and a new destination— eternity with Him.

Grace for Today

GOD'S WORD ENABLES YOU TO PURGE YOUR OLD FILES, SO
YOU CAN ENJOY YOUR NEW LIFE IN CHRIST—A GIFT OF GOD'S
GRACE.

ARE YOU JESUS?

No one has ever seen God; but if we love one another, God
lives in us and his love is made complete in us.
1 JOHN 4:12 NIV

The story is told of three businessmen traveling to an important meeting in a faraway country. Their first flight is delayed; so when they reach the airport for their connection, they must run to catch their plane. As they are running, they collide with a little girl who is selling oranges. The fruit is sent flying in all directions, rolling under seats and across the terminal. The three executives stop for a moment. The little girl is crawling around on her hands and knees, feeling for the lost fruit. She is blind. The three men look to each other, then two of them turn and break into a run again. The third man hesitates.

GRACE FOR TODAY

THE BEAUTY OF GRACE MAKES US LOOK LIKE JESUS.

He is on his way to a big meeting—his career is on the line. Yet, he can't move. As his colleagues call to him, he waves them ahead, sets his luggage down, and begins to gather the rolling oranges.

It takes several minutes to find all the escaped fruit. When they are finished, the young girl reaches her hand out to touch her helper.

"Thank you," she says in broken English, tears in her staring eyes.

"I'm sorry that we knocked them over. I was happy to help," the businessman responded, finding that, in spite of his missed flight, he really was happy. "Have a good day," he said in farewell.

Before he had walked very far, the girl called out to him. "Sir? Excuse me, sir?"

He turned. "Yes?"

"I wanted to ask you . . . I cannot see you, but . . . are you Jesus?"

Has anyone ever mistaken you for Jesus? There can be no higher compliment than to be told that we look like our Savior. May we keep our eyes wide open to see opportunities to show grace that even the blind can see.

TALK IT OUT

Be angry but do not sin; do not let the sun go down on
your anger, and do not make room for the devil.
EPHESIANS 4:26-27 NRSV

Comedian Phyllis Diller said this about marriage: "Never go to bed mad. Stay up and fight." Funny enough, there is some truth in that statement. The apostle Paul cautioned us to deal with anger before the sun goes down.

GRACE FOR TODAY

IN HIS WORD, GOD GIVES US THE TOOLS TO RESOLVE CONFLICT. THEN HE GIVES US THE GRACE WE NEED TO IMPLEMENT THEM.

Even people who love each other will disagree and get upset or even angry sometimes. But when hurts or disagreements are allowed to smolder and fester, they can grow into disproportionate monsters: and that's a problem. While it's a good idea not to say anything when anger is at its peak, silence during times of conflict never solves anything. Even though its message can't be heard by the human ear, silence can speak volumes and sometimes say much more than you mean or want it to. Paul's advice is simple: don't let anger settle in for a long haul at your house or in your heart.

When you think about it, what purpose do anger, resentment, and unforgiveness serve? They are destructive emotions that hurt you and others: and the longer they persist, the more damage they do. Dr. Archibald Hart defines things this way. "Forgiveness is me giving up my right to hurt you for hurting me."

Talking things out takes time, patience, commitment, and an abundance of energy. It takes God's grace to do it right. But the effort is well spent. Communicating your hurts and disappointments as soon as possible—in a nonthreatening way—is essential to healthy relationships. Get it out and look for ways to resolve issues instead of holding on to them. In marriage, praying individually and as a couple is an amazing way to share with each other and with God. Sometimes people need professionals to help them find the right verbal tools to express themselves. And that's okay.

Just remember: love talks.

GOD'S COMPASSION

You, O LORD, will not withhold Your compassion from me;
Your lovingkindness and Your truth will continually
preserve me.
PSALM 40:11 NASB

When Christ came to Earth, He became a man who experienced the same human emotion and feelings that we experience. His heart was moved with compassion whenever He encountered someone in physical or emotional pain. He didn't offer superficial answers or solutions, but He met people at the very heart of their suffering. He fed them, ate with them, listened to the cries of their hearts, and most importantly, He wept with them. Compassion was never a random act of charity or a kind gesture of obligation. Compassion was and is the very heart of God.

GRACE FOR TODAY

GOD'S COMPASSION BRINGS COMFORT TO YOU—AND TO OTHERS THROUGH YOU.

Today, we are the vessels God uses to pour out His compassion. He allows us, if we are willing, to be His hands, His feet, His eyes, and His heart. Compassion changes lives and brings healing to those broken places we all experience in this life.

Hands of compassion reach through the darkness and do what is needed without asking, "What can I do?"

The feet of compassion walk tirelessly with a friend down the road of suffering, no matter how far and winding the road.

The eyes of compassion share a friend's pain. With one wordless glance, a compassionate friend simply says, "I'm here."

The heart of compassion pours a gentle, healing balm of unconditional love over the wounds of the hurting.

God provides ways for us to be both givers and receivers of His great compassion. There may not always be answers to earthly pain, but you can be God's ambassador of compassion whenever someone who needs God's healing is placed in your path.

And if suffering invades your life, you can be certain God will see the flare for help that your heart sends to Heaven. As surely as a soft quilt warms you on a cold night, God will send an ambassador of His compassion to comfort you in your winter season.

QUIET TIME

Quiet down before GOD, be prayerful before him.
PSALM 37:7 MSG

GRACE FOR TODAY

PARTAKING OF GOD'S GRACE IS LIKE LEISURELY DINING IN A FINE RESTAURANT; IF WE SLOW DOWN TO RECEIVE IT, WE FIND THE EXPERIENCE LIFE-CHANGING.

Do you consider yourself to be too busy? Frazzled? In our fast-paced world, it is sometimes difficult to focus on one thing at a time. The term "multitasking" originally pertained to a computer rapidly alternating between several active tasks. Now we commonly hear of humans multitasking. It is common for families to eat dinner while watching television. Flow many times have you seen someone driving, talking on a cell phone, and munching on a snack?

With computers and life running faster, unfortunately we can be tempted to move quickly through our prayer life too. When life gets busy, does your time with God tend to get pushed aside? Often we do that to take care of other business that we think is really important.

It is ironic that the more timesaving devices and strategies we use, the more rushed we feel. No wonder many people long for a simpler, slower, and more meaningful life. There are times when we all need to just stop, be quiet and still, and rest in the presence of the Lord. When we do, we often find more than rest. We find God changes us in wonderful ways.

Take time to commune with God on a deeper level and enjoy the blessing of His presence. There you will find joy and peace, rest and refreshment. He is there all the time, just waiting for you to slow down and to receive the blessing He has for you today.

THE NEXT PLATEAU

By Evelyn Christenson

God always changes me to lift me to a higher level. Sometimes God's changing takes me through hot fires, deep valleys, grief, or suffering; but after a while the "God of all grace" makes me perfect, established, strengthened, and settled (1 Peter 5:10 KJV). These unpleasant experiences have prepared me for the next and higher plateaus of my life.

After an extremely deep valley in our family, I recorded in my Bible my cry to God, "O Lord, when is after a while?" But it was exactly a year later that I added the note, "Now is God's after a while! Great joy again!" It had taken a year for God to do His changing in me and turn that difficult circumstance back to normalcy.

When the violent learning season is over, God settles me down—but not where I was before. As I'm changed, according to His will, He places me on the next plateau that He has prepared. There's always an open door and always power to go through it when I am changed into what He wants me to be.[11]

HEAVENLY FATHER,

Thank You for the transforming work of Your grace in my life that changes me into Your image. As I continue to seek Your face, I pray that You will take me from one degree of glory to the next, that You will perfect, establish, strengthen, and settle me so that my life will be fully pleasing to You.

AMEN

We all, with open face beholding as in a glass the glory of the Lord, are changed into the same image from glory to glory, even as by the Spirit of the Lord.
2 CORINTHIANS 5:18 KJV

PLANS AND GOALS

The human mind plans the way, but the LORD directs the steps.
PROVERBS 16:9 NRSV

When Sir Walter Scott was young, his goal was to become a soldier. An accident, however, left him slightly lame; so he had to abandon his plan. He turned his energies to reading old Scottish histories and romances and became a master novelist himself. His works included classics such as *Ivanhoe* and *The Talisman*. He developed his characters in such a way that the reader becomes caught up in the violent, dramatic changes in history. His death in 1832 marked the end of the romantic age in English literature. In Scott's case circumstances forced a would-be soldier into the life of a novelist.

GRACE FOR TODAY

GOD IS BIGGER THAN OUR CIRCUMSTANCES, AND THE PLANS THAT HE HAS FOR US ARE FAR GREATER THAN ANY SETBACKS WE MAY SUFFER.

But circumstances couldn't stop Gladys Ayleward. A small and dark-haired woman who had no education to speak of in a time when women were not allowed to preach or evangelize, Gladys felt God's call to China. She tried various mission boards; and they told her that unless she had a nursing or teaching degree, she could not go. Undeterred, Gladys listened to the Voice within and left for China. Several months later she arrived and began an evangelistic ministry to travelers and orphans deep in China that God blessed.

What made the difference? God called Gladys, and His plans for her were greater than any circumstances.

Perhaps at some point in your life your own plans and goals were changed. Disappointment may be understandable, but when we invite God into the situation, we can trust that He will guide our steps and bring us into the ultimate plan He has for our lives. And His plan will happen—no matter what!

COME HOME

[Jesus said of the prodigal son,] "While he was still a long distance away, his father saw him coming. Filled with love and compassion, he ran to his son, embraced him, and kissed him."
LUKE 15:20 NET

He had really messed up. He had taken money that he hadn't earned and used it for fleeting pleasures that poisoned his very soul. Now he was alone, lost, and destitute. How had he let things get this bad?

He was afraid to go home. He had left so cocky and self-assured, vowing never to return. How could he go crawling back, penniless and pitiful? With a stab of fear, he realized that they might not even take him back. But he had no choice. He would have to go home and face the family he had betrayed.

The road home was long, and it provided him with plenty of time to think. Before he saw the hills of home rise before him, he had decided that he would go to his family with no expectations. He would ask only to be a servant since he was no longer worthy to be called a son.

GRACE FOR TODAY

IT'S NEVER TOO LATE TO COME HOME TO THE GRACE OF GOD.

He was suddenly shaken from his dark thoughts by the sight of a man running toward him. He squinted his eyes against the sun to better see who it was. His heart leapt into his throat when he realized that the runner was his father!

Before he could decide how to react, his father was at his side. The words of rebuke he expected did not come. Instead, he was smothered with kisses and wrapped in a warm embrace.

Did you know that this story isn't about some far-off people in a faraway land? This story is about you. No matter how badly you have messed up, no matter how much you have disappointed God, when you turn and head home, He comes running. Let His grace smother you with kisses and wrap you in His embrace today. Your Father is waiting—searching the horizon for His beloved child.

LOVE POSITIVELY

Keep your heart with all diligence, for out of it spring the
issues of life.
PROVERBS 4:23 NKJV

Your heart is like a battery. It slowly drains or charges with each exchange you have with others. People you interact with each day—from the guy who cuts you off on the freeway to the teller at the bank to the bus driver who drops off your children—have a positive or negative influence on your life. Your response, in turn, affects their "battery" as well as your own.

When you pay someone a compliment, offer a word of thanks, or encourage someone, you show the character and nature of your heavenly Father. You allow God's grace to flow through you. You freely pour out His love into the earth, and it fills you back up so that you're ready to give out again.

God is your key source of influence and power. You have an opportunity to fully charge through knowledge and understanding of the Bible and time spent in His presence. God will always provide a positive charge for your life, and You can go to Him anytime you need it.

Protect your emotional battery from being drained. You can choose to deny access to negative influences. On the other hand, when you are filled with the love of God, you are positively charged. You can decide to either contribute to or take away from the supply of others. But when you're filled with God's love, you just can't help but overflow with His goodness. Choose daily to love positively.

GRACE FOR TODAY

GOD'S GRACE FREELY CHARGES US WITH HIS LOVE.

GOD'S CALL

As Jesus went on from there, He saw a man called
Matthew, sitting in the tax collector's booth; and He said to
him, "Follow Me!" And he got up and followed Him.
MATTHEW 9:9 NASB

Never was there a more unlikely candidate for the office of apostle than Matthew. In those days, people had no tax charts, so they were never quite sure what they owed. Because of this, some unscrupulous tax collectors became wealthy through extortion.

Maybe Matthew had known about Jesus and knew he needed to make a change but believed it was too late to leave his old lifestyle and start again. At any rate, when Jesus called him, Matthew left everything and followed Him without a moment's hesitation. This split-second decision changed Matthew's life forever.

GRACE FOR TODAY

GOD HAS THE WONDERFUL ABILITY TO NOT ONLY SEE OUR PRESENT CONDITION, BUT ALSO WHAT WE CAN BECOME THROUGH THE INNER WORKING OF HIS GRACE.

Answering the call of God often requires paying a price, and this was certainly true for Matthew. The disciples who were fishermen could always return to their nets if things didn't work out, but for Matthew to leave his post meant no turning back. He could never return to this lucrative business with a clear conscience—nor would the Roman government have allowed him to.

Matthew did take one thing with him though—his skill at writing and record keeping. Ultimately, he used this attention to detail to compose what is likely the most quoted of the four Gospels in the Bible.

Jesus has the wonderful ability to see not only the present condition of a person, but also what that person can become through the inner working of His power. Matthew's story is a shining example of how Jesus can use whatever gift a person brings to Him. Matthew gave up a comfortable job, but he discovered his life's purpose.

Two other Gospel writers, Mark and Luke, refer to him as Levi, but he called himself Matthew, meaning "gift of God." Your name may not be Matthew; but if you accept God's calling and use your talents for Him, you, too, can become a gift of God and know true fulfillment.

TAKE IT PERSONALLY

Jesus himself stood among them and said to them, "Peace
be with you."
LUKE 24:36 NIV

GRACE FOR TODAY

JESUS' DEATH AND
RESURRECTION
DEMONSTRATE THAT
GOD'S LOVE FOR YOU,
THOUGH
INCOMPREHENSIBLE,
IS ENDURING AND
COMPLETELY
SELFLESS.

Mel Gibson's movie *The Passion of the Christ* has brought the Easter story to the forefront of the world's consciousness. It evoked a kaleidoscope of reactions. People took the movie very personally.

This isn't surprising because Jesus' crucifixion and resurrection is His personal sacrifice for all of us. Peter Marshall wisely commented, "The stone was rolled away from the door, not to permit Christ to come out but to enable the disciples to go in."

That morning of discovery is just as relevant today as it was thousands of years ago. Easter is a time for all of us to revisit the tomb and relive that moment in our hearts.

Sometimes we forget that surprise as we celebrate Easter each year in traditional fashion. Have we lost the wonder and complete joy that the women felt upon encountering the angel and the empty tomb? "So the women hurried away from the tomb, afraid yet filled with joy, and ran to tell his disciples" (Matthew 28:8 NIV).

But the story doesn't end there. "Suddenly Jesus met them. 'Greetings,' he said. They came to him, clasped his feet and worshiped him" (Matthew 28:9 Niv). What a beautiful, enduring image, which can prompt us to recover our own passion and love for the risen Christ! Seeing Jesus alive can be a personal event that gives us a glimpse of eternity. We can discover for ourselves that the depth of God's love is incomprehensible, enduring, and completely selfless. Jesus endured all to give us a love we did not deserve, but one that is given freely. And this same Jesus will be waiting at the end of time to greet each of us by name in a very personal and loving way. How will we greet Him? Think about that coming encounter this surprising and wonderful Easter.

SALVATION BY GRACE THROUGH FAITH

By Gene Getz

Philip P. Bliss, a well-known song-writer, understood the truth that we are saved by grace through faith. He wrote a poem and then set the words to music.

Free from the law – O happy condition!

Jesus hath bled, and there is remission;

Cursed by the law and bruised by the fall,

Grace hath redeemed us once for all.

Children of God – O glorious calling!

Surely His grace will keep us from falling;

Passing from death to life at His call,

Blessed salvation – once for all.

Once for all – O sinner receive it!

Once for all – O brother believe it!

Cling to the cross, the burden will fall –

Christ has redeemed us once for all![12]

HEAVENLY FATHER:

Thank You for the gift of grace You've poured out on my life. I reach out in faith, believing that it will cover all my failings, all my imperfections, all my sin, and make me worthy to abide in Your presence.

AMEN

Since we have been justified through faith, we have peace with God through our Lord Jesus Christ, through whom we have gained access by faith into this grace in which we now stand. And we rejoice in the hope of the glory of God.
ROMANS 5:1-2 NIV

OUT OF THE PIT

I waited patiently for the Lord; he turned to me and heard my cry. He lifted me out of the slimy pit, out of the mud and mire; he set my feet on a rock and gave me a firm place to stand.
PSALM 40:1-2 NIV

Katie looked up from her dinner preparations with a start. She was suddenly aware that it was too quiet. As a mother, Katie felt instinctively that quiet meant trouble. And the chill creeping into her heart wasn't signaling mischief, but danger.

GRACE FOR TODAY

JUST WHEN WE NEED HIM THE MOST, GOD REACHES DOWN TO RESCUE US.

She quickly headed outside. Nothing seemed out of place, but a small voice inside her mother's heart told Katie to continue investigating.

She jogged across the gravel drive and looked into the barnyard and pasture. The gate to the barnyard was open, and around the corner of the barn she could see the family's dogs huddled around something. Katie broke into a run, suddenly realizing where the dogs were—at the manure pit.

As she rounded the corner, her heart leapt—her four-year-old son, Sam, was stuck chest-deep in the full pit. She climbed frantically down to the edge and reached into the hole. Sam's slime-covered hand grasped for her as he cried, "Mom," noiselessly. He'd lost his voice calling for help. Katie pulled him up and into her arms, holding him tightly to her chest as she ran back to the house.

Katie would not stop shaking inside for a week, but Sam was soon happily washing off in a warm tub, the trauma all but forgotten. He knew he was safe.

Sometimes we find ourselves stuck in what feels like a slimy pit. Then, just when we need Him the most, our heavenly Father reaches down to us. He lifts us up and holds us close with no thought for the muck that covers us. His embrace cleanses us and we realize we are safe. Such is the wonderful grace of God. Call to Him and wait—and He will lift you up.

EXPAND YOUR VIEW

We are His workmanship, created in Christ Jesus for good
works, which God prepared beforehand that we should
walk in them.
EPHESIANS 2:10 NKJV

Sometimes it takes a challenge to push us beyond what we think we can do. We all have our carefully crafted lists of things we are good at. Yet there are other things we think are beyond our capability. Sometimes the problem is just a lack of knowledge.

Renowned humanitarians Jimmy and Rosalyn Carter are volunteers for Habitat for Humanity. Founder and President Millard Fuller's concept for the organization is simple—build homes for people who don't have them. But don't let that simple statement mislead you. The ideals behind this organization are enormous and global: "We must reflect Christ's love in our own lives by loving and caring for one another. Our love must not be words only—it must be true love, which shows itself in action."

Maybe you don't think you are handy with a hammer. Well, maybe you need to think again. Female crews are being recruited and trained to build homes for other families too. These crews have built hundreds of homes across the United States—women helping women.

The point is not whether you can build a house, but whether you have the courage to try something new and let God meet you there. Taking on challenges that seem foreign can be intimidating, but we can embrace them and perhaps learn something surprising and new about ourselves and how God works

GRACE FOR TODAY

GOD'S GRACE WILL ENABLE AND EQUIP YOU TO DO THINGS YOU HAVE THOUGHT IMPOSSIBLE.

through us. By pushing our present abilities, we can explore a whole new world of opportunities and a whole new way of serving God and our communities.

Allow the spirit of exploration and compassion to flow through you, and set an example for other women. If you show them that you have the courage to try something challenging, it will inspire them to venture in ways to which God is calling them.

HE KNOWS YOU BY NAME

[The Lord says,] "I have written your name on my hand."
ISAIAH 49:16 NLT

There's one thing about kids that hasn't changed much since we were in grade school: relationships. Kids still look to their peers for acceptance and affirmation. They still exchange notes in classrooms, expressing their feelings in friendships. Remember the notes you'd pass to say how you felt about someone? They often read something like this: "I like you. Do you like me? Circle your answer: 1) Yes; 2) Maybe; 3) No."

GRACE FOR TODAY

GOD'S WORD IS A LOVE LETTER AND TANGIBLE REVELATION OF HIS LOVE FOR YOU.

Of course it sounds childish today, but back then, the answers on those notes could send us crashing to the ground emotionally or lift us up to the clouds. Another popular schoolroom practice was to write the name of your boyfriend in the palm of your hand, like a closely guarded secret you might show only to a close friend.

Knowing someone cares is a very relevant need in a young child's life. Kids relate to visible affirmations, like a smiley face on their homework or a shiny star for perfect attendance. As adults, we still seek acceptance from our peers; but more importantly, as God's children, we all need the affirmation that He loves us. We long to know if He cares about our hopes, our doubts, our dreams, our fears, our joys, and our needs.

Are there days when you wish you could write God a note and get a tangible reply like one you received from a childhood friend? God longs to assure you that He knows you personally and cares about the deepest concerns of your heart.

God's Word is full of love notes to you. He's made sure that you will never question or misunderstand His love. He has no multiple-choice answers to your questions. His answer is always yes to the question of His love for you. He whispers your name, and it is forever engraved upon the palm of His hand.

WITH APPRECIATION

So speak encouraging words to one another . . .
Overwhelm them with appreciation and love!
1 THESSALONIANS 5:11,13 MSG

It is very likely that when you were a child you were taught to say "Thank you" when someone paid you a compliment or gave you a gift. Our busy lifestyles today offer little time to demonstrate our admiration, gratitude, and thankfulness as often as perhaps we want to.

Maybe that is why when someone does offer little words of encouragement, approval or acceptance, we are so captivated by their thoughtful gifts to us—someone buys your lunch, someone returns your lost sunglasses, another compliments you on the colors of your clothing. It can be a smile, a wave, or a simple little e-card that lets you know you were in their thoughts today. These freely given gifts are expressions of God's grace.

GRACE FOR TODAY

FILLING UP WITH APPRECIATION FOR GOD AND HIS GOODNESS AND GRACE WILL SPILL OUT INTO THE LIVES OF OTHERS.

Perhaps you really have to go the extra mile to make room to offer others that moment of appreciation. If it's difficult for you, start with someone easy to go to—your heavenly Father. It can be as simple as telling Him how much you enjoyed the sunrise this morning or the rainfall that allowed you to sleep late. As you share your gratefulness with Him, your heart will fill with His goodness and joy that comes from spending time with Him.

Then it will be easy for you to add a drop of appreciation into the lives of those around you. Offer a smile or cheerful hello. It can become contagious. You might be surprised who catches a taste of God's goodness and grace from you.

THE GRACE OF TRUE FRIENDS

Friends come and friends go, but a true friend sticks by
you like family.
PROVERBS 16:24 MSG

True friends are one of the most wonderful ways that God shows us His grace and love. Take a moment to think about some of your happiest or most meaningful memories. Most of them include friends! The gift of friendship makes our journey through this life a bit lighter — and a lot more joyful! There are so many ways in which God's grace can be seen through our friends.

When you can tell a friend anything, without fear, knowing he or she will keep your secrets and pray for your struggles, you see a glimpse of the God who listens and forgives completely. When a friend reassures you and renews your hope in the midst of anxiety, you experience God's love that casts out all fear.

When you are stressed out and overwhelmed, true friends not only listen and convey sympathy but they jump in and reduce the workload with a helping hand. And as you work side-by-side, you sense the grace of God's divine help.

Little notes, cards, phone calls, and e-mails seem to always show up when you need them most—a bad day becomes better when you know your friend is thinking of you. God wants you to remember that those messages mean that He is thinking of you too.

In emergencies large or small, friends are quick to drop everything to be by your side. They are the Lord's way of reminding you that He never leaves you and will see you through anything.

When we are reunited after time and distance has separated us from our friends, there is no gap, no awkwardness. There is only the joy of seeing that wonderful, smiling face again. Looking into the eyes of our friends is a lovely foretaste of the day that we will look into the eyes of our very Best Friend- knowing that we have all eternity to enjoy our friendship together.

DEATH-LIFE

By Warren W. Wiersbe

The Gospel gives life to those who believe, because of the work of Jesus Christ on the cross.

Paul was not suggesting that the Law was a mistake or that its ministry was unimportant. Far from it! Paul knew that the lost sinner must be slain by the Law and left helplessly condemned before he can be saved by God's grace. John the Baptist came with a message of judgment, preparing the way for Jesus and His message of saving grace.

Preachers who major on rules and regulations keep their congregations under a dark cloud of guilt, and this kills their joy, power, and effective witness for Christ. Christians who are constantly measuring each other, comparing "results," and competing with each other, soon discover that they are depending on the flesh and not the power of the Spirit. There never was a standard that could transform a person's life, and that includes the Ten Commandments. Only the grace of God, ministered by the Spirit of God, can transform lost sinners into living epistles that glorify Jesus Christ.

Paul's doctrine of the New Covenant was not something that he invented for the occasion. As a profound student of the Scriptures, Paul certainly had read Jeremiah 31:27-34, as well as Ezekiel 11:14-21. In the New Testament, Hebrews 8-10 is the key passage to study. The Old Covenant law, with its emphasis on external obedience, was preparation for the New Covenant message of grace and the emphasis on internal transformation of the heart.[13]

PRECIOUS FATHER:

I was helpless to save myself, but You reached beyond my unworthiness and made me worthy by Your grace. If You had not, I would have been lost forever, for I could never have kept the rules perfectly. I thank You for saving me by Your grace.

AMEN

[God] has made us competent as ministers of a new covenant—not of the letter but of the Spirit; for the letter kills, but the Spirit gives life.
2 CORINTHIANS 3:6 NIV

CHOW MUCH IS ENOUGH?

Remind each other of God's goodness and be thankful.
EPHESIANS 5:4 TLB

Consumerism is the grease that makes the industrial world go round, but it can also be the spiritual friction that slows us from experiencing contentment and instead creates an inner poverty. Our culture continually stimulates us to want and buy more. An average of seventeen minutes out of every hour of television is dedicated to advertising. We are being conditioned to want more. And we do!

GRACE FOR TODAY

GOD'S GRACE PROVIDES EVERYTHING WE NEED AND INSPIRES A LIFE OF THANKFULNESS AND CONTENTMENT.

We can blame society, materialism, or the idolization of the rich and famous. We can theorize that discontentment is a symptom of our modern age. But discontentment isn't a new condition. Remember the complaining Israelites wandering the wilderness with Moses? They were disgruntled because they forgot what God had rescued them from—a life of slavery. And they didn't trust Him to provide a prosperous future for them, in His good time. "The people spoke against God and against Moses, 'Why have you brought us up out of Egypt to die in the wilderness? For there is no food and no water, and we detest this miserable food'" (Numbers 21:5 NRSV). Does their attitude ring a bell?

The roots of discontentment are many, but perhaps ingratitude is the main source, despite our unrivaled prosperity. Are you thankful? Sam Lefkowitz said, "When asked if my cup is half-full or half-empty my response is that I am thankful to have a cup."

Being content is a state of mind, one the apostle Paul said that he learned to achieve. We can learn this too. It starts with a determined effort to focus on God's faithful provision. The result is freedom to enjoy and appreciate your present life, confident that God will take care of the future. It gives you permission to say that life is good now, just as it is. It compels you to say time and time again, "Thank You, God."

AMBASSADOR OF GRACE

God . . . reconciled us to himself through Christ and gave us the
ministry of reconciliation . . . We are therefore Christ's
ambassadors, as though God were making his appeal through
us.
2 CORINTHIANS 5:18,20 NIV

Did you know that as a believer, you have the special designation of "Ambassador for Christ"? Just as the State Department sends U.S. ambassadors all over the world to represent America, so Jesus sends us to the ends of the earth on a mission of grace.

The official definition of an ambassador is "an official of the highest rank, sent by one country as a long-term representative to another." As Christians, we are of "highest rank," being daughters and sons of the King of Kings. We are of another country: the Kingdom of Heaven. We are in this world, not as citizens of it, but as representatives to it. Our mission is long-term—it lasts a lifetime.

GRACE FOR TODAY

YOU HAVE THE GREAT
RESPONSIBILITY AND
PRIVILEGE OF BEING
AN AMBASSADOR OF
GRACE.

The designation as ambassadors of God's grace certainly means great responsibility. We are responsible to be loyal, above all, to our Sovereign, Jesus. We have the "ministry of reconciliation"—the obligation to share the love of God and His message of salvation. And we are called to serve each other and those who remain in bondage to the rules of this world.

But our status as Heaven's emissaries also brings great privilege. We are under the love, guidance, and protection of our great King. We are not bound by the rules of this world but live in the freedom of the citizens of Heaven. And one day, when our tour of duty is complete, we will be welcomed home with open arms by the Prince of the universe.

So each day, remember that you have a high and holy calling. Seek the guidance of your King and live with the joy of knowing that your citizenship in Heaven is secure. You are an ambassador of the grace that overflows from the Lord Jesus to you, His beloved representative.

IS FEAR YOUR MASTER?

[The Lord says,] "Don't worry, because I am with you. Don't be afraid, because I am your God. I will make you strong and will help you; I will support you with my right hand that saves you."
ISAIAH 41:10 NCV

GRACE FOR TODAY

GOD'S GRACE EMPOWERS IMPERFECT, FLAWED PEOPLE TO ACCOMPLISH HIS PERFECT WILL IN THE EARTH.

Every summer, if you visit a swimming pool, you're likely to see a child climb the many steps to the high dive and timidly place one foot in front of the other until he or she is at the edge of the diving board. The child looks over, panics, and then inches his or her way backward. What keeps this child from plunging into the water below? Fear.

Sometimes we teeter on the edge of a high dive, a spiritual one. God has a purpose for each of us to fulfill. Even though we know God has a job for us, we fear taking that first step. What if we fail?

In Matthew 25, we read a parable that Jesus told of a man going on a journey. He entrusted his property to his servants. The man who received five talents gained five. The one with two doubled them to four talents. But the man with one talent dug a hole and hid the master's money. When the master returned, he praised the first two servants. But the third man received harsh punishment because he didn't do as his master wished. And why didn't he? Fear.

Perhaps fear is keeping you from ministering in some way. Maybe perfectionism is holding you back. It helps to remember only One is perfect, and He uses plain, ordinary, flawed people. As our Master, God loves us and empowers us with His grace to do His work on Earth. We can trust Him to help us—in spite of our inadequacies.

Take that step of faith. Let's make it our quest to hear God say to us at the end of life's journey, "Well done, thou good and faithful servant."

BEARING THE FRUIT OF PATIENCE

Let patience have its perfect work, that you may be perfect
and complete, lacking nothing.
JAMES 1:4 NKJV

We live in a society based on demanding and getting what we want immediately. We thrive on the fast track of convenience. The result? The number of road-rage incidents has tripled in the past two years. People are all in a hurry to get somewhere without slowing down long enough to exercise common driving courtesies.

Modern lifestyles have left little room for patience. Yet there are some things in life and in our walk with God that simply can't be rushed. Someone once said, "Do not sacrifice the permanent on the altar of the immediate." When we try to rush ahead of God and His timing, we settle for a fast-food meal of short-term satisfaction rather than the nutritious and slow-cooked meal He'd like to serve us. There is such a thing as spiritual malnutrition. In time, it could do permanent damage to our souls.

GRACE FOR TODAY

THE GRACE OF GOD-GIVEN PATIENCE WILL ALLOW HIS PLAN FOR YOUR LIFE TO UNFOLD IN HIS PERFECT TIMING.

It's not without example and reason that God's Word lists patience as one of the fruits of the Spirit. In a self-serving world, we could take a refresher course in the art of patience and long-suffering. We want instant answers, even from God. Yet we see by example that God's chosen vessels have always gone through a process of testing and timing. Joseph endured rejection from his own family and was left for dead. There were no instant answers for him. Trusting God was all he had left. In time, God raised him up, honored him, and even gave him the compassion to help the very family who had abandoned and betrayed him.

God has a permanent plan for your life—and He will go to great lengths to make sure you don't sacrifice that plan on the altar of immediate solutions. Trust God's timing as He works patience in your heart.

THE ACTS OF PRAYER

Do not worry about anything, but pray and ask God for
everything you need, always giving thanks.
PHILIPPIANS 4:6 NCV

GRACE FOR TODAY

NOTHING IS
IMPOSSIBLE FOR GOD
. . . WHAT HE DID IN
THE OLD TESTAMENT
AND IN THE NEW
TESTAMENT, HE STILL
DOES TODAY. GOD
STILL ANSWERS
PRAYER
DRAMATICALLY AND
MIRACULOUSLY.

BON RUSSELL

Do you have a favorite place to pray? Some people have what they call a prayer closet that they retreat to. The important thing is not where we pray but that we find a place where we can be alone with God without distraction. There is no better way to get to know Him.

What should we pray about? The Bible instructs us to pray for those in authority over us. (See 1 Timothy 2:2.)

We can pray for our families and friends as well as the unsaved. We can—and should—even pray for our enemies and those who persecute us.

The acronym ACTS is a good guide regarding the different aspects of prayer. A stands for adoration. In this, we show our reverence and love for God as we honor and worship Him. C is for confession—our opportunity to confess our sins to Him and to receive forgiveness. T represents thanksgiving. We have so much to be thankful for, including the many answers to prayer He has given us as well as the other blessings He has bestowed. S is for supplication, making our requests known to God.

One thing to keep in mind is that it is important to always ask according to God's will, for it is then that He hears us and grants the petitions we ask of Him. (See 1 John 5:14.) His will is His Word, and we can stand upon the promises He has made regarding our situation. All of His promises are "'yes' in Christ" (2 Corinthians 1:20).

In short, prayer is simply conversation with God. Spend some time talking to Him today, and be sure to listen too. He wants to share His heart with you.

CHOICES

By Evelyn Christenson

People respond in various ways to God's answers to their prayers. Many different responses to prayer are recorded in the New Testament. There is the choice of witnessing. Anna prayed for many years to see the Messiah, and when God answered her prayers at Baby Jesus' circumcision, she went out and told everyone she had seen the Messiah. But Simeon's response was quite different. After praying the same prayer for a similar period, he, too, saw the Messiah. His response? "Now I am ready to die."

There is a reaction of disbelief. As the early Christians prayed for Peter's release from prison, they could not believe that God had answered their prayers, thinking it was his ghost knocking at the gate. There is the response of obedience. Peter's prayers on the rooftop were answered by God in a vision he did not understand at the time. But even so, when God did explain it, Peter obeyed immediately and brought the Gospel to the Gentiles.

We have to make a choice. Paul and Silas prayed and sang in the prison, and God answered by sending an earthquake that opened all the doors and broke the prisoners' chains.

But Paul chose to forgo immediate freedom in order to win the jailer to Christ. Perhaps one of the most difficult responses to God's answer to prayer was Paul's response of acceptance. Paul prayed three times for his thorn in the flesh to be removed, but accepted God's answer—no—relying at last on God's strength.

The Bible reveals myriads of different responses to God when He answered prayer—some good, some bad, some rebellious, some submissive, some joyous, some thankful, some angry. Our responses to God's answers to our prayers can be many and varied also. The decision is up to us.[14]

GOD,

I want to always respond to You with an eager and willing heart. When I find that difficult, extend Your grace to help me obey joyfully.

AMEN

If you are willing and obedient, you shall eat the good of the land.
ISAIAH 1:19 NRSV

TREASURE HUNT

[God] raised us up with him and seated us with him in the
heavenly places in Christ Jesus, so that in the ages to come he
might show the immeasurable riches of his grace in kindness
toward us in Christ Jesus.
EPHESIANS 2:6-7 NRSV

From *Treasure Island's* pirate gold to Indiana Jones' priceless artifacts, mysterious stories of hidden treasure have fascinated us for ages. We've probably all daydreamed about unexpectedly coming across something incredibly valuable—riches that have been lost and forgotten, just waiting for us to find them.

Perhaps this longing to seek out hidden riches is a God-given trait, for the Bible speaks often of ways we can find secret treasures. But the valuables that God's Word offers are more priceless than the finest diamonds, for these are the treasures of an otherworldly kingdom— treasures that will last for eternity!

The Bible says that through Jesus we can receive the "riches of God's grace"! These riches are described as "incomparable," "unsearchable," and a great mystery that has been revealed through Christ. Jesus, "though he was rich, yet for your sakes he became poor, so that you through his poverty might become rich" (2 Corinthians 8:9 NIV).

There are riches—eternal and beyond our wildest imagination in beauty and value—and this bounty is for us! When we accept the free gift of salvation through Jesus, we are handed the map that leads us to the treasures of the kingdom. Jesus gave up all these unfathomable riches, just so we could have access to them! What an incredible story of glorious treasure this is, a story worth sharing!

GRACE FOR TODAY

THE VALUABLES THAT GOD OFFERS ARE MORE PRICELESS
THAN THE FINEST DIAMONDS, FOR THESE ARE THE
TREASURES OF AN OTHERWORLDLY KINGDOM— TREASURES
THAT WILL LAST FOR ETERNITY!

IT'S ALL RELATIONAL

All this comes from the God who settled the relationship between us and him, and then called us to settle our relationships with each other.
2 CORINTHIANS 5:18 MSG

Most people would likely agree that their biggest problem in life is other people. Self-help books, talk shows, and reality TV all focus heavily on how we interact with each other. However, God didn't mean for relationships to be difficult.

When a teacher asked Jesus, "What is the most important commandment?" Jesus replied, "The first of all the commandments is you shall love the Lord your God with all your heart, with all your soul, with all your mind, and with all your strength. And the second is like it. You shall love your neighbor as yourself." (See Matthew 22:37-39.) This answer gives us a clear foundation upon which to build successful relationships.

GRACE FOR TODAY

GOD'S GRACE GIVES US THE ABILITY TO SEE AND LOVE OTHERS THE WAY HE SEES AND LOVES US.

First, we must love God and experience an ongoing exchange with Him. The second part—loving others like you love yourself—is where many of us have trouble. We live in an "all about me and what I want" society. In order to honor Jesus' command, we must go against the flow and embrace God's grace—His ability in us to love others the way He loves us.

It takes a commitment and a daily renewal to see others the way God does. If we emphasize the good things in the lives of those we share this world with, then we can more easily minimize the little things they do that annoy us. If we can enjoy our differences and celebrate those things in each of us that make us unique and valuable, then we can experience the love that Jesus said we should have for one another.

TOGETHER

In Christ we who are many form one body, and each
member belongs to all the others.
ROMANS 12:5 NIV

Who were the Inklings? A group of friends who met together to share and talk about their passions. Their passions just happened to make them household names—J.R.R. Tolkien, C.S. Lewis, Charles Williams, and others. As you might have guessed, their passion was Christian theology and the study of language, literature, and creative writing. Members like C.S. Lewis became Christian writers of great wisdom and global influence. But beyond that, their individual faith sustained and influenced each on his own personal journey with God. That faith also sustained a fellowship of friends who liked and supported each other.

GRACE FOR TODAY

GOD DESIGNED US TO ENJOY INTIMATE FELLOWSHIP WITH LIKE-MINDED BELIEVERS.

Fellowship: That's a pretty important word for all of us. The apostle Paul tells us to be devoted to one another in brotherly love. Devoted has some pretty interesting words related to it: loyal, dedicated, dutiful, faithful, constant, and committed. If we are to have devoted fellowship with others, that certainly sounds intimate and personal-like family. "See what love the Father has given us, that we should be called children of God; and that is what we are" (1 John 3:1 NRSV).

That's right, we're a family. Which doesn't mean that you have to spill your life out to every Christian you meet, but like the Inklings, you can commit to a small group of people whom you relate to. Like any relationship, close fellowship doesn't just spring out of thin air; it takes time to develop. You give of your time to listen and care for other people, and in return they offer their time to listen and care about you. Rick Warren in his book *The Purpose-Driven Life* reminds us that "a church family moves you out of self-centered isolation." That's right. We weren't designed to be an island unto ourselves. But, then, who really wants to be?

EVER INTERCEDING

Christ Jesus . . . is at the right hand of God and is also
interceding for us.
ROMANS 8:34 NIV

It's been said that dynamite comes in small packages, and sometimes that package is five little words: "I'll be praying for you!" You know what impact those words have if you've ever needed the prayers of a friend. On the giving end, we are compelled by our concern to speak words of intercession that will dynamite the debris Satan spills across the lives of our friends. Prayers of intercession defeat the enemy's tactics and schemes. Prayer lights the fuse that destroys discouragement, doubt, and despair.

Has there ever been a time in your life when you felt too weak to pray, only to find out that during that time a friend was praying for you? God places special people in our lives to intercede on our behalf. That's why when we feel that gentle nudging from the Holy Spirit to pray for someone, we need to stop and stand in the gap of their defenses for them as the Lord directs. The power of prayer pulls down fortresses raised by Satan in our lives.

GRACE FOR TODAY

GOD HAS GIVEN YOU ACCESS TO HIS THRONE OF GRACE THROUGH PRAYER.

After Jesus died on the cross, the veil was ripped in the temple where the priests were once the only ones allowed in the Holy of Holies. Hebrews 4:16 assures us that we are now able to come boldly before the throne of grace in our times of need. We are told that when we cry out to God, Jesus himself—sitting beside the Father—intercedes for us.

When you feel too weak to pray for yourself or to ask for prayer, remember that Jesus is as close as the mention of His name, ever interceding and petitioning the Father on your behalf.

95

BECOMING A BEAUTY

Let not yours be the [merely] external adorning with [elaborate]
interweaving and knotting of the hair, the wearing of jewelry, or changes
of clothes; but let it be the inward adorning and beauty of the hidden
person of the heart, with the incorruptible and unfading charm of a
gentle and peaceful spirit, which . . . is very precious in the sight of God.
1 PETER 3:3-4 AMP

GRACE FOR TODAY

THE RESTORING
TOUCH OF OUR
SAVIOR BEGINS AN
INCREDIBLE
TRANSFORMATION
THAT LEADS TO INNER
BEAUTY.

Women around the world spend millions — that's right, millions — of dollars a year trying to be beautiful. You know this because you probably feel like you spend at least a million all by yourself! With all the makeup, clothes, hair treatments, and weight-loss programs available today, you'd think we would all feel like beauty queens — and look like them too. Yet that's not always the case. Even if we do look great and enjoy compliments everywhere we go, we can feel ugly inside. Why?

Deep down in our hearts, we sense that we were made to be truly beautiful, that God created us for loveliness. But all the age-defying skin creams in the world can't touch our souls. Only the grace of Jesus can.

When we shift our focus from making ourselves beautiful on the outside to opening our hearts to the restoring touch of our Savior, an incredible transformation will commence. He will begin by healing our wounds and bringing wholeness to our hearts. He'll do a deep cleansing of our spirits — removing any sin, sorrow, or pain that hides our true beauty. And He will touch us with His glory, allowing us to shine with the light of Heaven. Nothing could be lovelier.

So don't give up on becoming beautiful. God made you with a longing to be captivating. Just remember to start your beauty program with your heart. Let the Creator of beauty do His work of grace there — you'll be amazed at the results.

When God Answers...
Have a Thankful Heart

By Evelyn Christenson

What happens when God answers? The ultimate, final response on our part should be to thank Him. No matter how God has answered our prayer, the one thing He expects from us is thankfulness. People tend to insert their thanksgiving at different places in the prayer process. Some never bother to thank God no matter how great and wonderful the answers He sends. Most people, but not all, are thankful when God answers the way they requested and has given them what they wanted. Then, some Christians have matured enough spiritually to thank Him in spite of how He has answered, trusting His divine wisdom.

But the Bible has an even greater requirement as to where the thanksgiving belongs in the whole prayer process. Philippians 4:6, surprisingly, reads, "Be anxious for nothing, but in everything by prayer and *supplication with thanksgiving* let your requests be made known to God" (NASB, emphasis mine).

It is rare indeed to find those who actually put their thanksgiving right in with the request. Few are able to be thankful while they are asking, because they are concentrating on the way they want God to answer. And the deeper the personal need or hurt, the more difficult it becomes to be thankful while begging God to intervene. Our minds usually are totally consumed by the problem, not with thanksgiving, during our wrestling and striving in prayer. It takes deep maturity indeed to be able to thank God before He answers, to be able to include the thanks with the request![15]

HEAVENLY FATHER,

I have so much to be thankful for. Forgive me for the times I've failed to thank You or have taken Your answers to prayer for granted. You know what I have needs of today, and because I trust in Your wisdom and goodness, I thank You in advance for Your answer.

AMEN

I will give thanks to the LORD because of his righteousness and will sing praise to the name of the LORD Most High.
PSALM 7:17 NIV

THE SACRIFICE

Live a life of love, just as Christ loved us and gave himself
up for us as a fragrant offering and sacrifice to God.
EPHESIANS 5:2 NIV

In the movie *Saving Private Ryan*, the military discovered that Private Ryan's mother had already lost three of her four sons during World War II. Captain John Miller was ordered to go behind enemy lines to find Private Ryan and bring him home. The feat was accomplished but with the loss of many lives, including the captain's own.

GRACE FOR TODAY

JESUS PAID THE ULTIMATE SACRIFICE FOR US AND HAS MADE SALVATION AVAILABLE AS A FREE GIFT WE NEVER HAVE TO EARN—THAT'S GRACE!

In the closing scene, many years later, Ryan took his entire family to France where Captain Miller had been buried. Standing over his mentor's grave, Ryan said, "I tried to live my life the best I could. I hope that in your eyes I've earned what all of you sacrificed for me."

Christ paid the ultimate sacrifice for us by dying on the cross. He doesn't ask us to earn our way as Private Ryan, tried to do for Captain Miller. God's grace and our salvation are free gifts. However, if we confess our sins and acknowledge Jesus as our personal Savior, like Private Ryan we will find we have become persons who want to live our lives in a manner worthy of that great sacrifice. God's grace brings about that change. He is better than a mentor who trains us. He brings about changes inside us that we could never induce by Bible reading or eloquent prayers.

In addition, God's grace makes it possible for us go beyond just the desire to be good and to actually live in loving ways that honor Him—and all for free.

I WANT TO BREAK FREE

[Jesus said,] "If the Son sets you free, you will be free
indeed."
JOHN 8:36 NIV

A recent commercial features a song that declares, "I want to break free—oh, how I want to be free." In the context of the commercial, they are talking about the freedom from carbohydrates in your soft drink. But the ad works well because the words and passion of the song catch your attention. We all want to break free.

GRACE FOR TODAY

JESUS CAME TO
BRING US TRUE
FREEDOM.

The images that accompany the song also touch on something deeper than just a "low-carb" lifestyle. The commercial features people dancing, riding tricycles through a maze of office cubicles, and playing with a hula hoop in the middle of a store. These people are showing pure joy—the joy of being free.

Unfortunately, though, soda isn't going to satisfy the longing to break free—free from the quiet desperation of everyday struggles, family tensions, addictions, and any number of other things that restrict us. Life can wrap us in some very heavy chains, and it takes a lot more than the right soft drink to break the bonds.

The good news is that there is hope for true freedom! Jesus came from His heavenly home to a world in bondage for just that reason. He said that He had come to proclaim freedom for the captives and release from darkness for the prisoners.

Do you want to break free? Take your chains to the foot of the cross. Ask, and the grace of the God of freedom will release the chains that bind you. Then you, too, can dance and sing for joy—the joy of being truly free!

INSPIRATION

Now there are varieties of gifts, but the same Spirit . . . To each is given the manifestation of the Spirit for the common good.
1 CORINTHIANS 12:4,7 NRSV

God's people are diverse. He endows us with varying talents and inspires us to do different things. Many are inspired to use their talents in a very public way as is true for painter and entrepreneur Thomas Kinkade. Some estimate that one in every twenty homes in America has some form of Kinkade's artwork in it. Although his critics may be harsh, he paints for an audience that adores his work. He is very open about the fact that God is his inspiration.

GRACE FOR TODAY

GOD NOT ONLY BESTOWS GIFTS AND TALENTS UPON US, HE ALSO PROVIDES THE INSPIRATION AND OPPORTUNITIES TO USE THEM FOR HIS GLORY AND FOR THE GOOD OF OTHERS.

Artists like Kinkade remind us that we all have a responsibility to share the talents that God has given us. That means putting aside our own agenda regarding our abilities and placing those gifts at God's feet. This may be a new concept for some, but remember, God is the one who gave you your talents; and He has a plan for how they can be fully utilized. He's certainly not going to waste them.

It comes down to a matter of trust. Vernon Patterson wrote, "There are always uncertainties ahead, but there is always one certainty—God's will is good." His plan to use the talents He has given you is a good one, one that will be fulfilling for you and a blessing for others.

Each day we use our gifts, whether it's in the arts, for the church, or in our workplace, we should ask God to give us inspiration and to direct and expand our opportunities. It is tempting to take credit for the fruit of our talents, but a close walk with God will keep us balanced and humble. Our gifts are simply a product of His grace, and our gift back to Him is to use those talents for His glory.

GIANT-CONQUERING COURAGE

[The Lord said,] "Have I not commanded you? Be strong
and of good courage; do not be afraid, nor be dismayed,
for the LORD your God is with you wherever you go."
JOSHUA 1:9 NKJV

In life's daily battlefields, it takes courage to begin each day with a smile on your face and a song in your heart. It takes courage to share your love, your home, your creativity, and your faith. It takes courage to face crisis, endure hardship, and keep going when you feel like giving up. But courage steps beyond the roadblocks and obstacles of life and dares to believe in victory.

When your cause is greater than your fear, courage prevails! Goliath laughed at David when he saw the young lad who had come to take him down. He underestimated David's courage. He forgot to factor in David's faith in God. He towered above little David, but he fell at the teenager's feet because David was a man after God's own heart and trusted that God would help him.

When God is on our side, all things are possible. When our faith connects with courage, the giants in our lives are no threat. God's Word assures, "I can do all things through Christ who strengthens me" (Philippians 4:13 NKJV).

No matter what giants you may be facing in your life, take courage. You don't have to be Wonder Woman in order to win your battles. When you're a child of God, life's battlefields are never walked alone. God has given you courage to fight on the front lines and the assurance that Jesus, the real hero of every battle, is walking beside you every step of the way, making sure you will be victorious.

GRACE FOR TODAY

GOD GIVES YOU THE COURAGE TO FACE EVERY GIANT IN
YOUR LIFE WITHOUT FEAR.

BELIEVE THE UNBELIEVABLE

Faith is the substance of things hoped for, the evidence of
things not seen.
HEBREWS 11:1 NKJV

When you were a child, you most likely experienced a desire for the invisible and unimaginable. You hoped against hope for the unbelievable. That is because you were born with creativity and imagination. The desire for more than what you see is an element of faith. When you received Jesus as your Lord and Savior, the unimaginable became possible. God had power to make it happen.

Abraham, in spite of his old age, hoped against hope. He believed that God would keep His promise to give him a son—and God did! The Israelites expected a deliverer, and Moses was born. He led them out of captivity, and they walked across the Red Sea on dry ground. Generation after generation dreamed of the Messiah, and Jesus came to Earth to set all men free eternally.

GRACE FOR TODAY

GOD GIVES YOU FAITH MIXED WITH HOPE—AN EARNEST EXPECTATION, WHICH DELIVERS THE TRUTH OF GOD'S WORD AND MAKES IT A REALITY IN YOUR LIFE.

God wants our passion for the supernatural part of Him that lives in us to grow to maturity. Fully developed, our love for Him and faith in Him can bring into reality every dream He places in our hearts.

Are you hoping today with earnest expectation? Do you dream and imagine fulfillment of the grand and wonderful plans God has for your life? He dreamed them first, and now your faith is the bridge that will take you to the place He destined for you all along. Believe the promises of God—no matter how unbelievable they seem—and you will eventually see evidence of what before, you could only imagine.

In His Presence

By Kathy Collard Miller

Focusing on who God is empowers us to release and relax. He is a big enough God to make happen whatever He wants to happen. We don't have to perform; we just need to cooperate with His plans. And if He's saying to just sit quietly, then He knows what He intends to do. We can trust Him.

How long can you sit in God's presence without getting edgy? I must admit that sometimes my limit is three minutes. Then I have to sing Psalm 46:10 as a chorus in order to concentrate again. I'm already wearing my robe of righteousness, and it doesn't need to be dry-cleaned. My crown of righteousness is already placed on my head, and I don't need silver polish to shine it. It's radiantly reflecting God's grace, because He gave me those royal duds, even though I don't deserve them.

The more you reflect, the more you'll have "the new self" that Ephesians 4:24 talks about. As a result, little by little, you'll not feel compelled to say yes to everything. You'll be able to laugh at mistakes and not feel as if everyone is criticizing you.

You'll be more able to reveal your less-than-perfect self to others, knowing that their attitudes and opinions about you pale in comparison to God's opinion of you.

When we arrive in heaven, we'll cast our crowns at Jesus' throne because we'll realize that we really didn't do anything to earn them, therefore we can't claim them as our own. (But I'm secretly hoping He'll let us keep our robes.)[16]

FATHER,

There is no place like Your presence. When I'm there, I am at peace because I trust You. Sometimes it is hard for me to sit still and be quiet. Give me Your grace at those times so that I can fully partake of the pleasure of Your company and become the person You've created me to be.

AMEN

You will show me the path of life; in Your presence is fullness of joy; at Your right hand are pleasures forevermore.
PSALM 16:11 NKJV

THE LITTLE THINGS

Casting the whole of your care [all your anxieties, all your worries, all your concerns, once and for all] on Him, for He cares for you affectionately and cares about you watchfully.
1 PETER 5:7 AMP

Jenna received a beautiful doll for her fifth birthday. She was completely in love with her new friend and took her everywhere. After several weeks of this, the new doll's arm came loose and fell off. Jenna was devastated. She went running to her dad who was busy working on the family finances.

"Daddy!" Jenna sobbed. She held up her doll in one hand and the detached arm in the other. Being a loving father, what did Jenna's dad say? "Oh, Jenna, grow up! It's just a doll! Can't you see I'm busy? Don't bother me!"

Of course not! Jenna's daddy loves her more than anything. What is important to her is important to him. So when she went to him with her broken toy, he turned his full attention to her. He gently took the little doll, slipped the arm back into place, and returned her to the loving arms of his daughter. Jenna's tears were dried; and she went back to her play, secure in knowing that her daddy cared.

GRACE FOR TODAY

OUR HEAVENLY FATHER CARES ABOUT EVERYTHING IN OUR LIVES— EVEN THE LITTLE THINGS.

If we lovingly tend to the small troubles of our children, even the relatively insignificant issues of their lives, then why do we fail to take all of our troubles to our heavenly Father? For some reason, as adults, we tend to stop asking for help. We think that we should handle the "little things" on our own and not "bother" God. But we need to remember that God is our Father—He loves us more than we can imagine. And He cares about everything in our lives—even the little things. So take your needs, big or small, to Him, knowing that in His grace and mercy He will not fail to give you His full attention. God is never too busy for you.

WORRY NOT

In all you do, I want you to be free from worry.
1 CORINTHIANS 7:32 TLB

Mary C. Crowley quipped, "Every evening I turn my worries over to God. He's going to be up all night anyway." As women we seem to excel at worrying, but we're in good company. The Bible is full of stories about anxious people, Mordecai worried about his cousin Esther. Hezekiah had enemies at his gate. The Psalms David are filled with his concerns and fears, and the disciples spent many otherwise happy hours fretting.

Jesus understood our nature and broached the subject during His Sermon on the Mount. Basically He said, "There's nothing to worry about. If God takes care of the birds, won't He take care of you? Aren't you worth more than they are?" (See Matthew 6:26.)

GRACE FOR TODAY

AN EXHORTATION FROM AN UNKNOWN SOURCE STATES, "DO NOT BE AFRAID OF TOMORROW; FOR GOD IS ALREADY THERE."

It is important to note that worry is not harmless. It actually changes blood chemistry and affects the way our minds and bodies function! Also worrying is trusting in Murphy's Law rather than God's. Worry expects the negative and is fearful.

Where does worry come from? Do we doubt our Heavenly Father's love and provision? Jesus assured us that the Father is well aware of our needs, that if we would seek God and His kingdom first, everything else would be taken care of.

Much of our worry consists of fear of the unknown, an uncertainty about the future. But can't you look back at some of the things you were concerned about and see that they turned out fine? We really have nothing to worry about. God has given us His Word that He will never leave us. He knows our future better than we know the past, and He is already working things out for our good. Our job is to trust that He will do what He said He would do.

Incessant worry never helped anything; incessant dialogue with God does.

A RIGHT ESTIMATION

Do not think of yourself more highly than you ought, but
rather think of yourself with sober judgment, in
accordance with the measure of faith God has given you.
ROMANS 12:5 NIV

Mary lived in a little-known village called Nazareth. She was probably around the age of thirteen when she became engaged to Joseph. Women in that day did not receive an education, and they became the property of their husbands after the betrothal took place, so Mary's circumstances were humble. She may have seemed the least likely candidate to become the mother of Jesus.

GRACE FOR TODAY

GOD'S GRACE IS NOT DEPENDENT ON OUR SOCIAL OR FINANCIAL STATUS, OUR RACE, OUR AGE, OR ANY OTHER THING. IT IS SIMPLY A GIFT—FREELY GIVEN, AVAILABLE TO ALL.

Yet during the betrothal, the angel Gabriel appeared to Mary and told her that she would give birth to a son, whom she would name Jesus. Her child would be called the Son of God. The angel went on to explain that the Holy Spirit would come upon her, and even though she was still a virgin, she would conceive.

Filled with grace and humility, Mary replied, "I am the Lord's servant . . . May it be to me as you have said" (Luke 1:38 NIV).

Soon after, Mary went to visit her relative Elizabeth. Upon Elizabeth's seeing Mary, her baby leaped in her womb, and Elizabeth was filled with the Holy Spirit. She confirmed for Mary how blessed she was to have the honor of carrying the Messiah. Mary glorified God for what He was going to do for the world through her.

Mary didn't think so highly of herself that she felt she deserved the honor. Yet, she didn't think so lowly of herself that she refused it either. Jt was simply a gift of God's grace.

If we struggle with poor self-esteem or are on the other end of the spectrum and could use a dose of humility, it is important that we see ourselves the way God does. In and of ourselves, we are nothing; but because of God's grace and because we are His children, we have infinite value.

THE CRY OF YOUR HEART

The LORD longs to be gracious to you; he rises to show you
compassion.
ISAIAH 30:18 NIV

Hannah had a good life. She lived in a comfortable home. Her husband adored her and treated her like a queen. She had a close relationship with God. Everything would have been perfect if not for one thing. Hannah wanted desperately to be a mother—but she could not conceive.

As each year passed, she struggled to understand why God had not answered her many prayers. It was with a heavy heart that she traveled with her husband to the annual festival to worship. She wanted to trust God, but it was becoming increasingly difficult as her sorrow grew.

And so it was that during the festival feast, her pain overwhelmed her; and she began to weep. She left the table and went to stand in front of God's temple. In her despair, she could not speak through her tears and simply mouthed the words of her prayers in silence, knowing that God could hear her heart's cry.

GRACE FOR TODAY

LIFT YOUR PRAYERS TO THE LORD AND WAIT IN EXPECTATION FOR THE GRACE OF HIS PROMISED ANSWER.

So passionate was her display that the priest who sat watching mistook her for a drunk. But when she told him her story, his heart softened and he blessed her, "Go in peace, and may the God of Israel grant you what you have asked of him" (1 Samuel 1:17 NIV).

When the festival came around the next year, Hannah did not attend. But her absence was not because of bitterness. God had heard her prayers—she now had a baby boy. Little Samuel was a gift from God and would be Hannah's gift in return to her Lord.

Lift the cry of your heart to your heavenly Father. Do not hold back. Be passionate and bold in His presence. Then wait in expectation, knowing that He will hear and answer your prayer—in His time and His way. The Lord longs to give you the desires of your heart, for He is ever gracious.

OUR HEAVENLY DWELLING

When this earthly tent we live in is taken down—when we die and leave these bodies—we will have a home in heaven.
2 CORINTHIANS 5:1 NLT

An evangelist arrived in a small town. With a local pastor's blessing, he erected a seventy-foot round tent to hold revival meetings. Wooden chairs, a makeshift platform, and a sound system filled the interior.

The fourth night of the revival, a ferocious storm blew in, and the top of the tent billowed as the winds picked up. Then the poles holding up the tent began to sway. The evangelist hurried to the platform to announce, "Folks, this tent is only a temporary dwelling. We need to file out in an orderly manner."

Did you know that you inhabit a temporary dwelling? You might slather on creams, exercise, and eat right to protect your health, but the body in which you live will not last forever, in spite of your best effort. The apostle Paul encouraged Christians to honor God with their bodies, for they are the temples of the Holy Spirit. You and I were not allowed to enter the ancient Holy of Holies, but with the Holy Spirit, the Holy of Holies has entered us through Christ.

Our bodies are only temporary habitations. At the end of our time on Earth, we won't exit in a "slow, orderly manner." No, in the twinkling of an eye, we will meet our final destiny. We mustn't get too comfortable in our own skin, for God has something far better in store. We look forward to having a glorified body and being able to dwell in the presence of the Lord in Heaven—our permanent home.

Are you ready for the transformation?

GRACE FOR TODAY

UNTIL WE GET TO HEAVEN, HEAVEN LIVES IN US THROUGH CHRIST.

PRECIOUS

By Kathy Collard Miller

God's view of us as precious isn't something that's easily transferred into our hearts. We can tell ourselves that we're precious in His sight, but to feel it in our hearts is a bigger mission, and sometimes it seems an impossible one. Yet God wants us to feel precious, regardless of whether anyone else does.

You might have difficulty believing and feeling that for several reasons. You may still believe you need to earn God's love and "precious standing" through good, even perfect, behavior. Or childhood trauma left you with a sense that you have no worth or value. Or maybe God seems to not value you because He hasn't answered your prayers for a husband. Or maybe you are married, yet your husband is cold and unaffectionate. He might not even say, "I love you," much less call you "precious." He might even be abusive. Or, the most curious situation of all, you might be married to a wonderful, loving man or have a terrific boyfriend who values you, yet you still don't consider yourself precious deep in your heart.

Regardless, God considers you so valuable that He would have sent Jesus to die for you if you were the only person alive on earth. Just you![17]

DEAR GOD,

It is hard for me to fully grasp my worth in Your eyes, so I pray that You will help me comprehend it. I know in my head that I don't have to earn Your favor, it is a gift of Your grace, but my life experience with people has often been the opposite. Heal my heart where it has been bruised and broken so that I can know down deep where it counts that I am precious to You just as I am.

AMEN

May your roots go down deep into the soil of God's marvelous love; and may you have the power to understand, as all God's people should, how wide, how long, how high, and how deep his love really is. May you experience the love of Christ.
EPHESIANS 3:17-19 NLT

THOUGH I FALL, I SHALL RISE

Rejoice not against me, O mine enemy: when I fall, I shall arise; when I sit in darkness, the LORD shall be a light unto me.
MICAH 7:8 KJV

When you fall, the feeling of failure is often visible to you in your heart, whether you're responsible for the fall or not. Perhaps you've had someone laugh or talk about your misfortune—rejoicing against you. It doesn't fee! very good and can make you want to hide. The fear of failing next time can discourage you and keep you from ever trying again.

However, there is hope! The Lord is your light. To His delight, when you fall—or fail—you can come up out of it. Don't join the pity party and become defeated. Come up out of the darkness and into His marvelous light. Your enemies might celebrate for a moment, but your mountaintop experience is ahead. God will not leave you in the midst of defeat. Deny failure an opportunity to gloat, and rejoice in what God is about to do.

Failure isn't permanent as long as you are willing to get back up and press forward. You are guaranteed success when you look to God. He is there, even when you fall. He is your help and encouragement: He will give you the grace to stand up and go again. When you fall, get up, dust yourself off, and press toward God's purpose. Wipe your tears, turn away from your enemies' taunts, and set your face toward God's goodness.

GRACE FOR TODAY

NO DEFEAT IS PERMANENT WITH GOD ON YOUR SIDE. HE SUPPLIES HIS GRACE SO YOU CAN ARISE AND GO FORWARD.

LILIES OF THE FIELD

[Jesus said,] "Why do you worry about clothes? Look at how the lilies in the field grow. They don't work or make clothes for themselves. But I tell you that even Solomon with his riches was not dressed as beautifully as one of these flowers . . . So you can be even more sure that God will clothe you."
MATTHEW 6:28-30 NCV

The beauty of flowers has been celebrated since the beginning of our world. God declared them good on the third day of creation after He called them to spread across the earth. For centuries, art of all kinds has been dedicated to the loveliness of flora. Today people spend millions of dollars to surround themselves with blossoms. God certainly displayed His artistry when He created these delicate plants. And in His care for even the tiniest buds, God shows us His amazing grace.

GRACE FOR TODAY

GOD'S GRACE TO HIS CREATION IS ABUNDANT— ESPECIALLY TO YOU!

God provides rain, sunshine, and nutrients for billions of flowers across the globe every day. He created unique and varied ways for other creatures to help the flowers pollinate. And He made them incredibly beautiful, with more colors than the rainbow, and gave many of them intoxicating scents. What beautiful grace God extends to His creation!

If God cares this much about flowers, what incredible plans must He have for us? His grace pours out on us every day, even when we don't notice or ask for it. Just like the flowers of the field, God wants us to be beautiful, to grow and flourish. But unlike a rose or a daisy, God wants us to have a personal relationship with Him—one that will last more than a day, one that will last for eternity.

So the next time you stop to smell the flowers, remember God's grace to them. But most importantly, remember His infinite grace and love for you. You are more precious to Him than the most perfect blossom, more beautiful than all the lilies of the field.

JUST LAUGH

[God] will yet fill your mouth with laughter and your lips
with shouts of joy.
JOB 8:21 NIV

Martin Luther said, "If you're not allowed to laugh in heaven, I don't want to go there." Nothing is as universal as laughter. Everybody laughs. It's a language we all understand. Often it is physiologically beyond our control—we just do it. God designed us that way.

There is much talk these days about humor therapy—a rediscovery that laughter is good for us. It boosts our immune systems, appears to reduce pain, and is great for our cardiovascular and muscular systems. When we laugh, our entire body takes part. The Bible tells us "a cheerful heart is good medicine" (Proverbs 17:22 NIV).

GRACE FOR TODAY

SO THAT WE MIGHT DISCOVER TRUTH, GOD SOMETIMES EMPLOYS UNEXPECTED METHODS.

Laughter energizes the mind and makes us more open to communicating with others. Victor Borge said, "Laughter is the closest distance between two people." Interestingly, science tells us that only a small percentage of our laugher is actually connected with humor. Most of our laughter is a form of communication. When we laugh together, we express our acceptance, happiness, and enjoyment. Clearly it disarms us and opens the door of communication. It seems to erase a lot of the negative emotions that we entertain too. It's hard to stay mad, stressed, depressed, bitter, or frightened when we're laughing!

When we encounter crisis, maintaining a sense of humor is a natural stress reducer. Sometimes finding humor in a situation is the first step to finding hope. If we can laugh at a situation, we can deal with it. Bob Newhart commented, "It allows us to step back from an event, deal with it, and then move on."

The next time you encounter a negative situation, stop, take a deep breath, and look for the humor in the situation. It will make you feel better inside. It will change your perspective and might rub off on the people around you. Laughter is a gift of God's grace. Use it often.

LETTING GO

So letting your sinful nature control your mind leads to death. But letting the Spirit control your mind leads to life and peace.
ROMANS 8:6 NLT

In many African countries, boys enjoy the sport of catching monkeys. Monkeys are fast and smart, but they have one weakness. That flaw makes catching them the easiest thing in the world.

An African boy dries and hollows out a gourd into which he cuts a hole just big enough for the monkey's hand to fit through. Next the boy puts an object in the gourd that the monkey will be attracted to, like a chicken bone. The boy ties one end of a rope around the gourd and the other to the base of a nearby tree, then the boy hides to watch and wait.

Monkeys are curious and aggressive. Soon a monkey finds the gourd, shakes it, and discovers the chicken bone. He reaches his hand into the gourd to grab the bone; but when he tries to remove it, he can't get it out because the chicken bone is wedged in the narrow opening. He pulls and pulls, but to no avail. Then because the monkey's sole concentration is on the chicken bone, the little African boy walks up and catches him. The monkey screams and screams, yanking on the chicken bone, but he won't let go of his prize. The monkey is caught.

Perhaps there is something in your life that is acting as your chicken bone. Are you hanging on to something that God wants you to let go of? He does not like to compete with other things for His children's attention. He wants to be our primary focus and for us to allow Him to be in control of our lives. He wants you to accept His gift of grace and hold tightly to Him.

GRACE FOR TODAY

GOD'S GRACE ENABLES US TO LET GO, SO WE CAN HOLD TIGHTLY TO HIM WHO CAUSES EVERYTHING TO WORK OUT FOR OUR GOOD.

COURAGE

Vindicate me, O LORD, according to my righteousness and
my integrity that is in me.
PSALM 7:8 NASB

Many stories in the Bible are stories of rescue from oppression. Are you one of those stories waiting to happen? New studies confirm that bullying can and does happen in the workplace. Bullies can be male or female, but either way their behavior is considered completely unacceptable. God doesn't want you to live like that.

GRACE FOR TODAY

YOU DON'T HAVE TO COWER IN FEAR. GOD WILL FILL YOU WITH HIS COURAGE AND STRENGTH.

Most define bullying as verbal or physical actions that are frequent and designed to isolate, intimidate, and devalue another person. These actions can include things like gossip, rumors, ostracizing, impeding someone's work, offensive jokes, persistent and unnecessary critique, unexplained and unjustified demotions or punishments, and hindering of advancement.

Do you dread going to work because of someone's behavior towards you? Just remember that your dignity is not optional in God's eyes. Here are some practical things to think about. First off, pray about it and get some advice from your pastor. Then talk to a superior or your union and outline your concerns. Don't be malicious; just clearly outline the behavior you feel is harassing. Make it clear that you want something done and that if it continues, you will file a formal complaint.

When bullying happens, be firm. Pray for courage and an attitude of love. Then tell that person calmly and professionally that his or her behavior is unprofessional and inappropriate. Keep a written record of events, outlining what happened and when. One thing bullies must understand is that their behavior is going to cause problems for them, not you. If your place of employment doesn't have bullying resolution policies, ask that they design a formal statement of policy.

Nobody has the right to make you feel bullied. Your courage, forgiveness, open-mindedness, and willingness to find a positive outcome will inspire others. Move on.

CATCH THE VISION

By Kathy Collard Miller

Does it scare you or make you incredibly excited to know that God has a specific and unique plan for you to serve Him? Ephesians 2:10 NIV assures us, "For we are God's workmanship, created in Christ Jesus to do good works, which God prepared in advance for us to do."

Isaiah 25:1 NIV has long given me great strength about serving God in His predetermined plans. "O LORD, you are my God; I will exalt you and praise your name, for in perfect faithfulness you have done marvelous things, things planned long ago." He's already got it planned. I just have to cooperate. Are you ready for that?

Both the Ephesians and the Isaiah verses give me great peace in believing that God knows exactly what He wants to do with me. And you, too! His plan is creative and unique for each one of us. He knew exactly what He wanted to accomplish when He designed you in your mother's womb. The Psalmist wrote about that perspective when he penned, "For you created my inmost being; you knit me together in my mother's womb. I praise you because I am fearfully and wonderfully made; your works are wonderful, I know that full well. My frame was not hidden from you when I was made in the secret place. When I was woven together in the depths of the earth, your eyes saw my unformed body. *All the days ordained for me were written in your book before one of them came to be*," (Psalm 139:13-16 NIV, italics added).

Are you catching the vision?[18]

DEAR GOD,

It is so comforting to know that You have a unique plan for me, on You planned long before I was ever conceived. There is no reason for me to fear it, because You are good and Your plans are good. Lead me day by day so that I may fulfill the destiny You have in mind for me.

AMEN

The plans of the LORD stand firm forever, the purposes of his heart through all generations.
PSALM 33:11 NIV

CHELP CYOURSELF

I myself no longer live, but Christ lives in me. So I live my life in this earthly body by trusting in the Son of God, who loved me and gave himself for me. I am not one of those who treats the grace of God as meaningless. For if we could be saved by keeping the law, then there was no need for Christ to die.
GALATIANS 2:20-21 NLT

"God helps those who help themselves" — right? Everyone has probably had this quoted to them at least once — and perhaps has quoted it to another as well. The saying seems logical — especially when we live in a world that values independence and self-sufficiency so highly. We just need to pull ourselves up by our bootstraps, hold our heads high, and muscle through on our own. That will make God proud of us, right?

GRACE FOR TODAY

GOD HELPS THOSE WHO CAN'T HELP THEMSELVES.

Contrary to what many people believe, the "God helps those who help themselves" line is not a verse from the Bible. It is actually a saying that comes from Aesop, the ancient Greek teller of fables. And the original saying was: "The gods help those who help themselves." Actually, the Bible teaches us that our relationship to God should be exactly the opposite of this famous saying!

We cannot help ourselves. If we could, Jesus would not have needed to come to earth; His death and resurrection would be meaningless. But because we are helpless — utterly incapable of breaking the bonds of sin and restoring our relationship with God — the Father sent His only Son to do it for us. This is the definition of God's grace!

Plus, God's grace for the helpless does not stop with salvation from sin. Our Father continues to give us grace and help every day — for issues large or small. So the next time you're struggling and someone quotes you that famous line — or you hear it rolling around inside your head — remember that it simply isn't true. Turn to the Lord whenever you need His help, because God always helps those who can't help themselves.

THE ENCOURAGERS

My mouth would encourage you; comfort from my lips
would bring you relief.
JOB 16:5 NIV

You've heard of the Untouchables? Well, God has called us to be the Encouragers! We are not just to make a difference in the world but in the lives of individuals. The apostle Paul exhorted believers to edify one another, to build each other up.

Encouragers have touched and impacted the lives of remarkable men and women, often at the moments of deepest crisis and failure. These heroes have stepped alongside and spoken words that have inspired others to greatness.

GRACE FOR TODAY

GOD'S WORDS ARE FILLED WITH HIS GRACE. EVEN WHEN HE CORRECTS US, HE EXPRESSES HIS LOVE AND ENCOURAGES US TO TRY AGAIN.

Paul should know about encouragement since he was heartened by a "son of encouragement," a man named Barnabas. Prior to his conversion, the apostle Paul had made a career of persecuting Christians. But after his amazing supernatural encounter with Jesus, he was ready to join the early Church. Understandably the disciples were wary and skeptical, and many opposed Paul. But Barnabas spoke to the apostles in Jerusalem and convinced them to accept Paul. We know the rest. Paul became one of the most inspirational figures of all time.

Then there was the young man named John Mark, who failed on his first mission trip. Once again, it was Barnabas who was willing to offer a second chance when others wouldn't. And again, his instincts proved right.

The role of encourager shines brightest during times of failure. An encourager has a willingness to listen and find ways to help. An encourager never gives up but rather sees others through till they win. An encourager helps people discover who God intends them to be. An encourager doesn't judge people by their failures but always believes the best. An encourager points people to God and trusts that He will work everything out for their good.

Does this describe you? It can. You can be counted as one of the Encouragers.

MERCY MAKERS

[The Lord] has told you what he wants, and this is all it is: to be fair and just and merciful, and to walk humbly with your God.
MICAH 6:8 TLB

GRACE FOR TODAY

THE THRONE OF GOD'S GRACE IS WHERE MERCY CAN BE FOUND.

People who do the unthinkable in the midst of the most incredible circumstances are viewed as heroes. Their stories of mercy, courage, sympathy, care, and consideration are told on the pages of inspirational books, hailed by the voices of motivational speakers, and spoken on the lips of many during encouraging conversational exchanges. It's very likely that their compassion, concern, and pausing to respond in kindness touched the heart of God.

Although most heroes consider themselves to have done no more than what anyone else in their situation would have done, the truth is, no one else did. They listened when everyone else kept talking. They gave when others saw no need. They offered hope and inspiration, which rekindled a fire and ignited passion. They forgave when others demanded repayment. They reached deep within themselves and found something perhaps they didn't even know was there—in order to change a life forever.

They are the exceptions—the mercy makers. And many do not even realize that they gave a gift—sowed a seed. But they will never lack in their own time of need.

Are there situations in your own life where you reached out to someone when no one else responded? Did you offer hope, comfort, and strength in someone's time of need?

God is the ultimate mercy maker. He is filled with compassion, and His mercies are new every day. We can all use some mercy—to give or to receive. God is the supplier of all things good. Take some time today and see where He would have you share a gift of mercy.

SHINE

Buy truth, and do not sell it; buy wisdom, instruction, and
understanding.
PROVERBS 23:23 NRSV

Recently the professors of a well-known college sat down to discuss ethics and integrity. It seems the students were stealing and sabotaging their competitors' projects. So the faculty designed a badly needed course on ethics and integrity. In fact, cheating, plagiarism, and dishonest collaborations have become rampant in our hallowed halls of learning. Some say the cheating rate is as high as 70 percent. Has our cultural drive to succeed completely trampled our desire for integrity? Albert Einstein said, "Try not to become a man of success but rather try to become a man of value."

As a student or professional, how can you shine honestly when the rest of your peers are using questionable means to get ahead? It may sound trite, but an honest heart will make you shine. Having honesty, integrity, and ethics combined with talent will make you different enough. If you don't think your superiors or professors will notice—they will. God designed us to be attracted to righteousness.

God will provide you opportunity to shine in the right ways when you have the right attitudes. Jesus said this, "When you are invited, go and sit down at the lowest place, so that when your host comes, he may say to you, 'Friend, move up higher'; then you will be honored in the presence of all who sit at the table with you. For all who exalt themselves will be humbled, and those who humble themselves will be exalted" (Luke 14; 10-11 NRSV).

GRACE FOR TODAY

GOD DESIGNED THE UNIVERSE TO SUPPORT RIGHTEOUSNESS AND INTEGRITY.

You know the person God wants you to be; you also know how to be that person of integrity in every situation. Sometimes making an ethical choice is hard, but in the end, you'll discover it's always the right one.

WHAT YOU DESERVE

Let your conversation be always full of grace.
COLOSSIANS 4:6 NIV

You've settled into your plush seat at a posh restaurant, ready to enjoy a delicious, although expensive, meal with a loved one. Forty-five minutes later you are still waiting for your food, and the only dinner conversation left is the rumbling of your stomachs. The waiter stops by, sheepishly apologizing for the delay. And you have a choice: You can say exactly what you feel—that you're hungry and irritated and you want your food . . . now!—or you can show grace.

Giving grace to others is not easy. When we feel wronged or slighted, we naturally want to defend our rights. We want what is entitled to us—the rebate, the discount, the apology, the restitution. In short, we demand justice. But what if we really got what we were asking for?

God made us, gave us spirits and free will so that we could fully love Him and enjoy a close friendship with Him. Plus, He placed us in a beautiful world full of everything we would ever need to thrive. And we chose to turn our backs on Him. We hurt and wronged our Creator. Did God demand justice? Yes. He doled out punishment for our crime— onto His own Son. Justice was done, and instead of getting what we deserved, we received grace.

GRACE FOR TODAY

JESUS DIED TO MAKE US HIS FRIENDS SO THAT WE CAN BEFRIEND OTHERS.

The definition of grace is unmerited favor. Grace is getting what you don't deserve. That's what God did for you. And you are most like your Father when you give others what they don't deserve—grace. So the next time your food is late to arrive or your friend lets you down, imitate your Father—be a grace-giver.

GROWING UP IN THE LORD

By Kathy Collard Miller

Years ago, I was a short-term missionary in Jamaica, and though I'd only been a Christian two years and was nineteen years old, I was appointed team leader over two other teenagers. One day I could choose what our team would do. I prayed and prayed, seeking God's mind for our assignment and believed I had finally heard Him say to go to a nearby town to pass out tracts in an open-air market. I felt confident I'd heard God's directive, even though I'd never really experienced a word from God before.

But the next morning as we prepared to leave, it started to rain. And then it poured! Since it rained frequently on that tropical island, that wasn't unusual; and we often went out anyway. But this was not the typical tropical rain. It was coming down hard, and I knew it was hard enough that no one would be in the uncovered market.

I was devastated. I prayed, "Lord, didn't I hear You?" I felt like a failure and wondered if I'd ever be able to learn to hear God's voice and take on His mind.

Now with over thirty years of experience as a Christian, I realize I didn't need to be discouraged. Having the mind of Christ doesn't necessarily mean we'll always know what to do. God wants each of us to develop the spiritual brain and heart muscle needed to see life with His perspective.

As with every aspect of Christian growth, we need to grow in our ability to hear His voice.[19]

DEAR LORD,

Sometimes I get so impatient with my spiritual growth. I am eager to serve you, but I have much to learn. Help me to grow in grace and wisdom so that I may discern Your voice, learn Your ways, and bear much fruit.

AMEN

We pray this in order that you may live a life worthy of the Lord and may please him in every way: bearing fruit in every good work, growing in the knowledge of God.
COLOSSIANS 1:10 NIV

PERFECT TIMING

When the bow [rainbow] is in the clouds and I look upon it, I will [earnestly] remember the everlasting covenant or pledge between God and every living creature of all flesh that is upon the earth.
GENESIS 9:16 AMP

Today we live in an electronic age of TVs, DVDs, VCRs, and computers. We can obtain information and entertainment instantaneously. We have instant tea and instant breakfast. We get antsy standing in front of the microwave oven waiting for the few minutes it takes to cook our instant dinner.

GRACE FOR TODAY

GOD ALWAYS KEEPS HIS PROMISES, AND HE HAS GIVEN US THE RAINBOW AS A VISIBLE REMINDER.

Since people today don't like to wait for anything or anybody, our timetable is often different from God's. However, God doesn't labor under the constraints of our self-determined schedules. He is not bound by time.

An example of this is the biblical story of Noah in Genesis 6-9. Many people think Noah and his family were in the ark for forty days, but the Bible says it rained for forty days. Water flooded the earth for 150 days, and Noah and his family were probably in the ark for over a year! God determined when it was time for Noah to come out.

Like Noah, you may feel that God has shut the door on you. You may wonder why He is not answering your prayers. If you have been going through a difficult situation for a long time, you are probably ready to come out of the ark. You may feel you have done all God has called you to do, yet He remains silent. Times like this test our faith and try our patience.

Yet, God remembered Noah and at the right time asked him to come out of the ark. Then He made a covenant with Noah. God's rainbow serves as a sign of His covenant with us as well. Every time we see His bow in the sky, we are reminded that He keeps His promises and will bring to pass His will in our lives—according to His timing.

JUST WHEN YOU NEED IT

Let us then fearlessly and confidently and boldly draw near to
the throne of grace . . . that we may . . . find grace to help in good
time for every need [appropriate help and well-timed help,
coming just when we need it].
HEBREWS 4:16 AMP

Brian and Jodi had sensed God leading them to a better way to live their lives. They wanted more than the 9-to-5 corporate grind had to offer. They longed to spend more time with their aging parents and extended family. They had a passion for ministry and didn't want it to always play second fiddle to career demands. So, after much prayer, they took a leap of faith, quit their corporate jobs, and started a home-based business together, trusting God to provide what they needed.

GRACE FOR TODAY

YOU CAN ALWAYS
TRUST GOD'S GRACE
AND PROVISION TO
COME THROUGH
WHEN YOU NEED IT
THE MOST.

During this transition, Brian and Jodi felt challenged to increase the amount that they were giving to their church. They decided to take the challenge, even in the midst of uncertain financial times. Then they waited in expectation for what God would do.

Having faith when it comes to finances is never easy. There were weeks that Brian and Jodi had to push back their fear and trust God for a check to arrive so they could pay the mortgage. This became especially trying when projects fell through at the last minute and unexpected expenses popped up out of nowhere. But the young couple kept praying and asked friends and family to pray with them for God's grace and provision.

Sure enough, just when things started to get desperate, God came through. Checks came in the mail, work was offered to them from the most unlikely places, and projects that they thought were no longer options suddenly became possibilities again. Best of all, Brian and Jodi felt their faith renewed in the grace of God's provision. The Lord knows what we need and will never fail to come through when we trust Him.

IN FULL BLOOM

The righteous flourish . . . In old age they still produce fruit;
they are always green and full of sap.
PSALM 92:12,14 NRSV

How do we as women come to terms with growing older? Remember what Robert Browning wrote: "Grow old along with me! The best is yet to be." Anna Mary Roberts certainly proved this out. Let her amazing career inspire you.

Anna was a farmer's wife who raised five children. She loved to embroider; but after her husband died, arthritis overtook her hands and prevented her from continuing that hobby. Not one to be kept down, Anne switched to painting. In 1938, an art collector was fascinated by the paintings he saw in a drugstore window—colorful scenes of country life. As a result, Anna Roberts was "discovered" and showed her first exhibit in New York when she was nearly eighty!

GRACE FOR TODAY

THERE IS NO EXPIRATION DATE ON GOD'S GRACE. IT IS AVAILABLE TO HIS CHILDREN, ALL THE DAYS OF THEIR LIVES.

Although you may not recognize her by her given name, you are surely familiar with Grandma Moses, one of the most famous folk artists of the twentieth century. She was still painting when she was a hundred and reportedly produced twenty-five works during the last year of her life! In all, Anna completed over fifteen hundred paintings in her twenty-year career as an artist. The motto? "Life is what we make it, always has been, always will be."

In God's eyes, our value doesn't diminish with age. Perhaps the secret of growing old gracefully can't be found in facial creams and tummy tucks, but rather by continually exploring and following the dreams God has given you. No doubt God's plan is that we continue to bear fruit in old age and never quit growing. His grace makes that possible.

Don't settle for the status quo. Claim God's promise that you will flourish even in your latter years. Truly the best is yet to be.

UNIQUELY BEAUTIFUL

Thank you for making me so wonderfully complex! It is
amazing to think about. Your workmanship is marvelous—
and how well I know it.
PSALM 139:14 TLB

Clergyman Jeremy Taylor said, "Know that you are your greatest enemy, but also your greatest friend." Tragically many people in our society hate themselves. They are their own critical enemy and fear there is no escape.

Look at the wave of interest in plastic surgery. This interest goes beyond just wanting to fix something that really makes you feel self-conscious. This craze feeds into a belief that we must all fit into a designed model of what beauty is supposed to be. We are a carbon-copy culture on a beauty quest.

GRACE FOR TODAY

GOD MADE YOU, AND YOU ARE UNIQUELY BEAUTIFUL.

But the amazing and wonderful thing about beauty is that it cannot be defined or caged. It changes with culture and time. What was considered beautiful a thousand years ago, two hundred years ago, or twenty years ago isn't what we think beauty is today.

There is something about beauty that radiates outwards and is a reflection of a million different faces and bodies. Sometimes the most beautiful women do not conform to what we think should be beautiful— yet the mystery is that they are. They are beautiful, unique, and defy definition. Perhaps beauty is not about perfect proportions. Perhaps a woman's beauty goes beyond that. Ralph Waldo Emerson wrote, "Though we travel the world over to find the beautiful, we must carry it with us or we find it not."

God made you, and you are beautiful. You carry your own unique beauty in a style that is indiscernibly wonderfully you. That beauty includes your personality and how you treat others. Your confidence in who you are is the most contagious beauty you can possess. When you are at ease with your own distinct beauty, so are other people. In fact, they are drawn to your confidence and happiness. God designed the world's beauty to be diverse, and that includes people. That includes you.

WINNING THE RACE

Let us run with patience the race that is set before us.
HEBREWS 12:1 KJV

Eric Liddell, a missionary to China, ran in the 1924 Olympics. He is quoted as saying, "I know that God has made me for a purpose; to be a missionary in China. But He also made me fast. And when I run, I feel His pleasure."

God made each of us for a purpose. When Eric left China to run in the Olympics, he stepped—or ran—into the will of God. The Lord used his athletic ability to witness to thousands. The movie *Chariots of Fire* chronicled his faith, influencing yet another generation for Jesus Christ.

You might feel as if you must be a preacher or teacher to be of service to God. In the body of Christ, all the parts are important. Perhaps your job is to fill a glass with fresh, ice-cold water and place it behind the pulpit for your pastor. Very few people might know you do this, but be faithful. It is a ministry.

Ask the Lord what He would have you do. Perhaps you wait tables or work on cars and have a difficult time imagining how this could be God's place for you, but God uses us if we are willing. When you honor God in all you do, He will honor your obedience with a life that counts for eternity.

Do you desire for God to find pleasure in your life? Jesus endured the cross "for the joy set before Him." During the Olympics, athletes keep their eyes on the prize—an Olympic medal. In our Christian walk, we strive for the prize of the high calling of Jesus Christ. We won't be awarded medals that soon pass away, but an eternal home in Heaven.

GRACE FOR TODAY

IT IS NOT THE POSSESSION OF EXTRAORDINARY GIFTS THAT MAKES EXTRAORDINARY USEFULNESS, BUT THE DEDICATION OF WHAT WE HAVE TO THE SERVICE OF GOD.

FREDERICK WILLIAM ROBERTSON

NO CONDEMNATION

By Kathy Collard Miller

There is a difference between condemnation and conviction. Yes, God does convict us of sin, but He doesn't condemn us. He will let us know when we've done something wrong, but we don't need to feel hopeless and burdened about it. We just need to confess our sins, and rejoice that we are forgiven.

Why is God so motivated to forgive us and make sure we don't feel condemned? I believe Isaiah 43:25 NASB holds a key: "'I, even I, am the one who wipes out your transgressions for My own sake; And I will not remember your sins.'" God wants to forgive us and restore fellowship with us "for His own sake." He desires our fellowship. He longs to have our attention and enjoy our company. Sin prevents that. And when we think we're condemned (though it's not true), we shy away from coming before our heavenly Father, expecting a sharp rebuke.

But God's voice is kind, understanding, and quick to offer forgiveness and cleansing.

What kind of voice do you hear from your Abba, or Daddy? He wants you to hear, "Daughter, I'm patiently helping you through this earthly process of growth. I forgive you and don't condemn you. Continue on in My power. I love you."[20]

HEAVENLY FATHER,

I love to serve You and please You, yet sometimes I feel guilty and condemned. When I err, help me to repent quickly and then resist condemnation when it tries to rob me of my freedom in You. There is no way I could ever deserve Your forgiveness, but because of Your grace, it is a gift that I receive with all humility. Thank You that condemnation is a thing of the past.

AMEN

There is now no condemnation for those who are in Christ Jesus.
ROMANS 8:1 NASB

GRACE-FILLED CONVERSATION

Conduct yourselves with wisdom toward outsiders . . . Let
your speech always be with grace, as though seasoned
with salt, so that you will know how you should respond to
each person.
COLOSSIANS 4:5-6 NASB

A Christian individual was talking to a colleague who was not a believer. The unbeliever said this of the man they were discussing: "You know, I've never heard him say a bad thing about anybody. I know because I notice these things."

It really made the Christian think about how people perceived him. Did he have as good a reputation? Do we? Gossip, speaking in unloving ways about people, is anything but Christlike.

Can you imagine God saying negative things about you behind your back? Of course not. And when His grace is at work in our lives, we become sensitive to unloving attitudes and our conscience is pricked when we are tempted to gossip. God's grace enables us to make a heartfelt choice to speak only those things that are loving, positive, and uplifting about others. Before we say one word about another individual, we should ask ourselves, Is what I am about to say loving? If not, mum should be the word.

God is love and utterly trustworthy with our lives. His words are full of grace. The more you spend time with Him, the more the same will be said of you. You will become His ambassador, and people will know they have spent time with the God of love when they have been with you.

Is your speech filled with grace? Spend time at the feet of Jesus, and it soon will be.

GRACE FOR TODAY

WHEN GOD'S LOVE SPILLS INTO OUR LIVES, HE CREATES A
PEOPLE WHOSE WORDS ARE ALWAYS FULL OF GRACE.

REVENGE IS FOR HOLLYWOOD

Depart from evil, and do good; seek peace, and pursue it.
PSALM 34:14 NRSV

Revenge is big in Hollywood movies today. Why? Vengeance is an incredibly strong emotional force that appeals to our sense of justice. But revenge doesn't make for a godly life, because revenge will hurt you—it hurts the person you're going to be in the future.

Swarming and beating others in response to perceived slights and jealousies has become all too common. Revenge can also take much more subtle forms like shunning others, spreading malicious rumors, and gossip.

Modern media fosters the belief that we are justified in taking action against others because it is our right to punish wrongs against us. That may be man's way, but it certainly isn't God's way.

GRACE FOR TODAY

AS WE WALK IN GOD'S FOOTSTEPS, WE FIND WE EXTEND GRACE TO OTHERS JUST AS HE HAS EXTENDED HIS REMARKABLE, DIVINE GRACE TO US.

God set the standard for those who would be like Him by bestowing grace rather than enacting revenge. Certainly we have wronged God, not once but many times, not just personally but also corporately. We have failed Him in every way. The Bible says that even as He hung on the Cross of Calvary, He could have called down thousands of angels to rescue Him. Certainly He could have taken revenge on those who beat, tortured, and murdered Him—but He didn't. Instead, He offered love and forgiveness.

In our lives, we all encounter injustice and cruelty. Others hurt us, and we hurt them. However, the more we spend time with God, the more our hearts change. As a wonderful result, we become people who use opportunities for revenge as opportunities to demonstrate to others the grace of God that we ourselves have experienced.

GOD HEARS US ALL

In my distress I called to the LORD; I cried to my God for help. From his temple he heard my voice; my cry came before him, into his ears.
PSALM 18:6 NIV

GRACE FOR TODAY

GOD HEARS AND ANSWERS WHEN HIS CHILDREN CALL.

Matt and Michelle were in love. They met in college and had great hopes for a future together. Matt graduated when Michelle was just a sophomore and soon took his first job in Chicago, two hours away. They were disappointed at the distance but knew that this job was part of their shared future. They trusted that God's grace would give them the patience to endure the separation until they could be married.

Four months after Matt went to Chicago, he was promoted to a position in St. Paul, Minnesota. He had been hoping for a position closer to Michelle, but it just didn't work out. After a very tearful good-bye, Matt moved to Minnesota—eleven hours from his future bride.

The young couple continued to grow in their relationship with nightly phone calls and a visit every six weeks, but it was difficult and painful for them both. After months of this, Matt and Michelle were at the breaking point. Michelle considered transferring to a school in Minnesota. Matt considered quitting his job. Neither option seemed wise; they felt trapped and confused. One evening they prayed together on the phone, crying out to God to intervene and provide a way out.

The very next day Matt got a call from his district manager. A position had opened up only an hour away from where Michelle was finishing college. God had heard their cry and granted the desire of their hearts—and in a way that was even better than they had hoped!

Matt and Michelle have been married for nearly eight years now. They find joy in remembering God's surprising grace to them; it continues to inspire them to trust. When hard times come, they know from experience that God hears and answers those who call to Him!

CHOOSING JOY

Rejoice in the Lord always [delight, gladden yourselves in
Him]; again I say, Rejoice!
PHILIPPIANS 4:4 AMP

Elizabeth was from one of the most important classes in Israel. She was descended from the priestly line of Aaron, and her husband, Zechariah, was a priest. They observed the Lord's commandments and were filled with His grace.

In spite of her honorable position, Elizabeth experienced a great sorrow. She was barren and thought herself too old to have children. Jewish society considered children to be a form of wealth, and parents counted on those children to assist them when they reached old age. To be childless was thought to be cursed by God.

Yet her sorrow turned to joy when she became pregnant. In her sixth month, she received a visit from her young cousin, Mary. When Mary greeted, her, Elizabeth felt the baby within her womb leap, and she was filled with the Holy Spirit. She said, "And how [have I deserved that this honor should] be granted to me, that the mother of my Lord should come to me?" (Luke 1:43 AMP).

GRACE FOR TODAY

GOD'S GRACE
MANIFESTS UNIQUELY
IN EACH PERSON, BUT
IT ALWAYS BRING
GLORY TO HIM AND
INSPIRES JOY IN US.

As member of the tribe of Aaron, Elizabeth could have envied her young, lowly cousin, a member of a lesser tribe, whose son would be greater than her own; but she didn't. She rejoiced with Mary.

When it was her time, Elizabeth gave birth to a son, whom they named John. And John the Baptist was chosen to "prepare the way for the Lord" (Matthew 3:3 NIV). John himself reflected the wisdom of his mother; and rejoiced to see Israel flock to Him.

It's tempting to envy people whom God has singled out. Yet we can rejoice with them, choosing joy over sorrow, because God uses each of us in the unique way He has chosen. God's grace is abundant for each of us, though in different ways.

No Coincidence

All our steps are ordered by the LORD.
PROVERBS 20:24 NRSV

Amazing things have happened in your life by the hand or heart of others. Perhaps you experienced a flat tire; and before you could even get out of your car, someone with a friendly set of helpful hands pulled up behind you with both the muscle and the equipment to send you on your way. Maybe it was the way someone lived his or her life that changed you, inspired you.

GRACE FOR TODAY

GOD ORCHESTRATES DIVINE APPOINTMENTS.

God often sends mentors into your life to demonstrate an element of character you need in your life as you journey forward. It could be someone you connected with who imparted a life lesson that changed you or caused you to experience an epiphany.

You may rack up such occasions to coincidences or wacky facts, when in reality God orchestrates them all. Some call them flukes, but such introductions are not happenstance. Their influence on your life is a result of calculated and direct planning on God's part to keep you on the right road toward your destiny.

It is said that hindsight is 20/20, and when you look back, you discover His fingerprints — evidences of His perfect design during key times in your life. When you suddenly recognize His influence in your everyday life, it will change everything in your heart. You may be surprised to see how God has truly ordered your steps for the plan He has for you. Look at how much of your life He has already touched through the hands, hearts, and voices of others whom He has brought across your path.

JESUS UNDERSTANDS

By Evelyn Christenson

This past summer I heard a prominent Russian pastor speak just two months after being released from a slave labor camp. He said, "I had to wear red stripes because I was considered the most dangerous kind of criminal in the camp. I was not allowed to fellowship with other prisoners. If the guards saw me talking to others, they would put us in separate barracks. Other prisoners were brainwashed against me as I was declared to be worse than a murderer."

But then he told us that no matter how segregated he was, he always had a great fellowship with his Lord. His captors could not take that away from him! Separated—but not from God's love and companionship!

Jesus also understands what it is like to be ostracized by those in authority. Throughout His public ministry, there was a running battle between Jesus and the religious leaders of His day. They called Him a liar, attempted to stone Him, took counsel together to put Him to death, delivered Him to the civil authorities unjustly—until they finally cried to Pilate, "Crucify Him, crucify Him" (Matthew 27:22-23). Ostracized by religious leaders—but not separated from His Father's love.[21]

FATHER,

I am so thankful for Your boundless, endless love. It is Comforting to know that nothing can separate me from it. It is also comforting to know that Jesus understands what I am going through. Thank You for Your grace that enables me to overcome. Your love never fails.

AMEN

I am convinced that neither death, nor life, nor angels, nor principalities, nor things present, nor things to come, nor powers, nor height, nor depth, nor any other created thing, will be able to separate us from the love of God, which is in Christ Jesus our Lord.
ROMANS 8:38-39 NASB

STEWARDSHIP

Give her the product of her hands, and let her works praise
her in the gates.
PROVERBS 51:31 NASB

The words "I'm going to the mall" invoke so many images, both negative and positive. The mall is where modern women go hunting and gathering without climbing trees or digging for roots. It satisfies our need to take things home to the cave. But Neolithic women never had to worry about charge card bills or blinking declined messages. The ease of purchasing may mean buying power actually deteriorates into powerful debt.

GRACE FOR TODAY

GOD HAS EQUIPPED WOMEN TO BE WONDERFUL MANAGERS OVER HIS PROVISION.

"Of what use is money in the hand of a fool, since he has no desire to get wisdom?" (Proverbs 17:16 NIV). It's pretty clear God's all for smart spending.

Contrary to masculine rumor, God knows women are wonderful managers. Proverbs 31 talks about a virtuous woman. "She considers a field and buys it; out of her earnings she plants a vineyard. She sets about her work vigorously . . . She sees that her trading is profitable, and her lamp does not go out at night." (Proverbs 31:16-18 NIV). This biblical woman clearly has business savvy and is money wise.

If she could do it before calculators, then make way for the rest of us! It doesn't matter if you're a stay-at-home mom or a high-powered executive: smart buying isn't a matter of how much but rather why and when. Smart spending starts by each day making informed choices with your money. It means doing a little research and a little education about your spending patterns and needs. It means going in with a clear vision of what you need, what you want, and how much you want to spend — gathering only the things you need and having good stewardship over what God's given you. It means breaking those stupid stereotypes about women and finances. It means not going into debt because we know what we're doing.

THE RIGHT PEOPLE AT THE RIGHT TIME

This service that you perform is not only supplying the needs of God's people but is also overflowing in many expressions of thanks to God.
2 CORINTHIANS 9:12 NIV

GRACE FOR TODAY

GOD USES HIS PEOPLE TO ADMINISTER HIS GRACE AND STRATEGICALLY PLACES THEM WHERE THEY ARE NEEDED MOST.

It was an impossible situation. Mara was a young, inexperienced store manager hired to run a Christian bookstore where all but five of the employees had quit. She had to hire six new people in a week and train them before the busy Christmas season just around the corner. The store's sales for the year were dismal. Mara was overwhelmed.

Throughout the next few weeks, Mara and her district manager prayerfully interviewed and hired six new people—all were excited and ready to devote themselves to their work. They learned to work well together as a team. They were flexible with their schedules, and they looked for opportunities to minister to their customers as well as their fellow employees. They all worked very hard and were exhausted at the end of the Christmas retail season, but God worked through them to touch many lives. They were a blessing to Mara and to her customers, a blessing that was nothing short of miraculous. God's grace in sending the right people was evident—and it didn't stop once Christmas was over.

The store began to turn its sales around. Its positive influence in the community blossomed—helping churches, families, and individuals grow in their relationships with God. The following year the store won awards. Mara was grateful for the recognition, but she never once forgot the grace of God that brought her the right staff at the right time. Without the Lord's help, she knew she would have failed. But through the miracle of divine grace, many lives were touched, and God's glory shone.

WHO DO YOU KNOW?

[My determined purpose is] that I may know Him [that I may
progressively become more deeply and intimately acquainted
with Him, perceiving and recognizing and understanding the
wonders of His Person more strongly and more clearly].
PHILIPPIANS 3:10 AMP

Every year in the spring, we celebrate various graduations. Many graduates from high school and college enter the job market only to be disillusioned by the difficulty in finding employment. Often people seem to get ahead in life, not based on their abilities or even by hard work, but rather on their connections. Sooner or later, fresh- faced graduates are tempted to mutter, "It's not what you know. It's who you know," followed by a long sigh.

This inequity of life can be frustrating, but there is one position we can all attain. Oddly enough it, too, is based on who you know. It is our place in the kingdom of God. Our position is assured when we know Jesus Christ as our Savior.

Knowing, really knowing, Jesus is better than any worldly connection. Think of it: David was made king by knowing God. Jeremiah was called to take messages to rulers and kings, as was Saul, who met Jesus on the way to Damascus. It wasn't what they knew that got them where they were supposed to be; it was Who they knew!

Consider this as you get to know Jesus and experience positive change in your life: knowing Him will open any door that is supposed to open. And knowing Him will make you the kind of person who can walk through that door.

GRACE FOR TODAY

THIS COMING TO KNOW CHRIST IS WHAT MAKES CHRISTIAN
TRUTH REDEMPTIVE TRUTH, THE TRUTH THAT TRANSFORMS,
NOT JUST THE TRUTH THAT INFORMS.

HAROLD COOKE PHILLIPS

GOD'S SERVANTS

I became a servant of this gospel by the gift of God's grace
given me through the working of his power.
EPHESIANS 5:7 NIV

Jimmy Carter has been called "the best ex-president that the U.S. has had since Herbert Hoover." In politics he emphasized ecology, efficiency in government, and the removal of racial barriers. As a born-again Christian, Jimmy stated, "The presence of my belief in Christ is the most important thing in my life."

Since leaving office, he has worked tirelessly through the nonprofit Carter Center in Atlanta that he founded and the Jimmy Carter Work Project (JCWP) for Habitat for Humanity International (HFHI). He has promoted human rights, education, agriculture, and health care—especially in Third World countries.

GRACE FOR TODAY

GOD'S GRACE EQUIPS US FOR SERVICE TO MEET THE NEEDS OF OTHERS EVERY DAY.

Each year, Jimmy and Rosalyn Carter donate a week of their time as well as their building skills to build homes and raise awareness of the critical need for affordable housing. When the former president left office, the White House staff gave him tools for his workshop. Rosalyn, on the other hand, didn't know how to swing a hammer, but she learned. Now she works alongside her husband.

The founders of HFHI said of Jimmy, "Whether he is swinging a hammer, resolving a conflict, stamping out civil rights abuse, lending a helping hand to a neighbor, or teaching Sunday school, it is obvious that Jimmy Carter takes great joy in being a servant of God."

You, too, can be God's servant, and you don't need to swing a hammer or change the international scene. You can help one person at a time—an individual who crosses your path at work, at church, or in your neighborhood. Let your prayer be, "Lord, give me the grace to bless someone each day."

GIVING YOUR LIFE

Even the Son of Man did not come to be served, but to serve, and to give His life a ransom for many.
MARK 10:45 NASB

GRACE FOR TODAY

KNOW THIS: WE SERVE THE HOLY ONE, TO WHOM OUR RESTLESS SOULS BELONG. WE HAVE OUR BREATH THROUGH GOD ALONE, LO WHOM WE RAISE OUR GRATEFUL SONG.

RUTH C. DUCK

On January 20, 1981, Ronald Reagan was sworn into office as the fortieth president of the United States. Only sixty-nine days later, after Reagan had given a speech to AFL-CIO members, John Hinkley Jr. fired six shots at the president. Although none hit him directly, it was determined later that one bullet ricocheted off the limousine and pierced his chest under his left arm.

Though it was not immediately obvious that Reagan had been shot, he soon began coughing up blood. The bullet had stopped within inches of his heart. The chief surgeon said that if it had taken the president five more minutes to arrive at the hospital, he would have died.

Once the president returned to the White House, he was visited by Cardinal Cooke on Good Friday. Reagan told the cardinal, "I have decided whatever time I have left is for Him."

Ronald Reagan made a commitment to God and to the people he served. Upon his death, all of America—and many all over the world—had a chance to reflect on how President Reagan lived his life, exhibited God's grace, and kept his promises.

His wife, Nancy, wrote, "As I saw the people lining the motorcade routes and heard the special tributes in communities across the country he loved so dearly, I realized once again how Ronnie touched so many of us."

We, too, can make a commitment to serve our Lord with the time that we have left, and none of us knows how long that may be. But God's presence in our lives can make us a blessing to the world. We can dedicate ourselves to serving God and serving others through His grace as did our fortieth president.

GOD'S GRACE CHANGES US

By Gene Getz

"As apostles of Christ, we could have been a burden to you," but, said Paul, that was not true. Rather, "we were gentle among you, like a mother caring for her little children" (1 Thessalonians 2:7 NIV, emphasis added).

What a contrast! Could this be the same man who several years earlier was "breathing out murderous threats against the Lord's disciples" (Acts 9:1 NIV), and now used a nursing mother to illustrate his style of ministry? What an example of God's grace! Paul was a changed man— a man of sensitivity and compassion.

It intrigues me that a man so tough, so rigid and unbending, reflected this kind of gentleness. No relationship better personifies gentleness than a mother who is nursing a baby. Yet Paul was not ashamed to identify with this analogy. This confirms the depth of change that had taken place in him.

This does not mean that Paul was unwilling to be frank, straightforward, and uncompromising. He never hesitated to confront wrongdoers— especially those whose motives were totally selfish (for example, see Titus 1:10-16). But Paul resorted to this methodology when he saw no hope, or when he saw Christians being deliberately led astray by false teachers. He believed that his initial approach should be a gentle one.

By the time Paul arrived in Thessalonica, he learned a great deal about gentleness. And this Timothy observed in Paul's own ministry. With gentleness and tenderness he encouraged these Christians in their new life in Christ.[22]

FATHER GOD:

Change me by Your grace. Make of me the person You created me to be–a person who is pleasing to You and of service to others.

AMEN

By the grace of God I am what I am, and his grace to me was not without effect.
1 CORINTHIANS 15:10 NIV

THE GRACE OF GENTLENESS

> As apostles of Christ we . . . were gentle among you, like a
> mother caring for her little children.
> 1 THESSALONIANS 2:6-7 NIV

Lily had just lost her beloved little calico cat. Her friend Angela was not a cat-lover—in fact, she really didn't like felines at all. But when Lily called, her voice shaking with emotion, Angela spoke words of sympathy and understanding. The passing of a cat didn't mean much to Angela, but her friend's broken heart did—so she gave Lily the grace of gentleness.

GRACE FOR TODAY

THE GENTLENESS OF GRACE LIFTS US ALL UP WHEN WE'RE FEELING LOW.

Carrie had a big decision to make. Fran gave her some wisdom that came from experience. In the end, though, Carrie chose her own way and ended up failing. It would have been easy for Fran to say, "I told you so." But Fran thought about how she would feel in the same situation. She chose to be gentle—listening with an open heart to Carrie's regrets and offering friendship and encouragement.

When you're feeling vulnerable, it is so comforting to confide in someone who will be gentle. Gentle people show us Jesus, who called everyone who was tired, disappointed, and full of regrets to come to Him. Even when we've sinned, He promises to accept us gently with love if we will only seek His forgiveness. When we feel broken, we can rest, knowing that Jesus will not beat us down further but will lift us up. Isaiah 42:3 NIV says, "A bruised reed he will not break, and a smoldering wick he will not snuff out."

With the promise and security of God's gentle grace in our lives, we can overcome the temptation to say, "I told you so" and "Get over it," and instead heal hearts with "I'm sorry" and "I'm praying for you." When we do, we'll find that our hearts are encouraged too.

MENTORING

These older women must train the younger women to love
their husbands and their children, to live wisely and be
pure, to take care of their homes, to do good, and to be
submissive to their husbands.
TITUS 2:4-5 NET

Mentoring is usually defined as a long-term relationship in which an experienced person agrees to advise and train another individual. There is something profoundly special about a commitment like this, and the Bible is full of examples. The apostle Paul mentored Timothy, his young son in the faith. Even today we can benefit from their relationship as we read Paul's New Testament letters to Timothy.

GRACE FOR TODAY

JESUS WAS THE
ULTIMATE MENTOR,
AND HE WILL HELP
YOU MENTOR
OTHERS.

The prophet Elijah found his student and successor plowing a family field. Elisha never hesitated in accepting the honor of being mentored by the great prophet and gave no thought to the dangers that surrounded them. He was wholly devoted to Elijah and became a great prophet in his own right.

Jesus, of course, was the ultimate mentor when He walked the earth. A significant factor in His relationship with His disciples was that He loved first and taught second. You might call it servant leadership. We can understand that it is easy to receive from someone when you know that the person has your best interest at heart. No doubt this played a role in their devotion to Him even after He had ascended to the Father. Everything Jesus did and said served to teach and guide the disciples, and we are still being mentored by Him through His Holy Spirit dwelling in us today.

In a world greatly lacking leaders with a spiritual and moral compass, we need godly mentors now more than ever. Are you willing to step up to the plate? You don't have to have "arrived." All that is needed is a heart full of love and a willingness to share what Jesus has taught you. God himself will help you do it.

THE PRECIOUS GIFT OF TIME

Lord, let me know my end, and what is the measure of my
days; let me know how fleeting my life is.
PSALM 39:4 NRSV

Donna couldn't believe her eyes. Her three-year-old daughter stood next to the coffee table, scissors in hand. Blond curls lay on the floor and coffee table. "Oh, Chelsea," she moaned. "I've told you never to touch the scissors." Taking the scissors from her daughter's hand, Donna turned her around. The back was untouched, but around the face, Chelsea had snipped at random, including her bangs.

Almost every mom has gone through this situation with her child, sometimes more than once. It seems to be a toddler's rite of passage. Even grown women have taken the scissors to their hair and quickly regretted it. Who hasn't had a bad haircut in a salon? Not fun. But the wonderful thing about hair is that it always grows back. A few weeks, and all is well again. Unlike hair, time, once lost, is lost forever. We cannot relive yesterday or add back days to our lives.

In the New Testament, James described life as a vapor that appears for only a little while and then quickly vanishes. Life is fleeting. In light of eternity, we live but a moment here on Earth. And each second, each minute, each day amounts to a once-in-a-lifetime opportunity, available only to you.

Treat each day as a precious gift of God's grace. Live it with gusto. Don't waste time being angry, longing for what you can't have, or being preoccupied with hopelessness and depression. See your time as the irreplaceable treasure it is.

SWEET-SMELLING SAINTS

Live a life of love just as Christ loved us and gave himself
for us as a sweet-smelling offering and sacrifice to God.
EPHESIANS 5:2 NCV

A friend brought Liz a plant similar to a cactus. Before long, a maroon, star-shaped blossom about eight inches in diameter appeared. It was beautiful; but the flower emitted a strong and fetid odor, resembling what would come from a decaying animal carcass. How could something so pretty smell so rotten?

When Liz asked her friend about the stench, she told Liz, "The name of the plant is Carrion. Now you know why."

It's surprising how much emphasis the Bible puts on the sense of smell. Unholiness is a stench in the nostrils of God. In Genesis 19:13 NLT, the angel of the Lord said of Sodom and Gomorrah's sin, "We will destroy the city completely. The stench of the place has reached the LORD, and he has sent us to destroy it."

> ## GRACE FOR TODAY
>
> GOD'S GRACE FILLS US WITH A SWEET-SMELLING FRAGRANCE THAT DRAWS TO CHRIST ALL WHO COME INTO CONTACT WITH US.

It is recorded in the Old Testament that when the Temple became offensive, it had to be cleansed by sacrifice. Before Christ came, the burning of incense and the sacrificing of animals were referred to as a sweet fragrance in the nostrils of God.

Jesus became the perfect sacrifice for our sins, and now there's no need for another. His blood makes it possible for us to repent and be saved. True repentance of sin is indeed a sweet aroma to God. Not only that, but the transformation of our lives also is a sweet aroma.

We do want to be beautiful like the Carrion as a display of the grace of God, but the Carrion flower's appearance is deceptive. It's important for our spiritual life to match our appearance, so we may attract others to God through our witness.

Let's not only look like Christians, but be sweet-smelling saints, diffusing the aroma of Christ. How do you smell to God and the world?

BE CREATIVE!

God has given each of you some special abilities; be sure to use them to help each other, passing on to others God's many kinds of blessings.
1 PETER 4:10 TLB

What is your passion? What do you love to do? Perhaps you like to paint or draw. Maybe singing lifts your heart to the Lord like nothing else. Or it could be that you get excited just thinking about leading a team of people to pull a big project together? Did you know that God gave you this passion? It isn't an accident that you feel the most alive when you're writing or sewing or organizing or whatever your particular passion may be. You are the only one with your unique abilities and gifts — God created you that way!

GRACE FOR TODAY

THE WORLD NEEDS THE UNIQUE CONTRIBUTION YOU CAN MAKE THROUGH GOD'S GRACE!

Our special creativity is a form of God's grace to us — and to the world. God is a Creator — the most creative being ever — and He made us in His own image. Just as He delights in what He created, so we find joy in making our own unique contributions. We are all blessed with certain talents that we can use to share God's grace and love with the world. And no matter what your ability, you can be assured that what you do is vital and important. You are the only one who can do what you do; and if you don't use your talent, no one else can do it for you!

So take some time today to reflect on your gifts. What are you passionate about? What makes you come alive? Your answer to these questions will lead you to your God-given role in this world. Offer these talents to the Lord and see what He does with them. You will find some of your most cherished dreams coming true when you seek to glorify God in your own unique way. So sing, draw, paint, organize, write, dance, play — rejoice that you are an absolutely unique child of God!

STOP! THIEF!

By Warren W. Wiersbe

"Paul's doctrine of grace is dangerous!" cried the Judaizers. "It replaces law with license. Why, if we do away with our rules and abandon our high standards, the churches will fall apart."

First-century Judaizers are not the only ones afraid to depend on God's grace. Legalists in our churches today warn that we dare not teach people about the liberty we have in Christ lest it result in religious anarchy. These people do not understand Paul's teaching about grace, and it is to correct such misunderstanding that Paul wrote the final section of his letter (Galatians 5—6).

Paul turns now from argument to application, from the doctrinal to the practical. The Christian who lives by faith is not going to become a rebel. Quite the contrary, he is going to experience the inner discipline of God that is far better that the outer discipline of man-made rules. No man could become a rebel who depends on God's grace, yields to God's Spirit, lives for others, and seeks to glorify God. The surrendered Christian who depends on the power of the Spirit is not denying the law of God or rebelling against it. Rather, that law is being fulfilled in him through the Spirit (Romans 8:1—4).[23]

FATHER IN HEAVEN:

I've made a mess of working to keep Your rules. No matter how hard I try, I just fail. Therefore, Lord, I throw myself on Your mercy. Pour out Your love and grace on my life, and make me the kind of person who will live a life that's pleasing to You.

AMEN

We through the Spirit eagerly wait for the hope of righteousness by faith. For in Christ Jesus neither circumcision nor uncircumcision avails anything, but faith working through love.
GALATIANS 5:5-6 NKJV

A PROMISE KEPT

A generous man will prosper; he who refreshes others will
himself be refreshed.
PROVERBS 11:25 NIV

In 1987, Christian real estate agent Oral Lee Brown walked into a class of first-graders from the violence-plagued flatlands of East Oakland, California, and made a promise—stay in school, and I'll see you through college. Brown then began setting aside $10,000 a year in a trust fund out of her $45,000 annual income.

GRACE FOR TODAY

GOD IS ABUNDANTLY GENEROUS WITH US; AND IN TURN, WE REFLECT HIS GENEROSITY TO OTHERS.

With this promise Oral Lee gave twenty-three children, whom few expected to amount to anything, a glimpse of something better to strive for. She tutored them weekly and bought them Christmas presents. When they were old enough, she took them to visit colleges.

Statistically, three out of four students who started as freshmen at the local high school dropped out before graduating, but Oral Lee's kids beat the odds. Twenty out of her twenty-three students graduated from high school, and nineteen enrolled in colleges.

LaTosha Hunter became the first student from that first-grade class to earn a college degree, a bachelor's in accounting, and Oral Lee was there to hug her after LaTosha crossed the stage and received her diploma.

LaTosha said, "I don't know what I would be today if I hadn't met Miss Brown. It's just her inspiration. It's carried us so far."

A colleague once warned Oral Lee, "You can't change the world," but that person was wrong. Through God's grace and her generosity, Brown is changing the world, one student at a time. Today she has renewed her promise to sixty more students through the Oral Lee Brown Foundation.

Through God's grace, you, too, can give of your time and financial resources to change the world, one child or one needy adult at a time.

RESURRECTION LIFE

If the Spirit of Him Who raised up Jesus from the dead dwells in
you, He Who raised up Christ Jesus from the dead will also
restore life to your mortal (short-lived, perishable) bodies through
His Spirit, Who dwells in you.
ROMANS 8:11 AMP

When we are sick, we often go to the doctor's office for medicine to treat the symptoms of the ailment. Do you realize that the very One you need for your spirit, mind, and body—your medicine—already lives and resides in you? He does. You are power-packed with the same Spirit—the same power—Who raised Jesus Christ from the dead!

God's very nature and goodness dwell in you through the power of the Holy Spirit. He's been there all along. Just like your physical heart pumps blood throughout your body giving you life, when your spirit yields to the Spirit of God, resurrection life is pumped throughout your entire being—spirit, soul, and body!

When you become aware of God's presence residing in you, His very power and life can bring health and healing to your spirit, mind, will, emotions, and body. You can yield to that resurrection life so that it fills you with His strength. All you have to do is tap into it. The Bible says that "the Spirit of Him Who raised up Jesus from the dead dwells in you." He's already there. Connect to God through prayer and become more aware of the power He's given you. If that same power can raise Jesus from the dead, it can restore your life—no matter what you need.

GRACE FOR TODAY

GOD HAS PLACED WITHIN US THE SAME POWER THAT RAISED
CHRIST FROM THE DEAD.

SURPRISING GRACE

You have turned my mourning into joyful dancing. You
have taken away my clothes of mourning and clothed me
with joy.
PSALM 30:11 NLT

They were two women with few options—but they did have each other. Naomi and Ruth faced devastating loss and sorrow together when both were widowed. Naomi decided to deal with her situation by going home to Bethlehem, in hopes of finding someone to provide for her needs. She urged Ruth to go back to her hometown as well—she was still young and deserved to find love again among her own people. But Ruth refused to be parted from her mother-in-law. With a passionate plea, Ruth convinced Naomi that they should remain together and face whatever was to come, side-by-side.

GRACE FOR TODAY

EXPECT THE
UNEXPECTED
WHEN IT COMES
TO GOD'S
GRACE—HE WILL
SURPRISE YOU
WITH JOY!

And so began a beautiful story of grace—grace given and received between two grieving women—and the providential grace of God, who turned their sorrow into joy. Naomi found comfort in the love and friendship of her daughter-in-law. Ruth found strength and wisdom in Naomi's gentle guidance. In the end, God blessed them both for their faithfulness by giving them a new family. Ruth found love again and became the mother of a son. Naomi's bitter disappointment was turned to delight as she held this precious new life. Centuries later, the grace of God through Ruth and Naomi continues, because it was through their family line that Jesus came to earth!

God's grace is truly amazing and often comes to us in unexpected ways. God used two poverty-stricken and grieving widows to become the ancestors of the Messiah. Just think of what His grace can do in your life today. Look to the Lord. Give Him your disappointment, your sorrow, and your grief. Expect the unexpected. Grace is going to surprise you!

EVERY REASON

A man will leave his father and mother and be united to
his wife, and they will become one flesh.
GENESIS 2:24 NIV

Relationships aren't cars. But couples often say that they want to live together to test-drive the relationship. If they want to share each other's daily lives—sounds pretty emotionally invested already. Don't need a license to prove their love? Why do they need a convenient exit door?

Perhaps today's couples don't understand how much marriage is an expression of God's grace. Jesus often used the imagery of a bride and groom to teach us about God's loyal commitment to us. Marriage at the heart is all about respect, love, friendship, dependability, admiration, care, and, most of all, lasting commitment. But couples often fear they won't be able to come through in a marriage. God says that through His grace, they can.

> ## GRACE FOR TODAY
>
> MARRIAGE ISN'T EASY, BUT BY GOD'S GRACE IT CAN BE ALL HE INTENDED IT TO BE.

Why? Weddings are spiritually significant. Cecil Myers wrote, "Successful marriage is always a triangle: a man, a woman, and God." In a marriage you are asking God to enter in with you. He is a partner to your marriage and is more committed to your love than even you are. One of God's graces that a Christian can depend on is the ability to love like God, even over the long run.

The Bible says that "marriage should be honored by all" (Hebrews 13:4 NIV). You're not just making a public declaration of your special and exclusive love. You're telling the world, "By the grace of God, marriage is possible." Your marriage demonstrates the miracle of changed lives to the watching world.

There's deep significant meaning in the promises you speak during a marriage ceremony You can't test-drive those meanings. You have to step out in faith and commit yourself to God's promise that you can keep this commitment to love "'til death do you part."

149

Special Stove

He himself bore our sins in his body on the tree, so that we might die to sins and live for righteousness; by his wounds you have been healed.
1 PETER 2:24 NIV

Michelle didn't notice when her son, Chase, slipped into the room while she talked with the contractor. She was remodeling her kitchen, and as they discussed which stove to buy, four-year-old Chase piped up with his opinion. "Mommy, you have to get one just like Grandma's!"

Michelle asked him why, to which he replied, "Because everything that comes out of it tastes so good!"

Chase gave the stove far too much credit. His Grandma Shirley would think so too, since she was the one who created the scrumptious concoctions that went into it.

Grace for Today

A MIRACLE IS A WORK EXCEEDING THE POWER OF ANY CREATED AGENT, CONSEQUENTLY BEING AN EFFECT OF THE DIVINE OMNIPOTENCE.

ROBERT SOUTH

In the Gospel accounts, Luke refers to some form of the word "heal" in connection with Christ's ministry more times than any other writer. As a physician, Luke knew his limitations, so it adds credibility to the accounts he records. He would have been able to verify the authenticity of Jesus' healings.

We might go to the doctor, but God created our bodies to fight off disease and heal wounds. He's the one who gave doctors the knowledge for modern medicine as well as traditional cures. We may have someone pray for us, but still, it is God who miraculously heals us through prayer. Just as the stove is a vessel used only to cook a meal, people are only vessels used by God. Ultimately it is through Jesus' death upon the cross of Calvary that we can receive healing in our lives.

As Chase credited the stove with creating the meals, at times we credit humans with our healing. Let's instead give credit where credit is due—to the Healer himself, the Lord Jesus Christ.

FREE FOR ALL

By John Wesley

The grace or love of God, whence cometh our salvation, is free in all, and free for all. It is free in all to whom it is given. It does not depend on any power or merit in man; no, not in any degree, neither in whole, nor in part. It does not in anywise depend either on the good works or righteousness of the receiver; not on anything he has done, or anything he is.

Receiving God's love and grace does not depend on a person's endeavors. It does not depend on his good temper, or good desires, or good purposes and intentions; for all these flow from the free grace of God; they are the streams only, not the fountain. They are the fruits of free grace, and not the root. They are not the cause, but the effects of it.

Whatever good is in man, or is done by man, God is the author and doer of it. Thus is His grace free in all, that is, no way depending on any power or merit in man, but on God alone, who freely gave us His own Son, and with Him freely giveth us all things.[24]

FATHER GOD:

Thank You for saving me when I could not save myself. I know that I don't deserve Your love and grace but You have given it to me despite my unworthiness. I know that anything good in me is from Your grace. I will call upon that grace every day as I walk out my salvation.

AMEN

God is able to make all grace abound to you, so that in all things at all times, having all that you need, you will abound in every good work.
2 CORINTHIANS 9:8 NIV

LIFE SPRINGS FORTH

[Jesus said,] "I am the vine, you are the branches; he who
abides in Me and I in him, he bears much fruit, for apart
from Me you can do nothing.
JOHN 15:5 NASB

When Jesus walked the earth, He used practical applications to teach people. Sometimes He used the wonders of nature as examples common to those He taught, so they could understand His teaching.

On the night before His death, Jesus compared us to branches that cannot bear fruit except we abide in the vine. He said that He is the vine. If we abide in Him and stay closely connected to Him, we receive life from the Vine. Without Jesus, we would be as dead branches ready to be consumed by the fire. But with Jesus, we not only live, we bear fruit.

In Jeremiah 20, Jeremiah said that God's Word felt like a burning fire shut up in his bones. It literally burst forth from within him like flames of fire. As you look around, see all the beautiful flowers and trees bursting forth with new life each spring, because they spent the winter with roots growing deep into the ground. Purpose in your heart that the good news of God's grace will burst forth from you as you spend time leaning on Jesus and abiding in Him.

Have you ever heard the saying, "Bloom where you're planted?" Let's be planted in the Lord, growing and developing the flowers and fruit of the Spirit.

GRACE FOR TODAY

SPIRITUAL GROWTH IS A GRACE FROM GOD. THE MORE WE
RELY ON JESUS, THE MORE FRUIT WE WILL BEAR.

BURNOUT

There is a time for everything, and a season for every
activity under heaven.
ECCLESIASTES 5:1 NIV

Sometimes we confuse our desire to always say yes to God with a need to say yes to everything people ask us to do. Sometimes saying no is the answer God wants you to give, the answer you need. There's no shame in that. Then why do we feel so guilty? Most people want to please others. But does saying yes make others happy but you and your family miserable? That is a sign you may be out of God's will.

GRACE FOR TODAY

WITHIN GOD'S GRACE
IS REST FOR THE
WEARY SOUL.

Jesus said that His burden is easy and light. If yours is heavy, maybe He didn't ask you to pick it up. Sometimes we burn ourselves out doing God's job, and no wonder!

Burnout is the disastrous process of falling into total exhaustion. Sometimes we don't even realize it. But our families can certainly smell the smoke. Here are signs of burnout:

- Your family sleeps; you lie horizontally and mentally organize/agonize for long periods of time in the dark.
- You cry hysterically when someone actually offers to help you.
- When the phone rings, you're afraid to answer.
- PMS symptoms never go away.
- You have increasingly negative thoughts about everyone and almost everything.
- Everybody is a jerk.
- You no longer view friends, colleagues, or church members as people, but rather life-sucking parasites.
- You wonder if you can have Duracell batteries surgically implanted in your body.
- Perfectionism is replaced with a "whatever" attitude.
- Disillusioned@myhouse.com is now your e-mail address.
- Nobody understands you except for the dog, and he drinks out of toilets.

It doesn't have to be like this. You can take on Jesus' yoke and live in His timetable. He can lead you by still waters. Want to go?

LET YOUR LIGHT SHINE

[Jesus said,] "You are the light of the world. A city on a hill cannot be hidden. Neither do people light a lamp and put it under a bowl. Instead they put it on its stand, and it gives light to everyone in the house."
MATTHEW 5:14-15 NIV

GRACE FOR TODAY

GOD IS LIGHT, AND HE HAS CHOSEN TO LET THAT LIGHT SHINE THROUGH US TO ILLUMINE THE DARKNESS ON EARTH.

A story is told of an uneventful flight from Washington, D.C., to Chicago. Upon landing, the plane taxied halfway to the terminal and stopped in the middle of the runway with its engines idling. Many of the passengers looked anxiously out the windows and started fidgeting in their seats.

Then the pilot made an announcement that defused the tension. "I flew this multimillion dollar aircraft from Washington, D.C. at night and found Chicago O'Hare International Airport on my first try. However, now I have to wait until a guy with a couple of ninety-nine-cent flashlights shows me how to park it."

We may laugh at this example; but it shows how important lights can be, whether they are runway lights, a cockpit panel, or ninety-nine-cent flashlights. Have you ever experienced a blackout? Total darkness can be frightening. Yet Scripture tells us, "God is light; in him there is no darkness at all . . . If we walk in the light, as he is in the light, we have fellowship with one another" (1 John 1:5,7 NIV).

God is our guiding light who illuminates the road or runway we are to travel. We may not fly multimillion-dollar planes or even wave ninety-nine-cent flashlights, but He has a purpose for each of us. If we are filled with His grace and have fellowship with Him, we will not walk in darkness but will be filled with His light. Then that light can shine through us so that we may illumine the way for others to discover God's plan for their lives.

TRAVELING COMPANIONS

Two people can accomplish more than twice as much as
one . . . If one person falls, the other can reach out and
help.
ECCLESIASTES 4:9-10 NLT

Young Dorothy was restless. She dreamed of something more than humdrum everyday life. What was she missing? Where was the adventure she longed for?

Dorothy found adventure when she was swept away to the colorful, and sometimes dangerous, world of Oz. This strange place introduced the Kansas farm girl to things she had never even imagined. Yet, from the moment she touched down in Oz, Dorothy realized that her deepest longing wasn't for exotic places and strange creatures—in her heart of hearts, she just wanted home.

GRACE FOR TODAY

GOD'S GRACE IS
MEANT TO BE
SHARED—SO DON'T
TRAVEL ALONE.

And so, little Dorothy set off on a journey to find her way back. Along the way she gains some traveling companions. Just like her, they are all searching for something that is missing in their lives. And just like Dorothy, they all need help—they all need grace.

The Scarecrow is wobbly and often needs support to remain steady. The Tin Man cries himself rusty and needs help to get moving again. The Cowardly Lion is, well, a coward. He needs the others to help him overcome his fears.

When you think about it, we're all on a similar journey. We're all searching. In the end, what any of us really want to find is our heart's true home. Along the way we meet others on the same journey. As we travel together, we find that we all need grace—from each other and from God.

None of us should take this long road alone. We need each other—for support when we're weak, to dry our tears when we're hurting, and to help us face our fears when our courage fails. God's grace is meant to be shared. So take a lesson from Dorothy and don't travel alone. May you and your companions discover your heart's true home, God's healing presence, together. There is no place like it.

TASTE THE MIRACULOUS

You are the God who performs miracles; you display your
power among the peoples.
PSALM 77:14 NIV

What constitutes a miracle, a wonder, or a marvel? Consider the Seven Wonders of the World. Although most people know they exist, few can name them. Like the ancient times in which they were built, for most of us the details remain hidden in history books. Yet we have the honor and privilege to witness miracles from God first, hand, every day.

We are not very different from the children of Israel. God's presence amazingly went before them as a cloud by day and a fire by night. He was always with them. All they had to do was look up. Everywhere they went, they experienced His power, from walking on the bottom of the dry Red Sea floor to the daily provision of manna God supplied for food. Our days are also filled with the wonders of God's presence.

Each one of us is actually a wonder of God, a miracle in many ways. Perhaps you were that premature baby that lived. Maybe you escaped a car crash unscathed. You beat the odds and survived cancer. When you look back over your life, you probably see many instances in which God's hand worked miracles on your behalf.

Celebrate today the very fact that you are breathing. He is as close as the air you inhale. Refuse to allow the wonders of your life to become a faded memory. Recall the events of your life and look for His marvels. Without Him we can do nothing, but with Him, nothing is impossible.

GRACE FOR TODAY

EVEN THE SMALLEST DETAIL OF YOUR LIFE IS A MIRACLE OF
GOD'S GRACE.

The God Who Raises the Dead

By Luis Palau

Despair seems to have several different forms. The most common type occurs when a person is beset by "external" troubles—such as financial difficulties or poor health. People who experience this particular form of despair usually are convinced that if only their external circumstances were better, they'd feel fine.

On the other hand, some people experience inner despair even though their external circumstances are ideal. They have all the money they want, all the friends they need, all the education they can stand—but an inexplicable emptiness still haunts them. This type of despair may well be the worst; its source is not definable, and it's suffered alone.

We often consider Paul to be the dynamic, unquenchable apostle, but he too suffered from inner despair. Paul's despair, however, was not due to "external" failures or the emptiness that accompanies the quest for personal gain.

Rather, his resulted from difficult circumstances he faced in the fulfillment of his ministry. Yet Paul found comfort and victory in the God who raises the dead—a comfort we can find too!

Perhaps you've gone through an experience similar to Paul's. Believe it or not, that could be the most exciting moment of your life—a moment of real victory, when Christ can step into the situation that is troubling you. He can take over the haunting, inner despair of your heart that you share with no one. He can cleanse you and transform you. He can fill you with His Spirit and give you peace.[25]

HEAVENLY FATHER:

I want to exchange my despair for Your comfort. I reach out to you now, expecting this to be a turning point in my life. May I experience the joy that comes from You.

AMEN

In our hearts we felt the sentence of death. But this happened that we might not rely on ourselves but on God, who raises the dead.
2 CORINTHIANS 1:9 NIV

FINDING YOU

Jesus said, "Your Father in heaven is not willing that any of
these little ones should be lost."
MATTHEW 18:14 NIV

The animated fish flick *Finding Nemo* was a box-office hit. Kids loved it. Parents loved it. Pretty much everyone loved this clever tale of a lost little fish and his father's quest to bring him home.

> ## GRACE FOR TODAY
>
> ---
>
> GOD IS ON A RESCUE MISSION TO FIND US AND BRING US HOME.

Nemo's dad, Marlin, knew all too well the dangers of the ocean. He lost his wife and all but one of his children in the beginning of the film. Nemo is all that is left of his family, and Marlin protects him fiercely — too fiercely for Nemo's adventurous spirit. One day Marlin's deepest fears are realized when little Nemo ventures off alone and ends up in a dentist's aquarium.

So Marlin musters up all the courage he can and faces the wide and treacherous ocean to save his beloved son. It is a beautiful story of the bond between a father and son, and the lengths to which a parent will go for the sake of a precious child.

When you consider the theme of this animated tale, it is no wonder that it was such a hit. We have all ventured far from home and found ourselves lost. We don't know how to get back to our Father. And so, because He loves us so much, God comes to Earth to search for us. He gives up the comfort and safety of His home in Heaven and travels through the treacherous world on a rescue mission — all for us. In the ultimate act of grace, He gives up His own life that we might be able to return home again.

So look around in expectation. Your Father has arrived. He has set you free, and you can go home. God's grace is all about finding you.

TECHNOLOGY AND YOU

My mouth shall speak wisdom; the meditation of my heart
shall be understanding.
PSALM 49:3 NRSV

"Back up my hard drive? How do I put it in reverse?" "Who's General Failure, and why's he reading my disk?"

Does this sound like you? Technology can be a new and scary thing. Still thinking an attachment has something to do with stapling? You burn a DVD? And why isn't that a bad thing?

Every generation has faced new technology, but never before in as accelerated a speed — or with results so accessible and freeing. We can view technology as a monster or as our new best friend. We may not have a desire to learn, but we do have an obligation to explore the tools which God has made available to us.

GRACE FOR TODAY

TECHNOLOGICAL PROGRESS IS FROM GOD. IT CAN AND MUST LEAD TO HIM.

Why do we need to keep current? We can reach the world in so many different ways today. We can communicate God's truth through the Internet, e-mail, computer programs, DVDs, CDs, digital and cellular technologies. The Gutenberg Bible may have been a result of one of the first steps into technology, but we continue that journey today.

Pope Pius XII said, "The Church welcomes technological progress and receives it with love, for it is an indubitable fact that technological progress comes from God and, therefore, can and must lead to Him."

How can we be effective communicators if we can't figure out new ways to communicate? That's a solvable problem. "If the iron is blunt, and one does not whet the edge, then more strength must be exerted; but wisdom helps one to succeed" (Ecclesiastes 10:10 NRSV). So is your technological iron a little blunt and dry? Time to sharpen your mental edge? Why not take a class, read a book, or get a friend to help you.

Just remember what the CEO of IBM, Louis Gerstner, said; "Computers are magnificent tools for the realization of our dreams, but no machine can replace the human spark of spirit, compassion, love, and understanding." With God's help you can put all of that into your technological world.

THE LIVING-WATER CYCLE

[Jesus said,] "If any man is thirsty, let him come to Me and drink!
He who believes in Me [who cleaves to and trusts in and relies on
Me] as the Scripture has said, From his innermost being shall
flow [continuously] springs and rivers of living water."
JOHN 7:37-38 AMP

GRACE FOR TODAY

WHEN YOU RECEIVE GOD'S GRACE, YOU BECOME PART OF THE LIVING-WATER CYCLE.

Do you remember learning about the water cycle in school? The rain comes down and fills up the streams that flow into rivers that flow into the ocean. Water evaporates from the streams, rivers, and oceans back up into the clouds where eventually it comes back down again as rain. Then the whole process starts over again.

We can see God's great wisdom in a process like the water cycle. Living things are watered and nourished without the amount of water in the cycle being diminished. The water just keeps recycling—it is never lost.

God created a spiritual water cycle too. Through His infinite resources, He offers us living water through Jesus. When we receive it, we are filled to overflowing. We can then share that living water with others through love and kindness and the good news of Christ. But when we pour what we've received onto others, we don't lose anything—because we are full to overflowing. When others receive that life, they then overflow to still other people who need renewal. Finally that living water overflows in thanks and praise back to God! The living water is never lost because it continues to flow from God to us, from us to others through Jesus, and from believers back to God.

So the next time it rains, imagine those drops of water as God's grace falling on you. Let Him fill you so that you overflow to those around you. Be nourished and nourish others, without fear of losing anything. Be a part of the living-water cycle!

GRACE AND GALAXIES

Thus the heavens and the earth were completed in all
their vast array.
GENESIS 2:1 NIV

One night in 1609, Galileo Galilei turned his telescope to the heavens above the Italian countryside and changed astronomy forever. Telescopes revealed stars that no one had previously imagined. Today, the Hubble Space Telescope, a large reflecting telescope designed by NASA and set into orbit in 1990, has brought us breathtaking images of the moons of Jupiter and the rings of Saturn. The ultimate goal of this space mission is to gain an understanding of how our universe began.

David also wrote about creation in the eighth Psalm. "When I consider your heavens, the work of your fingers, the moon and the stars, which you have set in place, what is man that you are mindful of him, the son of man that you care for him?" (verses 3-4 NIV). Consider the wonder of the universe that David beheld that night. He had an advantage that most modern astronomers lack—the simple faith to believe that the God who made it all cared for him.

GRACE FOR TODAY

AN INFINITE GOD CAN GIVE ALL OF HIMSELF TO EACH OF HIS CHILDREN.

A.W. TOZER

The indescribable beauty of a night sky causes us to reflect upon its Creator. Out of this infinite, dark expanse, God focused on us that He might express His love. Jesus himself was made a little lower than the angels for the suffering of death. The Creator of the Universe became subject to His creation and suffered at their hands. By this we see that God loves and values us more than all the massive suns and galaxies that He created. He created us and came to save us. He chose to redeem us. Even while we were still sinners, Christ gave His life for us.

The Creator of this vast universe, the One who molded the stars and gave them light, loves us so much that He has redeemed us. Tonight, look up at the stars and thank God for His provision.

MESSAGES OF GRACE

The LORD is close to the brokenhearted.
PSALM 34:18 NIV

Just two days before Rick and Rachel's wedding, Rachel's grandmother passed away suddenly. The whole family was in shock, but agreed that Grandma would want the wedding to go on and for the happy couple to keep their honeymoon plans. So with a mixture of grief and joy, Rick and Rachel became man and wife on a blustery April day. The next morning they boarded a plane and flew to the Colorado Rockies for a ten-day honeymoon.

GRACE FOR TODAY

GOD WHISPERS TO OUR HEARTS THE WORDS WE NEED TO HEAR.

On their way into Rocky Mountain National Park, they stopped at a music store. Their rental car had a CD player, so they thought it would be nice to have some driving music. A hauntingly beautiful song was playing over the speaker in the store, and Rick asked what it was. The clerk found the CD for him, and he decided to buy it on a whim. They jumped back into their car, popped the CD in, and headed for the mountains.

As they drove, enjoying the music and the majestic scenery, Rachel's thoughts turned to her grandmother. She knew that Grandma was now rejoicing in Heaven, but losing her still left an ache in Rachel's heart. As a tear crept down her face, the words of the song that was playing reached her ears. Like a distant chorus from Heaven, it sang, "When I'm gone don't cry for me, for in my Father's arms I'll be." Rachel turned to Rick with tears running down her face—tears of both sadness and joy. God had provided just the right message at just the right time.

Sometimes, when we least expect it, God sends us messages of grace. Whether it be through His Word, through the love of a friend, or even the words of a song, God is always speaking to our hearts. His grace surrounds us and whispers the words that we are desperate to hear. Listen today for His still, small voice. He is speaking words of grace.

IT IS DIVINE

By John MacArthur Jr.

To put it simply, peace is an attribute of God. If I asked you to list the attributes of God, these are the ones that would probably come most readily to mind: His love, grace, mercy justice, holiness, wisdom, truth, omnipotence, immutability, and immortality. But do you ever think of God as being characterized by peace? In fact, He is peace. Whatever it is that He gives us, He has and He is. There is no lack of perfect peace in His being. God is never stressed. He never fears. God is never at cross purposes with Himself. He never has problems making up His mind.

God lives in perfect calm and contentment. Why? Because He's in charge of everything and can operate everything perfectly according to His own will. Since He is omniscient, He is never surprised. There are no threats to His omnipotence. There is no possible sin that can stain His holiness. Even His wrath is clear, controlled, and confident. There is no regret in His mind for He has never done, said, or thought anything that He would change in any way.

God enjoys perfect harmony within Himself. Our Bibles call Him, "the Lord of peace," but in the Greek text a definite article appears before the word translated "peace," meaning He literally is "the Lord of the peace." This is real peace—the divine kind—not the kind the world has. Paul's prayer is that we might experience that kind of peace. Its source is God and God alone.[26]

HEAVENLY FATHER:

I need Your peace in my life. I need Your calm, Your serenity, Your contentment. I want to experience perfect harmony. I ask You to pour out Your grace on me, Lord–Your grace and Your peace.

AMEN

May the Lord of peace himself give you peace at all times and in every way.
2 THESSALONIANS 3:16 NIV

PERSONAL COMPUTERS

[Jesus said,] "I have called you friends."
JOHN 15:15 NIV

GRACE FOR TODAY

JESUS IS A FRIEND WHO STICKS CLOSER THAN A BROTHER OR ANY EARTHLY FRIEND. HE IS UTTERLY RELIABLE AND WILL NEVER LEAVE YOUR SIDE.

"Personal computers" have become an integral part of our lives. Almost every home has one. Yet, they are poorly named. They may be computers, but they aren't personal. They are cold, heartless, and detached. Their main component is called a hard disk, and even the shell is hard. Just when we think we have the programs inside the machine mastered, a new version of software comes out, and we have to learn all over again.

The biggest problem with computers is that they do exactly what we command, even when we mean to do something different. If we inadvertently hit the "Caps Lock" key, giant letters appear as we type; and we have to go back and correct the problem. Even worse, if we hit the "Delete" key at the wrong time, an hour's worth of work may disappear. We can "Undo" some things if we catch them in time, but often we don't see the problem until it's too late to reverse the damage.

Wouldn't it be nice if our PCs were more like personal friends? Then they would instinctively know what we mean and not give to us quite so literally what we command. There wouldn't be the danger of making a mistake and causing irreversible damage; it would forgive our blunders and make things right. A computer like that, however, would be too good to be true.

Yet, we do have a friend who is greater than our wildest dreams. He is our PS—our "Personal Savior," and our PF—our "Personal Friend." Jesus died on the cross and made us His friends. We do not have to follow the letter of the law and push exactly the right buttons to win His approval, nor does He dismiss us if we hit a wrong key. All He asks is that we accept His gift of grace. It's not what we do—it's what He did.

CRITICAL NATURE

She opens her mouth with wisdom, and the teaching of
kindness is on her tongue.
PROVERBS 31:26 NRSV

Logan Pearsall Smith wrote, "Don't tell your friends their social faults; they will cure the fault and never forgive you." We love to be overly critical of famous people. It's practically a national sport. The first thing to remember is that life isn't a movie and we're not the critic. Having a critical personality is not the way to have a winning social life.

Jesus had a lot to say about a critical spirit. "Don't pick on people, jump on their failures, criticize their faults — unless, of course, you want the same treatment. That critical spirit has a way of boomeranging" (Matthew 7:1-2 MSG). So God's going to be as critical of us as we are with other people. Isn't that a horrifying thought? But Jesus tells us this because He wants us to experience the free, uncritical grace of God and to share it with others.

Being critical is damaging to others, but it robs us of enjoying people, places, events, and life. If we can only see things in sour tones, what kind of satisfaction can we have in life? What kind of thankfulness can we show God? So what purpose does being critical serve if it robs us personally, distances us from others, and goes directly against the way God wants us to be? It's just a no-win situation.

GRACE FOR TODAY

THE EYES OF GRACE SEE THE BEAUTY IN PEOPLE AND THE WORLD.

Focus on the beauty in your world and the people around you. After all, Jesus loves you — and the people around you. He sees a beautiful you, and them, within a very human shell. Follow His example with others, and you will find more than God's blessing — you'll find Him.

A WEB OF HOPE

The needy will not always be forgotten, nor the hope of the
afflicted perish forever.
PSALM 9:18 NASB

In 1966, after Mao Tse-tung launched his Great Proletarian Revolution in China, Nien Chaing was beaten, imprisoned, and left in solitary confinement for more than six years. Her crime? She worked for Shell Oil Company.

While lying on her cot one afternoon, a spider crawled into her cell and methodically climbed up one of the iron bars of her window. In her book *Life and Death in Shanghai* Nien wrote that she watched with fascination while the tiny creature scaled its mountain to the top. After it reached the summit, the spider swung off the bar and slid down on a silken thread spun from its body. Once it had secured the thread to the bottom of the bar, it crawled back up the bar and swung out on a new track.

> ## GRACE FOR TODAY
>
> GOD'S FINGERPRINTS LEAVE EVIDENCE ALL AROUND TO HELP US LOOK PAST OUR CURRENT SITUATION AND FIND A TREASURE OF HOPE IN HIS HANDS.

Nien's cell was no longer a prison as she stared at the spider's feat with admiration. How did it know, without hesitation or mistake, what to do next and where to attach the next thread? Once the spider had made the outside frame, it proceeded to fill in the middle with its intricate web.

Questions continued to bombard her mind. Who taught the spider to make its web? Was it only an evolutionary skill as the communists taught? Or did God give the spider its abilities? Ultimately, she decided that it was God who was in control, not only of a tiny spider, but of her life as well. At that thought, Nien said, "I felt a renewal and a hope surge inside me."

No matter your circumstances, God has not forgotten you. Look around you for God's fingerprints. If He can use a tiny spider to give one small Chinese woman hope in a prison cell, don't you think He can do the same for you?

RETURN TO AFRICA

Consider it pure joy, my brothers, whenever you face trials
of many hinds, because you know that the testing of your
faith develops perseverance.
JAMES 1:2-3 NIV

With the firm belief that God had called him to the mission field in Africa, young Peter Cameron Scott set sail from England. His main goal, along with his seven-member team, was to preach the Gospel from the eastern shore of Kenya all the way to Chad in the central part of the continent.

But shortly after their arrival in 1895, where they established the Africa Inland Mission, Scott and many others contracted severe cases of malaria. Several died, and because of his poor health, Scott went home to England to recuperate. But he was determined to return to Africa after his recovery.

> ## GRACE FOR TODAY
>
> GOD GIVES US PERSEVERANCE TO FULFILL HIS PLAN FOR OUR LIVES.

On his second voyage, his brother John accompanied him, but again the dreaded fever struck soon after their arrival in Kenya. John died, leaving Scott all alone. Still mourning his loss, Scott recommitted himself to God's mission and vowed to stay. Once again, though, his health declined; and he was forced to return home. Where would he ever find the strength to complete God's work in Africa?

One day Scott quietly entered Westminster Abbey and knelt in prayer before the tomb of David Livingstone, another man who had pledged his life to Africa. The inscription on the stone reads: "Other sheep I have which are not of this fold; them I also must bring."

When Scott arose, God birthed new hope in his heart. He would return to Africa for a third time. The Africa Inland Mission, which had such a tragic beginning, not only survived, but continues to flourish today with more than 850 active missionaries.

Most of us could never imagine battling hardship and disease on the mission field. But God has called each and every one of us to fulfill His plan for our lives. Can we persevere in the face of trouble? Only with God's help.

GOD'S CLEAR DIRECTION

If you leave God's paths and go astray, you will hear a Voice
behind you say, "No, this is the way; walk here."
ISAIAH 30:21 TLB

Traveling on vacation by car requires a good map. Anytime you venture down the highway into unknown territory, you need to study and highlight your driving path.

GRACE FOR TODAY

GOD WILL ALWAYS SHOW YOU WHICH WAY TO GO WHEN YOU CALL ON HIM FOR DIRECTION.

But even great planning for your destination doesn't always prepare you for what's not on the map—things like unforeseen detours. Our sense of direction can be greatly altered by anything that is not clearly marked on the map.

When Moses led the children of Israel through the wilderness, he didn't have a paper map to rely on. Can you imagine leading thousands of people into unknown territory without knowing anything about the terrain? It was certainly no vacation having to rely on heavenly food to feed the masses of people, or on the cloud by day that kept them from scorching in the sun, or the fire by night to keep them warm. God provided everything that was needed for the journey through the wilderness; yet, some still doubted God's power and strength when they heard giants were waiting in the Promised Land. But Moses trusted God's direction; and regardless of what happened along the way, He remained on God's path.

God's grace is boundless towards you on every level. His Word is the roadmap that provides counsel, comfort, and confidence that you will never be alone on your journey. Even when life's bumps in the road cause you to veer off His chosen course, He will redirect your path.

Like navigation systems that are built into many new cars to help guide you to your destination, God is your heavenly navigator, always on call, waiting to steer you in the right direction for your life. Throughout your journey, you can trust God's still small voice to guide you out of the darkness and into the light.

TABLES OF STONE–HUMAN HEARTS

By Warren W. Wiersbe

When God gave the Law, He wrote it on tables of stone; and those tables were placed in the Ark of the Covenant. Even if the Israelites could read the two tables, this experience would not change their lives. The Law is an external thing, and people need an internal power if their lives are to be transformed. The legalist can admonish us with his "Do this!" or "Don't do that!" but he cannot give us the power to obey. If we do obey, often it is not from the heart—and we end up worse than before!

The ministry of grace changes the heart. The Spirit of God uses the Word of God and writes it on the heart. The Corinthians were wicked sinners when Paul came to them, but his ministry of the Gospel of God's grace completely changed their lives. (See 1 Corinthians 6:9-11.) Their experience of God's grace certainly meant more to them than the letters of commendation carried by the false teachers. The Corinthian believers were lovingly written on Paul's heart, and the Spirit of God had written the truth on their hearts, making them "living epistles of Christ."[27]

LORD GOD,

Thank you for changing my heart through Your ministry of grace–Your unmerited favor. No matter how hard I tried, I could never be good enough to deserve to be in Your presence. But You overruled the law and received me by an act of Your sovereign grace. Teach me to walk in the gift of grace You've given me, and in return I will give You all my praise.

AMEN

You were washed, you were sanctified, you were justified in the name of the Lord Jesus Christ and in the Spirit of our God.
1 CORINTHIANS 6:11 NRSV

PRESENCE, NOT PERFECTION

Contribute to the needs of God's people [sharing in the necessities of the saints]; pursue the practice of hospitality.
ROMANS 12:13 AMP

GRACE FOR TODAY

WHEN IT COMES TO HOSPITALITY, WE ARE FREED BY JESUS TO BE LOVING AND SAY, "IT IS YOUR PRESENCE, NOT MY PERFECT HOUSE, THAT REALLY MATTERS.

Doesn't it feel great to be invited into someone's house—to be told to "make yourself at home"? You don't notice the color of the carpet or the worn chairs. You feel warm and special knowing that someone cared enough to invite you in. And frankly, if there is a little dust on top of the bookshelf, you don't mind—at least you know you're not alone in your battle with the stuff.

So when it's our turn, why do we struggle so with inviting others over? For most of us, lots of house-cleaning, cooking, and maybe even some redecorating must predicate any invitation. Those mismatched chairs are a travesty—we have to wait until we can buy new ones! That ketchup stain on the family room rug has to be scrubbed! Every last dust bunny must be captured!

Did you know that Jesus himself said that it is not important to have a perfect house? Really—it's in the Bible. Some friends named Mary and Martha invited Jesus and His disciples over to their house. While Mary sat with Jesus and enjoyed His company, Martha scurried frantically around the house, trying to make things perfect. Finally, she got too frustrated to keep silent anymore. She wanted Jesus to tell her sister, Mary, to get up and get moving—there were things to be done!

Jesus did not respond the way Martha had hoped He would. He said, "Only one thing is needed" (Luke 10:42 NIV). He told her, in essence, to "chill out." Things did not need to be perfect. All He really needed was her love, her friendship—her presence with Him. And isn't that what we all want when we're visiting someone? Fancy meals and perfect decor aren't what matter most. The grace of hospitality—genuine love and warmth—these are what make memories that last.

170

SHAKE IT OFF

[The Lord said,] "I have chosen you and have not rejected you."
ISAIAH 41:9 NIV

We all want to be admired, liked, respected, and accepted—but it's a big world out there, and not everybody is going to like you. That's a fact. The reasons may vary, but the feeling of rejection is always the same—painful. The important thing to remember is everybody has felt rejected at one point or another—everybody—from the famous to the ordinary person beside you.

Understanding that rejection is universal and probably inevitable helps us to put it into perspective. Did you know that Jesus was rejected by the majority of the world and understands your feelings of pain, anger, and frustration?

Jesus had some advice on how to deal with rejection. This is what He told His disciples: "If any place will not welcome you and they refuse to hear you, as you leave, shake off the dust that is on your feet as a testimony against them" (Mark 6:11 NRSV). To put it in our terms—just shake it off and walk away. Don't try to convince them of your worth or try to prove your value. Remember, you're a jewel in God's eyes.

> ## GRACE FOR TODAY
>
> I AM AS MY CREATOR MADE ME AND SINCE HE IS SATISFIED, SO AM I.
>
> MINNIE SMITH

Think of it this way. It's a big world out there, and you've got things to do, places to see, and undiscovered friends to meet. Jesus didn't try to transform himself to fit the world, and neither did His disciples. They were who they were, and people could choose to accept or reject them. That's confidence combined with faith.

God loves you, and He would never isolate you from friendships. Think of rejection as a process of elimination that helps you find true friendship. And it is waiting for you because God loves you.

No One Can Take It From You

Rejoice and exult in hope; be steadfast and patient in
suffering and tribulation; be constant in prayer.
ROMANS 12:12 AMP

Almost everyone wonders what it would be like to suffer for their beliefs. What if we were to wake one morning and find our liberty gone and our lives at the mercy of godless men? Could we stand up for what we believe? For two thousand years, Christians around the world have taken a stand for their faith, and many have lost everything—even their lives—as a result. You may think that you would never have the courage to do what they did. And in your own strength, you would be right.

GRACE FOR TODAY

GOD'S GRACE ASSURES US OF HIS PRESENCE, HIS POWER, HIS STRENGTH, HIS PEACE, HIS COURAGE, AND HIS COMFORT IN THE MIDST OF OUR GREATEST TRIALS.

But many of those who have suffered for their faith speak of a remarkable provision in the midst of their trials. They discovered that God's grace was more than enough for them. They felt His mighty hand lifting them up, making them strong in their weakest moments. They learned that God truly was there to walk with them through every painful step on their path. And they soon discovered that no one could separate them from God's love or the eternal reward waiting for them in their Father's kingdom.

No matter what you face in this life, no matter what your losses, you will have the strength and the courage you need just when you need it. God will see to that! You will have more than enough of His presence, His wisdom, and His love—enough to see you through your trial, and enough to share with others. Those are things that no one can take from you.

THE QUILT MAKER

[God] has made everything beautiful in its time.
ECCLESIASTES 3:11 NIV

Have you ever watched someone piece together a quilt? In the beginning, that quilt is just a pile of scraps and some spools of thread. It doesn't look anything like what it will become. But through hours of skilled stitching, the pieces come together to make a beautiful work of art.

Sometimes our lives seem like a pile of mismatched rags and random threads. We look at all these pieces and wonder how they will ever come together to make a meaningful life. We try a stitch here, and things end up tangled. We try another and end up tearing the prettiest strip of cloth. We sink deeper into frustration, wondering how this mess can ever be made into something of worth.

GRACE FOR TODAY

GOD IS WEAVING THE PIECES OF YOUR LIFE INTO A BEAUTIFUL CREATION.

But just like a beautiful quilt, our lives need to be put into the hands of Someone who knows what the finished work should look like. When we give God the "raw materials" of our lives, He begins weaving the thread together in a masterful way. Soon you'll begin to look back and see a pattern emerging out of the chaos. The beautiful person that you were created to be will begin to appear from the cloth and thread.

Take some time today to survey the stitches that God has made in the fabric of your life so far. What situations seemed pointless and painful at the time but turned out to be great seasons of growth? Who are the people who have been woven into your life that have helped you become better and more like Jesus? Can you see the pattern taking shape? God's grace is shaping you into the magnificent creation He always meant you to be. Continue to hand Him the pieces of your life and just watch what He will do!

NAVIGATING THROUGH LIFE

All Scripture is given by inspiration of God, and is profitable for doctrine, for reproof, for correction, for instruction in righteousness.
2 TIMOTHY 3:16 NKJV

Running late to pick up her friend, Cheryl hurried to her brand-new car. As they headed to an unfamiliar area to shop, they talked incessantly and ended up lost. As they tried to figure out where to turn, Cheryl's friend began to laugh. "Cheryl, you have a navigational system right here on the dash."

GRACE FOR TODAY

THE BIBLE IS GOD'S CHART FOR YOU TO STEER BY.

Many new cars come equipped with a Global Positioning System. GPS can provide useful information about the car's position and the best travel routes to a given destination by linking itself to a built-in digital map. When Cheryl looked down at the small screen with a map right in front of her, she joined in the laughter. She'd forgotten about that feature.

The modern system uses satellite signals. Early navigators used the stars, the sun, and the moon to guide them across thousands of miles of open ocean. What is your standard as you navigate the seas of life?

The psalmist said that God's Word was the lamp that lit his way. The Scripture will illuminate your every step, one at a time, and help you as you navigate along the path of life. God's Word teaches us how to live lives that are pleasing to Him so that we can enjoy a relationship with Him. In times of crisis, the Bible holds hope and encouragement. When we lack wisdom, it answers questions and gives direction; and if we have a question about what's right, it helps us discern the truth.

Have you lost your way in life? Memorize Scripture, meditate on it, and hide it in your heart. The Word of God is the best navigational system of all to guide you successfully through life.

WE LIVE BY GRACE

By Warren W. Wiersbe

We must never forget that the Christian life is a living relationship with God through Jesus Christ. A man does not become a Christian merely by agreeing to a set of doctrines; he becomes a Christian by submitting to Christ and trusting Him. You cannot mix grace and works, because the one excludes the other. Salvation is the gift of God's grace, purchased for us by Jesus Christ on the cross. To turn from grace to law is to desert the God who saved us.

Keep in mind that God's grace involves something more than man's salvation. We not only are saved by grace, but we are to live by grace (1 Corinthians 15:10). We stand in grace; it is the foundation for the Christian life (Romans 5:1-2). Grace gives us the strength we need to be victorious soldiers (2 Timothy 2:1-4). Grace enables us to suffer without complaining, and even to use that suffering for God's glory (2 Corinthians 12:1-10). When a Christian turns away from living by God's grace, he must depend on his own power. This leads to failure and disappointment. This is what Paul means by "fallen from grace" (Galatians 5:4) — moving out of the sphere of grace into the sphere of law, ceasing to depend on God's resources and depending on our own resources.

Paul explains the relationship between the grace of God and practical Christian living. He shows that living by grace means liberty, not bondage (sale); depending on the Spirit, not the flesh (5:13-26); living for others, not for self (6:1-10); and living for the glory of God, not for man's approval (6:11-18). It is either one series of actions or the other — law or grace — but it cannot be both.[28]

HEAVENLY FATHER:

I choose to live this day by Your grace–Your goodness, Your sinlessness, Your strength, and Your truth.

AMEN

If it is by grace, it is no longer on the basis of works, otherwise grace would no longer be grace.
ROMANS 11:6 NRSV

IN HOT PURSUIT

> Where can I go from your Spirit? Where can I flee from your presence? . . . If I rise on the wings of the dawn, if I settle on the far side of the sea, even there your hand will guide me, your right hand will hold me fast.
> PSALM 139:7,9-10 NIV

Jonah did not want to do what God wanted him to do. So he refused. He was not about to go to Nineveh to preach salvation to those people. In Jonah's mind, they were rotten, evil people. Frankly, he really didn't want them to be saved from God's destruction. So Jonah skipped town. But what he forgot is that you can't hide from God.

GRACE FOR TODAY

GOD IS IN HOT PURSUIT—OF YOU. WHEN YOU STOP RUNNING AND TURN TO HIM, YOU'LL FIND GRACE.

God followed him—out of town, out to sea, and into the belly of a fish—until Jonah understood that he could not escape the Lord. In spite of Jonah's disobedience, God never lost faith in him—and He never stopped pursuing him until Jonah understood the depth of His love and grace. It was a love and grace that extended not only to a disobedient prophet, but also to the people of Nineveh.

Many times in life we, too, run from God. We fear what He will make us do. Or perhaps we fear that we're just too rotten for Him to save. Our humiliation and fear keep our backs turned to God. What we don't realize is that God is patiently and lovingly waiting for us to stop and surrender. When we do, we will be enveloped by His grace—not by condemnation.

God is the ultimate, faithful friend. He won't stop pursuing us. He never loses faith in what He knows we can become. He sent His one and only Son so that we could stop running. Will you choose to stop, lift your burdens to the Lord, and experience the healing power of grace today? He will be there with open arms when you do.

DESTINED TO ACHIEVE

Body and soul, I am marvelously made! . . . You know
exactly how I was made, bit by bit, how I was sculpted
from nothing into something.
PSALM 139:14-15 MSG

Society's perspective is "If you don't like yourself, change." People encourage you to choose from diet pills, creams, exercise machines, or gym memberships. What once seemed extreme is becoming the norm. Today we can suck it out, add it in, move it around, lift it, or tuck it!

But your heavenly Father created you body and soul by His own design. He equipped you with everything you need in every area of your life. He started with nothing and made you something unique and extraordinary.

The world may judge you by its temporary standards, but God knows what He had in mind when He made you. And He knows that what lies in your heart is much more a beauty issue than your hair color. You know beautiful people made ugly by inner fear or bitterness. And you know people made beautiful by a grace within that makes you fall in love with them.

Look to God for your makeover. Change starts small, step by step, moment by moment. God knows the pace that you need to run your race. He knows where you are and how far it is to the finish line. Follow Him closely, and you'll discover the champion He created you to be.

GRACE FOR TODAY

GOD PROVIDES THE GRACE FOR A CHANGE ONLY HE CAN
ARRANGE, ONE STEP AT A TIME.

DISAPPOINTMENT

[The Lord says,] "Forget the former things; do not dwell on the past. See, I am doing a new thing! Now it springs up; do you not perceive it?"
ISAIAH 43:18-19 NIV

GRACE FOR TODAY

GOD CAN CAUSE OUR GREATEST BLESSINGS TO SPRING FORTH FROM LOSSES AND DISAPPOINTMENTS.

We all have moments of profound disappointment, times when everything seems to spiral down into a feeling of shock. Missionary William Carey was a linguist who translated the Bible into forty-two Asian languages and dialects. He contributed some of his own life's savings to build a paper mill and printing press in Serampore, India.

In 1812, a fire started in the printing room, destroying most of the equipment, library, and printing supplies. Tragically, Carey's irreplaceable completed Sanskrit dictionary, grammar books, and many translations of the Bible were also consumed by the fire. Carey reportedly wept at the sight, years of work destroyed. But then he remarked, "We are cast down but not in despair." The team simply went back to work. Sometimes, in the midst of our biggest losses and disappointments, our biggest blessings spring forth. People all over the world learned of the tragic fire, and their donations allowed Carey to not only rebuild but to expand.

When disappointment hits, talk to a friend and vent a little. Then stop and take your disappointments to God in prayer. Sit down and look at what really happened and what you've learned from it. Find positive things that can actually come out of this disappointment—how to do things differently next time or how to build and learn from what happened. Then continue in the faith that God will make your disappointment make sense and redeem your loss, in time. Trust that His grace is there, and then act on that trust.

A FRESHLY BAKED COOKIE

Thanks be to God, who always leads us in triumph in
Christ, and manifests through us the sweet aroma of the
knowledge of Him in every place.
2 CORINTHIANS 2:14 NASB

Freshly baked cookies are wonderful, especially on a chilly fall afternoon. Your mouth waters the minute you start to mix the ingredients in the bowl. Stirring the batter takes some effort, but you know it will be worth it. As the cookies bake, the whole house fills with the delicious aroma. Any person within smelling distance comes running with a smile, hoping for a warm cookie. And that first bite — it's almost like Heaven! It fills your mouth with warmth and makes every taste bud sing. I'll bet you can't eat just one!

Grace is like one of those cookies. We crave it. We long to experience the warmth and comfort it brings to our souls. When we receive grace, we savor it. And like a batch of great cookies, grace has key ingredients — time spent with God through His Word, fellowship with Him in worship and prayer, plus our belief in Jesus and acceptance of His gift of salvation. Grace, too, fills our home with warmth and makes it inviting. Being filled with God's grace heightens all of our spiritual senses, and we experience a peace we've never known before. Grace then overflows to those around you. They sense the fragrance of its joy — and they want to know it as well.

GRACE FOR TODAY

GOD WANTS TO
FILL YOUR LIFE
WITH THE WARMTH
AND FRAGRANCE
OF HIS GRACE.

God wants us to experience His grace. He created that craving inside each of us, and He wants to make it a key ingredient of our lives. He surrounds us with people who will offer us the grace they've received. And then, when His grace fills us, its inviting presence draws others. Just like a batch of freshly baked cookies, God's grace brings joy and is best when shared!

179

THE BEST LOVED NEIGHBOR

May our sons flourish in their youth like well-nurtured plants. May our daughters be like graceful pillars, carved to beautify a palace.
PSALM 144:12 NLT

During childhood, Fred Rogers dreamed of being a pastor; but when television came on the scene, he decided it could be used as a medium to nurture children and teach them wholesome values. So upon graduation from college, he was hired by NBC, where he worked on a number of TV shows. He eventually graduated from seminary, though, and was ordained as a Presbyterian minister.

Fred returned to his native Pennsylvania in 1953 and helped launch the first community-supported public television station in the country. At one point a major network considered syndicating his local children's show, but they wanted to know what kind of costume he planned to wear.

GRACE FOR TODAY

THE HOLY SPIRIT TRANSLATES OUR BEST EFFORTS INTO WHAT NEEDS TO BE COMMUNICATED TO OTHERS IN THEIR PLACE OF NEED.

Mr. Rogers said he didn't need a funny costume to communicate with children. The network passed on the opportunity, but his show was picked up by the Public Broadcasting Service. Almost nine hundred episodes of *Mister Roger's Neighborhood* have aired, and the show is the longest-running program on PBS. Fred wrote each episode in longhand on a yellow legal pad, and each was dedicated to his mission of broadcasting "grace."

Mr. Rogers said, "Every time I walk into a studio, I pray, 'Let some word that is heard be Yours.' The Holy Spirit translates our best efforts into what needs to be communicated to that person in his or her place of need."

Fred believed that the children and parents who watched his program were his God-given congregation. And his manner of nurturing children and building their self-esteem in a deliberate, repetitive, one-on-one approach sets an example for us all.

EXPRESSIONS OF WORRY

By John MacArthur Jr.

The word worry comes from the Old English term *wyrgan*, which means "to choke" or "strangle." That's appropriate since worry strangles the mind, which is the seat of our emotions. The word even fits the notion of a panic attack.

We're not much different from the people to whom Jesus spoke. They worried about what they were going to eat, drink, and wear. And if you want to legitimize your worry, what better way than to say, "Well, after all, I'm not worrying about extravagant things; I'm just worrying about the basics." But that is forbidden for the Christian.

As you read through the Scriptures, one thing you learn is that God wants His children preoccupied with Him, not with the mundane, passing things of this world. He says, "Set your mind on the things above, not on the things that are on earth" (Colossians 3:2). To free us to do that He says, "Don't worry about the basics. I'll take care of that." A basic principle of spiritual life is that we are not earthbound people. Fully trusting our Heavenly Father dispels anxiety. And the more we know about Him, the more we will trust Him.

I believe in wise planning, but if after doing all you are able to, you still are fearful of the future, the Ford says, "Don't worry." He promised to provide all your needs, and He will.[29]

HEAVENLY FATHER:

I thank and praise You for the miracle of Your grace–grace enough to provide everything I need. I exchange my worries for Your provision, my anxiety for Your peace.

AMEN

You can be sure that God will take care of everything you need, his generosity exceeding even yours in the glory that pours from Jesus.
PHILIPPIANS 4:19 MSG

Steps to Mom

Love is patient, love is hind. It does not envy, it does not
boast, it is not proud. It is not rude, it is not self-seeking, it
is not easily angered, it keeps no record of wrongs.
1 CORINTHIANS 15:4-5 NIV

GRACE FOR TODAY

GRACE IS UNMERITED FAVOR. IT SEEKS TO BLESS OTHERS, WITH NO STRINGS ATTACHED.

There's a whole lot of advice for stepmothers for the simple reason that loving your husband's children is tough. You pray your stepchildren will love you back, but being a stepmom can become a search for approval. It's a challenge to rise above critical eyes. There are so many to please—children, husband, ex-wife, old friends, and in-laws. That's why you'll need to draw on God's love and love like He does.

The funny thing is, your husband's a nice man, so why would he marry a witch? Of course the image of the wicked stepmother is only a myth in fairy tales. But experts warn that many stepmothers have unrealistic fantasies about what the cottage in the woods is going to be like.

The fact is, the cottage can be a pretty lonely place because the happy little elves aren't really that happy about having a stepmother in the first place. But don't take the rebuffs or negativity personally. They probably would have had a hard time accepting anybody as their father's new wife.

Building a relationship with your stepchildren takes patience. It can be a balance between learning to take a backseat and getting involved. Maybe that means cheering on the sports field when they don't seem to hear—but they do care. It could mean being available to listen or not sweating the little stuff by focusing on the important battles. Haim Ginott said, "If you want your children to improve, let them overhear the nice things you say about them to others." That's all part of being a stepmom too.

Sure it can be a thankless job, but that's parenting. Expect and be on the lookout for God's grace. He can knit your hearts together and make your house a home.

BEING GRACEFUL

The grace (unmerited favor and blessing) of our Lord
[actually] flowed out superabundantly and beyond
measure for me, accompanied by faith and love that are
[to be realized] in Christ Jesus.
1 TIMOTHY 1:14 AMP

Do you consider yourself a graceful person? Or do you tend to stumble and bump into things? Many of us struggle with being less than ballerina — like! The American Heritage Dictionary defines grace as "seemingly effortless beauty or charm of movement, form, or proportions." We admire people who portray this kind of grace — dancers, models, and women of rank and status. They train themselves to move and speak with seemingly effortless grace. They are recognized the world over for that special kind of charm. It might seem that this kind of grace is reserved only for those special few. They make being graceful look so easy.

What a joy it is to realize that God's grace isn't reserved for just a few. It is open to anyone willing to accept it. You don't have to exhibit special skills or speak in a certain way or have the beauty and movement of a ballerina. In fact, it's even okay if you tend to be a klutz. All God asks is that you admit that you need Him and His forgiveness. Believe in the name of His grace-filled Son, Jesus. Accept God's free gift. It is truly that simple.

So whether you glide through the room with the grace of a supermodel or feel like you have two left feet, you, too, can be full of grace — God's infinite grace!

GRACE FOR TODAY

YOU CAN BE GRACE-FULL THROUGH THE GRACE OF GOD.

FIRST THINGS FIRST

[Jesus said,] "He will give you all you need from day to day
if you live for him and make the Kingdom of God your
primary concern."
MATTHEW 6:33 NLT

"First things first" is a phrase often used when someone wants to convey the message of putting and keeping priorities in order. So often, as women, we get caught up in the busyness of our careers, households, kids' schedules, and deadlines. We barely have time for ourselves, much less any quality time to spend with the Lord. We try to fit Him into our schedule, rather than fitting into His. We mistakenly think our place on the pew fills that Sunday slot of priority. It's one thing to spend time in church—and quite another to spend intimate time with Jesus. The statistics are staggering concerning ministers who have become estranged from their families because they placed their position in the church above their position as husband or parent.

GRACE FOR TODAY

GOD'S WAY OF
PRIORITIZING
PROVIDES
EVERYTHING WE
NEED TO LIVE WELL

God is a jealous God, who wants first place in our lives. Putting Him first includes spending quality time with Him—and an adequate quantity of it. He longs for our visits and conversations. He's the kind of friend with whom we can sit and share our innermost hearts. He's the kind of God who sings over us, finds His delight in us as He waits to be invited into our busy lives.

Do you long to hear God's gentle voice of affirmation and love? Putting God first is not a Sunday choice, but a daily choice. He promises that when we put Him first, everything else we require will fall into place. It is His divine order that we put Him first, then family, then our work (in order to care for our families), and then our church duties and ministry.

First things first: Prioritizing God's way brings refreshment, everlasting peace, and everything you need to balance your daily life.

ROAST NOT, LEST YOU BE ROASTED

[Jesus said,] "Judge not, that you be not judged."
MATTHEW 7:1 NKJV

Have you ever felt judged by someone? You may have muttered, "Here I am, doing the best I can to live the Christian life, and even my best isn't good enough for some people." Or perhaps you've judged someone by standards that you've established for your own Christian walk.

GRACE FOR TODAY

THE GRACE OF GOD IS LOVING AND KIND TO ALL.

At times we find ourselves with judgmental attitudes where extremes affect our thoughts and actions. The strong Christian might think unkind thoughts about a so-called narrow-minded one, whereas the weak person might think the strong one isn't compassionate. The command not to judge others doesn't mean we can't see the sinfulness of certain actions, but we are to be careful not to become harshly judgmental, looking for faults and taking the opportunity to look down on others from our position of self-righteousness.

Jesus did not come to live among us to benefit himself or for personal gain. He became the ultimate and perfect sacrifice. He didn't come to be ministered to, but to minister to others. As our example of self-sacrifice, He gave His life's blood for our sins and provides the strength and grace we need to love other Christians, even ones who judge us.

Paul states in Romans 15:5 that God gives endurance and encouragement and will grant us a spirit of unity. He implored believers to show gentleness and consideration to fellow Christians. We can consider other people's interests before our own because of God's provision of the fruits of the Holy Spirit. (See Galatians 5:22-23.) Let's treat each other with love and avoid condemning one another. Let's be willing to give up our rights and criticism for the welfare of our brothers and sisters in Christ.

185

INDEPENDENCE DAY

We depend upon the Lord alone to save us. Only he can help us.
PSALM 33:20 TLB

GRACE FOR TODAY

DEPENDENCE ON GOD PRODUCES A GRACE THAT CAN HANDLE ANYTHING.

The day is going great. All your planning and hard work for your ten-year-old son's family birthday party is about to pay off as guests begin to arrive. Suddenly your nearly sixteen-year-old sucks every ounce of joy from the room as he loudly defies your gentle refusal to allow him to miss his younger brother's party.

Thoughts of what to do swim against the angry current in your mind. Choose your battles. Is this one of the big ones? Should I just let him go? How did I raise such a selfish child? A soft answer turns away wrath. Perhaps the party would be less confrontational without him.

Suddenly you feel hot tears slowly sliding down your face. What happened? When he was two years old, I was his world. Now, he pushes me away, struggling for independence. God, I need a little help here!

God in His great love is the ultimate restorer. He knows your heart and the heart of your child. Suddenly your boy's face softens at the sight of your tears. "Mom, I didn't know it was such a big deal. I'm sorry. Here, let me help you with the cake."

When it seems the relationship is hanging by a thread, God's grace is enough for both of you. Dependence on God produces a strength that can handle anything. You realize you can no longer hold on and must let go; God's grace will catch him and carry him from boyhood to manhood. And His mercy will teach you how to make the transitions as you become increasingly dependent on God.

LIVING FOR CHRIST

By Warren W. Wiersbe

Eternal life through faith in Jesus Christ, this is our experience of salvation. He also died that we might live for Him, and not live unto ourselves (2 Corinthians 5:15). This is our experience of service. It has been well said, "Christ died our death for us that we might live His life for Him." If a lost sinner has been to the Cross and been saved, how can he spend the rest of his life in selfishness?

In 1858, Frances Ridley Havergal visited Germany with her father who was getting treatment for his afflicted eyes. While in a pastor's home, she saw a picture of the crucifixion on the wall, with the words under it: "I did this for thee. What hast thou done for Me?" Quickly she took a piece of paper and wrote a poem based on that motto; but she was not satisfied with it, so she threw the paper into the fireplace. The paper came out unharmed! Later, her father encouraged her to publish it; and we sing it today to a tune composed by Philip P. Bliss:

I gave My life for thee,
My precious blood I shed,
That thou might ransomed be,
And quickened from the dead.
I gave, I gave, My life for thee,
What hast thou given for Me?

Christ died that we might live through Him and for Him, and that we might live with Him![30]

———

HEAVENLY FATHER:

Thank You for Your grace that allows me to live through Your son Jesus Christ. Strengthen and guide me as I learn to live for Him.

AMEN

In this the love of God was manifested toward us, that God has sent His only begotten Son into the world, that we might live through Him.
1 JOHN 4:9 NKJV

THE BAG LADY

Let everything you say be good and helpful, so that your
words will be an encouragement to those who hear them.
EPHESIANS 4:29 NLT

In 1980, Emilie Barnes organized a group of homemakers to meet for a neighborhood Bible study. She asked Florence Littauer, a vivacious speaker and gifted Bible teacher, to lead it. The number of attendants grew until Emilies home could no longer hold them.

Then the two friends came up with a plan to reach larger audiences — "Feminars," seminars with a feminine touch. At one of the first of these gatherings, Florence thought of a way to break the ice. She suggested, "Emilie, why don't you show the ladies your purse?"

GRACE FOR TODAY

NONE OF OUR SKILLS OR LIFE'S EXPERIENCES ARE WASTED BY GOD. HE USES ALL OF THEM TO MINISTER HIS GRACE TO OTHERS.

Emilie obliged and began pulling out an array of neatly organized little bags. Emilies method of organization captivated the group; and she realized she could help women organize their purses, their homes, and their lives. Her speaking ministry grew.

Then Florence suggested, "Emily, why don't you write a book?"

But Emilie replied, "I wouldn't know the first thing about writing a book, and besides, I only have a high school education."

But God had other ideas, and the result was a book, which is still in print, titled *More Hours in My Day*. Emilie has now authored over sixty books. While stricken with non-Hodgkin's lymphoma four years ago, she wrote two books to help other cancer victims, telling of God's grace and faithfulness throughout her illness. God has used all the events in Emilies life to touch the lives of hundreds of thousands of women.

If you have a particular skill, share it with others. Or if you have suffered illnesses, losses, and tragedies, these can be used to help other women who are experiencing a similar situation.

ELDER-CARE GIVING

Even to your old age and gray hairs I am he, I am he who will sustain you. I have made you and I will carry you; I will sustain you and I will rescue you.
ISAIAH 46:4 NIV

Millions of people every day are taking on the loving challenge of caring for aging parents. The Bible encourages us to "Listen to your father, who gave you life, and do not despise your mother when she is old" (Proverbs 23:22 NIV). When the time to help comes, there are some important things to consider. You should really have a good understanding of why your parent needs help. Are there medical, financial, or emotional reasons that need to be addressed? How do they feel emotionally about receiving your assistance? What will be the different support roles of other family members?

GRACE FOR TODAY

GOD PROMISES TO PROVIDE FOR THE ELDERLY. HIS GRACE WILL ENABLE YOU TO DO YOUR PART.

Making life-changing decisions is always difficult and emotional. Try to make plans for the future when your parent feels empowered, healthy, and in control- before there is a crisis. Remember the safety and well being of your parent is the most important thing. Discuss ways to preserve as much independence as possible while achieving the goal of maintaining both a good lifestyle and a safe one. There are many options out there to help you make informed and positive choices from day care, home support, senior housing, to long-term care. There are also support groups available to help guide and assist you.

But there's another aspect to consider: the impact on you and the rest of the family. Each member of the family must consider their limitations, lifestyles, and needs. If you decide to become a primary caregiver full time, make sure resources are there to help you avoid exhaustion, frustration, and emotional burnout. You want your love to bring dignity, honor, respect, and joy to your parent. What form that takes is completely unique to each family and situation, but God's grace can help you do it.

SEASONS OF THE SOUL

Blessed are those who trust in the LORD and have made the LORD their hope and confidence. They are like trees planted along a riverbank, with roots that reach deep into the water. Such trees are not bothered by the heat or worried by long months of drought.
JEREMIAH 17:7-8 NLT

GRACE FOR TODAY

————————————

THE SEASONS OF THE SOUL DEVELOP THE DEPTH OF OUR ROOTS IN THE GRACE OF GOD.

Fall is such a beautiful time of the year. We go from hot, hazy summer days and sticky, humid nights to crisp, bright days and cool, clear nights. The trees change from their summer green to a rainbow of color. In areas that have the most extreme temperature differences between day and night, the colors are especially brilliant. The kaleidoscope of yellow, red, and orange is breathtaking.

This burst of color is the prelude to a season of rest for the plant world. While the bare limbs of trees in the winter may look desolate and dead, this dormant time allows them to renew themselves for the next year's canopy of green. It is a critical and vital stage in the life cycle of the plant that helps it become deeply rooted and increasingly strong.

Isn't our walk with Christ similar? We begin our walk as new Christians, and everything is like springtime—new and fresh and full of possibilities. Our time with God comes naturally and easily. As we move into new seasons of growth, we encounter uncomfortable weather of the soul. Hot and dry summer seasons cause us to cry out for the refreshment of God's living water. The autumn seasons of change bring us to the throne of grace for direction. The cold and dark winter times draw us closer to the light and warmth of God's love.

Seasons of the soul are necessary to help us grow as followers of Christ. If we take the time to see the beauty of God's grace in each, we will learn to rejoice in the depth of our roots and the strength of our faith.

KEEPING THE PACE

I press on toward the goal for the prize of the upward call
of God in Christ Jesus.
PHILIPPIANS 5:14 NASB

In some health clubs, the treadmills are situated in the front windows. All of the members line up, sweating, walking mile after mile. Do you sometimes feel as if you're stuck on a treadmill, running and running and getting nowhere? How many people feel like this could be a metaphor for their lives?

Our Christian life should not be compared to a wind sprint but to a marathon. In a wind sprint, you run as fast as you can for a short distance, with speed being of utmost importance. But in a marathon, endurance is the critical factor. The writer who spoke to the Hebrews advised them to run with patience the race set before them. Paul told the Philippians to continue to hold tightly to God's Word so that when their race was done, they would not have run in vain.

GRACE FOR TODAY

THE MASTER, WHO
LOVED MOST OF ALL,
ENDURED THE MOST
AND PROVED HIS
LOVE BY HIS
ENDURANCE.

HUGH B. BROWN

Our stride needs to be true and sure—a steady pace to the finish. As we make our way through life, we endeavor to fulfill the purpose that God has for us. Our purpose drives our persistence. When we endeavor to fulfill God's plan for our lives, we will not have labored in vain.

The members of the health club press on, hoping to be rewarded with a healthier body. We press on in our service to the Lord, knowing that one day we will be rewarded with eternal life. Jesus told us that those of us who endure to the end would be saved. Don't lose heart. Don't become discouraged. Don't quit. Keep running the race.

CALLED TO SERVE

Serve one another in love.
GALATIANS 5:13 NLT

There is no more beautiful picture of servanthood than when Christ met with Elis disciples to celebrate the Passover the night before He was betrayed. With a towel and a basin of water, He knelt before His followers and washed their dirty feet. "I have set you an example, that you should do as I have done for you. I tell you the truth, no servant is greater than his master" (John 13:15-16 NIV).

How we serve Christ and serve others is up to us. We are not robots, but we have the freedom to freely choose how we serve God and mankind. Paul tells us, "You have been given freedom: not freedom to do wrong, but freedom to love and serve each other" (Galatians 5:13 TLB). Until we find that purpose and place to serve others, a longing and void will remain within our hearts.

GRACE FOR TODAY

GOD QUALIFIES YOU BY HIS GRACE AS YOU DEVELOP A HEART OF SERVANTHOOD.

Have you found your place of service as a woman of God? Are you waiting until you think you are more qualified, more settled, more refined? God is the qualifier—and He is looking for our availability more than our capability. The Bible is full of men and women whom God used but whose lives weren't perfect. Despite their shortcomings, they heeded His call to serve. If you think God can't use you until you have a perfect resume, consider David, Moses, Naomi, Abraham, Peter, Thomas, and a whole list of others. God saw beyond their inadequacies and used them to build His kingdom.

With a heart willing to serve, equipped with God's qualifying grace, He will use you to touch and change lives.

A SISTER OF JESUS

By John MacArthur Jr.

The Bible says that God's will is that people be saved, and that is where it all starts, Jesus made this clear in Mark 3:31-35. He was already teaching inside a building when His brothers and mother arrived. The multitude was sitting on the inside, and it was so crowded that His family could not get to Him. Someone said to Him, "Jesus, Your mother and brothers outside seek You."

He answered, "Who is My mother, or My brethren?" (verse 33).

I am sure the crowd's reaction was something like: What kind of question is this? Everybody knows His mother and brothers!

If Jesus' first reaction did not shock them, His next words did. "He looked round about on them which sat about Him, and said, 'Behold My mother and My brethren!'" (verse 34).

Each person probably looked at the other and thought, Who, me?

Then He qualified it. "For whosoever shall do the will of God . . . is My brother, and My sister, and Mother" (verse 35).

What was Jesus saying? He was teaching that in order to be related to Him, one has to do the will of God. Turn it around. To do the will of God one has to be related to Jesus.[31]

HEAVENLY FATHER,

To be considered the sister of Jesus is almost more than I can comprehend, yet it is true. The only qualification is that I obey You and do your will, which is my heart's desire. At those times when I find that difficult, I ask You to give me an extra dose of grace. I'm willing to be made willing.

AMEN

[Jesus said,] "They who have my commandments and keep them are those who love me; and those who love me will be loved by my Father, and I will love them and reveal myself to them."
JOHN 14:21 NRSV

GET OUT OF THE ZONE

This expectation will not disappoint us. For we know how dearly God loves us.
ROMANS 5:5 NLT

Have you reached a plateau and found life easy or just really comfortable? It's nice to enjoy that place for a season; but over time, like water that hasn't moved in a while, you can grow stagnant. Your growth may become stunted. The comfort zone can become a dangerous place to live. You might prefer to cruise through life smoothly, but seldom is that the case.

GRACE FOR TODAY

GOD IS CHEERING YOU ON TO THE NEXT LEVEL.

God created all of us to grow on a continual basis. You have a natural desire to gain knowledge and understanding of everything around you. It's important to expand your horizons and experience new things. Challenges in life stretch you and cause you to realize there are many new horizons yet to explore.

If you perceive the challenges you face in life as opportunities to grow, you will begin to recognize that God is always there, cheering you on to the next level. He stands ready to console and comfort you as you work to climb the next mountain and travel through the next valley toward His destiny for your life. He will stand you back up if you fall, and He will encourage you to take another step forward.

A life with God is filled with His great expectations for you. It's His way to take the ordinary and make something extraordinary. If you're willing to step out of the comfort zone, He'll help you climb to the top where you will find unlimited God-given opportunities awaiting you.

THE GRACE OF GUIDANCE

Whether you turn to the right or to the left, your ears will hear a voice behind you, saying, "This is the way; walk in it."
ISAIAH 30:21 NIV

Vic had just been accepted into a prestigious program at work for top employees. His wife, Jane, expected long hours and more stress for Vic than ever before. But she also knew that this would be a rewarding opportunity for her husband.

So, Jane threw herself into the role of cheerleader. The further he got into the assignment, the more she tried to encourage and be supportive. But the more Jane gave, the more deeply she felt Vic's growing distance from their family.

GRACE FOR TODAY

GOD GIVES THE GRACE OF HIS GUIDANCE THROUGH THE WISDOM OF HIS WORD.

Jane's chipper demeanor masked the sadness she began to feel. She was being such a supportive wife. When was Vic going to see that and reward her with some quality time together? She felt the resentment begin to build. Then, Jane realized that she hadn't talked to her husband about her feelings. But she was afraid to let down her cheerleader facade. He doesn't need any more stress right now, especially from me, she worried. So she began to pray and asked some trusted friends to join her in asking God for help.

That very week, during Jane's Bible study, she read the story of Ananias in Acts 9. Ananias was called to restore the sight of the newly converted Paul. Once Paul was filled with the Spirit, God sent him away for three years of preparation.

Jane saw a message from God in the story of Ananias. She needed to speak to her husband about her feelings (to restore his sight). She also needed to be patient as God's plan was fulfilled in his life (his time of preparation). Through the prayer support of good friends and God's grace and guidance, Jane and Vic worked through the struggles of this intense time. And through it they found that God's Word will always show the way if they are willing to follow.

ALL YOU NEED

Pray that I will he given the message to speak and that I
may fearlessly explain the mystery about the good news.
EPHESIANS 6:19 CEV

GRACE FOR TODAY

NO NEED IS SO GREAT
THAT IT CANNOT BE
SUPPLIED BY GOD'S
GRACE. IN CHRIST WE
HAVE IT ALL.

At the beginning of their relationship, Kay was drawn to Tom's sensitive nature. Yet, after they married she became aware that he was a moody, unhappy man who constantly criticized her. In time a divorce resulted, and Kay's life spiraled downward.

One night at a party, a friend asked her a question that radically changed her life. "Why don't you quit telling God what you want and tell Him that Jesus Christ is all you need?" The next morning Kay knelt beside her bed and committed her life to Christ. In the days that followed, she developed a ravenous hunger for God's Word.

Kay's zeal for the Bible led her to attend a Bible college in Chattanooga, Tennessee. In the campus ice cream shop one evening, she and her boys met Jack Arthur, a missionary to South America. Three months later lack and Kay were married.

In the late sixties, Kay Arthur started a Bible study for teenagers in their living room. By 1970, the teens were meeting in a barn they had cleaned out and patched up. Soon adults were coming too, and it became obvious that an expanded ministry center needed to be constructed. Today, Precept Ministries International has exploded into thirty-five different Bible studies, which are used in all fifty states and in over one hundred countries.

Kay Arthur has touched thousands of lives through her writing and teaching of God's grace. Perhaps you can touch a life, as Kay's friend did here, by telling a hurting soul that, "Jesus Christ is all you need."

NOW

> The LORD is merciful and gracious, slow to anger and
> abounding in steadfast love.
> PSALM 103:8 NRSV

We've spent years talking to our children, but with teenagers we have to learn to talk with them. Family therapist Virginia Satir stated, "The greatest gift I can receive from anyone is to be seen by them, to be heard by them, to be understood by them, and to be listened to." Give that gift to your teenagers.

The Bible advises, "Children, obey your parents in everything, for this is your acceptable duty in the Lord. Fathers, do not provoke your children, or they may lose heart" (Colossians 3:20-21 NRSV). Biblically teenagers must obey us, but we are the keepers of our children's self-esteem and hearts; and that's a bigger responsibility. So, how can we achieve a good relationship with our teens?

GRACE FOR TODAY

GRACE RESPECTS, LISTENS TO, AND LOVES ITS RECIPIENT.

Pope John XXIII said, "See everything; overlook a great deal; correct a little." Your teenager must start making his or her own decisions about life and the future, and your job is to stand alongside and help them make good choices. You may not always agree with them, but you must revere their right to express their feelings in a civil and productive manner. You're there to listen and care, but respect both ways is essential.

Being the example to your teen is important. That means being honest about your feelings, apologizing when you need to, and trying to keep destructive emotions and words out of your conversations.

Remember, your teenagers watch how you deal with family, co-workers, and the world. They study how you overcome challenges and setbacks. They learn to be excited by goals and the future by how you embrace those types of things. Your attitudes, faith, and values will be their guidepost. And God's will be yours. So let love be the biggest thing you show them, no matter the situation.

One Foot in Front of the Other

I follow close behind you, protected by your strong right arm.
PSALM 63:8 TLB

Remember the game Follow the Leader? Everyone wanted to be the leader. While that was fun during childhood, in real life we still need a leader. As children of God, we are chosen to follow the greatest leader of all-our heavenly Father. All through our lives, He leads the way. Although we may not know what it is, He has a preplanned destination for our lives. We're on a fabulous journey. And we can rest assured that no matter what opportunities lie before us—life's biggest challenges are no match for our fearless leader. God is bigger and more powerful than anything we face, and when we follow Him, He always causes us to triumph in Christ.

GRACE FOR TODAY

WALKING IN GOD'S GRACE IS A STEP-BY-STEP JOURNEY OF FOLLOWING IN HIS FOOTSTEPS.

There is not one single mountain we can't overcome if we stay close to Him. We can cross the ocean during even the most phenomenal storms, knowing He will guide us safely through. Even when the day seems dark and we can barely make out the path in front of us, we know our steps are perfected as we follow Him.

When we have questions, He has the answers. If we take Him a problem, He has the solution. He's bigger than anything that concerns us. We don't have to look forward and worry about what might happen in the miles ahead. All we have to do is take it step by step, putting one foot in front of the other, walking a step or two right behind Him.

SALVATION FOR ALL

By John MacArthur Jr.

Talking about sin and salvation is offensive to some people. Who wants to hear about sin? Most people mask it. Sin is not sin. Oh, no. Sin is "a prenatal predilection," psychologists tell us. Sin is an "idiosyncrasy of individuality." Sin is "poor secretion of the endocrine glands"!

But God's will is that people be saved! And basic to salvation is the recognition of sin. This lays it right at your feet. Either you are not saved from your sin and you need to come to Christ because that is God's will, or you are saved and need to reach others with the message of salvation. There is a world out there that needs Jesus Christ. God wants them to be saved, and you and I are the vehicles for the transportation of the Gospel. That is God's will.

You say you do not know what God's will is, but I'll tell you what it is. First, that you know Christ and then that your neighbors hear about Christ. So often we sit around twiddling our thumbs, dreaming about God's will in some far distant future when we are not even willing to walk down the street and do God's will right now.

God so desired that men be saved that He gave the One whom He loved most, His Son, and sent Him to die on a cross. That is the measure of His love, and that indicates how much He wills that men be saved![32]

FATHER GOD,

Your Word says that You want all to be saved, and You've asked us—me—to spread this Good News to everyone. Lead me to those who are ready to receive salvation and by Your grace, grant me the boldness I need to be an effective witness.

AMEN

[God] longs for all to be saved and to understand this truth: That God is on one side and all the people on the other side, and Christ Jesus, himself man, is between them to bring them together.
1 TIMOTHY 2:4-5 TLB

UNCLOGGING YOUR PIPES

We know that God causes everything to work together for
the good of those who love God and are called according
to his purpose for them.
ROMANS 8:28 NLT

No amount of plunging was going to unclog the sink. Donna would have to call a plumber. The extra cost and inconvenience were not what she had wanted. But the minute that Donna learned that the plumber could come right away, she sensed God had a plan. While the plumber cleared the clog, Donna chatted with him about some exciting things happening at her church. Before he left she had invited him and his family to Sunday services. Unclogging her pipes led to a divine appointment with a seeker of grace.

On another occasion, Kathy had her shopping list set, all the various stops planned for her day; and she headed out to her garage to leave. But the garage door would not open. It wouldn't budge. Kathy felt trapped and frustrated. Normally she would not have accepted defeat and would have done just about anything to get that door open, but her Bible study group had recently discussed the fact that God has a plan for every setback. She sensed that she should call her husband and ask him to come home early, picking up their daughter on the way. She then willingly settled into the house for the day.

GRACE FOR TODAY

INCONVENIENCES AND SETBACKS MAY BE GOD'S GRACE IN DISGUISE.

Not long after that, she received a phone call. Her husband had recently submitted a resume to a company for a new job. Because of the garage door incident, her husband would be home in time to return the call and discuss the new opportunity. God had not delayed in giving Kathy His reason for the day's setback. When we unclog our brains of our own will and fill it with God's, we are able to see all the wonderful things He is doing in our lives.

FLIGHT

Strength and dignity are her clothing, and she laughs at
the time to come.
PROVERBS 31:25 NRSV

Authors Karen Savage and Patricia Adams wrote, "Adolescence is perhaps nature's way of preparing parents to welcome the empty nest." In the frenzy of raising teenagers, you may have dreamed about peace and tidiness. But now that day has come, and you're experiencing the dreaded empty-nest syndrome.

Erma Bombecfe quipped, "Graduation day is tough for adults. They go to the ceremony as parents. They come home as contemporaries. After twenty-two years of child-rearing, they are unemployed." Actually being your child's contemporary is a pretty good volunteer position.

GRACE FOR TODAY

GOD WILL USE YOUR EMPTY NEST AS THE LAUNCHING POINT FOR THE NEXT CHAPTER IN YOUR LIFE.

Defeating the empty-nest syndrome is all about looking at things in the positive. Spend some time asking God what plans He has for you in this next step of your life. He may have planned for you to use the freedom you gain to rediscover the wonderful man you married. Explore what you have in common, and let God reveal things you haven't tried. If you're a single parent, He may have you take up a new hobby, get more involved at church, or maybe start a Bible study.

The last thing you want to do is stay at home feeling lonely. If your kids haven't left yet, prayerfully plan some new and exciting events or goals now so that you have positive things to look forward to. Get with a group of empty nesters and do things together.

Maybe God has given you the desire to go back to school, change careers, or join an organization that wants and needs your experience and talents. There's nothing to stop you from exploring financial and personal changes with God leading you.

And remember: your children haven't dropped off the planet. They still need you, but in new and exciting ways. Journalist, Art Buchwald commented, "There isn't a child who hasn't gone out into the brave new world who eventually doesn't return to the old homestead carrying a bundle of dirty clothes." The good news: You get to pick which new ways to help.

Growing Through Discipline

The Lord disciplines those he loves.
HEBREWS 12:6 NLT

GRACE FOR TODAY

GOD LOVES US SO MUCH, HIS CHASTENING IS ALWAYS FOR OUR BENEFIT.

Discipline is defined as "training intended to elicit a specified pattern of behavior or character."[33] As parents, we teach our children obedience primarily for their own protection and character development, knowing that it will serve them all of their lives. In our efforts to train our children, discipline is an essential and necessary part of their growth and learning.

Small children have no concept of danger, but we know how dangerous a tiny finger in an electrical socket can be — or what consequences result from tender hands touching a hot stove. We also prepare our children for another level of learning they will experience when they attend school. Obeying classroom rules, doing homework, and respecting their peers and leadership all require the kind of obedience that Webster's Dictionary describes as: "compliant, conformable, and tractable."[34]

As adults, we may think ourselves long past needing discipline or having to learn obedience: but in the spiritual sense, we never stop learning and growing. We have a heavenly Father whose desire it is to protect us and equip us for all we need in life. Our experiences of discipline are for the ultimate purpose of bringing us into the character and likeness of Christ. Studying Hebrews 12:8-11 will give you a more in-depth explanation of the benefits and results of discipline from God's perspective.

God loves you enough to be your parent and heavenly Father. He has blessed you with a spirit that is sensitive to His instruction and correction. He sees your potential, much like parents see the potential in their own children. Rejoice when you feel God's caution or rebuke, knowing it is your loving Father caring enough to keep you from harm or danger.

AN AUDIENCE OF ONE

The LORD is watching everywhere, keeping his eye on
both the evil and the good.
PROVERBS 15:3 NET

Have you ever felt you don't accomplish much? You may teach a Sunday school class, or perhaps you clean the church but wonder if your students remember any of the lessons or anyone notices the carpets have been vacuumed. At times you may even ask yourself if you do these things to glorify God or to generate praise for your effort.

In the twelfth chapter of Mark, we read an account of offerings given to the temple. Jesus sat across the way and observed the people as they put their money into the treasury. The rich people gave large amounts, making quite a spectacle of themselves to draw attention to their generosity.

Then came a poor widow. She dropped in two very small copper coins worth only a fraction of a penny—hardly worth the effort in the eyes of many. But the eyes of many weren't watching. She had an audience of one.

Jesus called His disciples to Him to comment, "I tell you the truth, this poor widow has put more into the treasury than all the others. They all gave out of their wealth; but she, out of her poverty, put in everything—all she had to live on" (Mark 12:43-44 NIV).

GRACE FOR TODAY

GOD IS CONSTANTLY OBSERVING US—NOT TO POINT OUT OUR FAULTS, BUT TO REWARD THOSE WHO PUT HIM FIRST AND LIVE LIVES THAT HONOR HIM.

Countless people through the ages have read these comments made by Jesus. A widow who thought she'd accomplished so little has been held up as a model of unselfishness and obedience. God knows our hearts. Just like the widow, all of us are being observed. At the end of the day, what does God say of our efforts? It's easy to get caught up in the comments and compliments of many, but we live for an audience of one—our Lord Jesus Christ.

MOUNTAIN MIRACLE

Spread your protection over them, that those who love
your name may rejoice in you.
PSALM 5:11 NIV

Spring break had finally arrived! Ruthie and four friends were driving through the Canadian Rockies on their way to vacation on Vancouver Island. They were driving a massive late-seventies Chrysler that resembled a tank. Doug, the owner of the car, drove as if he thought it was a tank too. He seemed to think that it didn't matter how crazy he was behind the wheel — this Chrysler was indestructible.

GRACE FOR TODAY

GOD'S GRACE
INCLUDES PHYSICAL
PROTECTION!

The first half of the trip was mostly uneventful. There was one "passing a car on a hill" moment on the way to Banff, Alberta; but after a couple of deep breaths, things were okay. Soon after dark, as the group headed deep into the mountains of British Columbia, a sudden spring snowstorm hit.

Ruthie was in the back seat, trying to help Doug see where he was going. Between the failing light and blowing snow, conditions were quickly becoming treacherous. Suddenly Ruthie felt impressed strongly with the notion that they were no longer on the road. She squinted into the darkness. Her hunch was right. The mountain road had veered off to the left; and they had continued straight ahead, blinded by the snow.

"Doug, stop! We're heading off the road!" At Ruthie's shout, Doug slammed on the breaks. The car slid sideways, hit a large snow bank, and tilted precariously downward. The friends suddenly realized how close they were to going over the edge of the mountain. One by one they climbed out of the car on the left side.

Four shaky college students peered over the edge where the car was perched. A small tree was keeping the tank of a car from plummeting down a seventy-foot drop-off. They looked at each other, knowing that they had just been part of a miracle. They never forgot God's grace of protection on that snowy March night.

YIELDED TO THE SPIRIT

By John MacArthur Jr.

A Fizzie is a small tablet used to make a soft drink; it's sort of a flavored Alka-Seltzer. Put it in a glass of water, and its flavor is released throughout the water. This concentrated, compact power pill is no good as long as it sits on the bottom of the glass. It has to release its energy to fill the glass, and then it turns the water into something new.

If it is a grape Fizzie, you get a glass of grape drink. The flavor of the tablet determines the flavor of the water.

In a measure, that pictures how the Spirit of God operates in a human life. He is in the Christian all the time as a compact, concentrated, powerful force of divine energy. The question is, has He ever been able to release that power, to fill your life so that you can become what He is? A Christian not yielded to the Spirit does not manifest the Christ-life. The Spirit of God has to permeate a life if that life is to radiate Him.

We cannot do anything apart from being filled with the Spirit.

If I say to a glove, "Play the piano," what does the glove do? Nothing. The glove cannot play the piano. But if I put my hands in the glove and play the piano, what happens? Music! If I put my hand in a glove, the glove moves. The glove does not get pious and say, "Oh, hand, show me the way to go." It does not say anything; it just goes. Spirit-filled people do not stumble and mumble around trying to find out what God wants. They just go![35]

HEAVENLY FATHER,

It is so good to know that I don't have to live the Christian life on my own. You have filled me with Your spirit. Teach me to recognize His prompting and how to yield myself completely to Him.

AMEN

They were all filled with the Holy Spirit, and they spoke the word of God with boldness.
ACTS 4:31 NKJV

ATTITUDE IS A CHOICE

All your waves and billows have gone over me, and floods of
sorrow pour upon me like a thundering cataract. Yet day by day
the Lord also pours out his steadfast love upon me, and through
the night I sing his songs and pray to God who gives me life.
PSALM 42:7-8 TLB

Zig Ziglar, famous for his motivational training seminars, addresses something called "stinking thinking." He believes our well-being, our successes, our failures, and our relationships are all established by how and what we think.

GRACE FOR TODAY

GOD'S PROMISES PROVIDE THE SUBSTANCE NEEDED FOR A POSITIVE AND EVER-HOPEFUL ATTITUDE.

As women, we have the awesome responsibility of helping shape how and what our children think. If we demonstrate healthy attitudes and responses to life's challenges, more likely than not, our children will develop at least a portion of those same attitudes.

People with an optimistic attitude never lose their sense of wonder. They seem to be filled with awe no matter what bends or turns life's roads may bring. They look for the best in every situation, believing that somehow it will turn out for the greater good. Are optimists ever disappointed? Certainly. Life is full of disappointments and circumstances that can cause any of us to become jaded and pessimistic about living, but as surely as the sun rises each morning, God gives new mercy and a new vision for living.

In Psalm 51, when David became downcast in his soul, he cried out for God to renew a right spirit within him and to restore his joy. The secret of David's optimism was his trust and faith in God. David's attitude reflected an undaunted trust in God. By choice, as in Psalm 42, He praised God as his source of life and love.

No matter what you may be facing today, ask God to direct your thoughts to those pure and lovely things that fill your life. Count your blessings and praise God for walking with you through every challenging circumstance.

SHINE BRIGHT

You were once darkness, but now you are light in the Lord.
Live as children of light.
EPHESIANS 5:8 NIV

A little boy ran to his mother's car, beaming with excitement after his first day of school. "Did you have a good day?" his mother asked.

"Oh, yes!" the little boy replied as he bounced into the backseat. "I asked everyone in my class if they knew Jesus, even my teacher; and then I only played with the boys and girls that knew Him."

The mother was shocked to discover that her son thought he should only associate with "Christian" children. Amazingly many Christians today make the same mistake by choosing to have as little contact as possible with those who are without God.

As followers of Jesus Christ, we are called to draw all men — everyone — to Him. We are the only light that shines in a world of darkness. Light has no fear of darkness. No matter what wattage the bulb is, when turned on, the light overtakes the darkness. We have no reason to fear the influence of the world if we are connected to our source of light and life.

Jesus said we are not of this world, but we are called to live in it. We are to direct our lives in such a way that our light shines so brightly that it draws others to Him. Darkness can never overtake us because we are the light — the only light — in the world.

So choose to let your light shine into all the world — showing God's grace to all men.

GRACE FOR TODAY

THE LIGHT OF THE WORLD SHINES BRIGHTEST WHEREVER THERE IS DARKNESS.

THE TENTMAKERS

Live your life in a manner worthy of the gospel of Christ, so that . . . I will know that you are standing firm in one spirit, striving side by side with one mind for the faith of the gospel.
PHILIPPIANS 1:27 NRSV

Priscilla and her husband, Aquila, were Jewish tentmakers who lived in Rome during the First Century. Emperor Claudius issued an edict expelling all the Jews from Rome, so Priscilla and Aquila moved to Corinth, a city full of wealth and immorality. This was the world that surrounded them as they once again built up their tentmaking enterprise.

Paul came to Corinth discouraged from his experiences in Athens. Because he was a tentmaker too, he stayed and worked with Priscilla and Aquila. The three of them became an effective team, and when Paul left Corinth, he took them with him. Although he went on to Jerusalem, he left Priscilla and Aquila in Ephesus to carry on his ministry there. They established the church at Ephesus, which met in their home and became one of the most influential churches of that century.

GRACE FOR TODAY

GOD'S TEAM—THE BODY OF CHRIST—IS COMPOSED OF MANY MEMBERS. HIS GRACE ENABLES US TO FLOW TOGETHER AS ONE TO ACCOMPLISH HIS WILL IN THE EARTH.

Priscilla's name appears with her husband's six times in Scripture. In New Testament times, it was customary to list the most important person's name first. Interestingly, Priscilla's name is mentioned first in four of these references.

Moving means uprooting a person's life. Yet, Priscilla seemed to adjust easily. Perhaps it was because her roots were sunk deep into Christ rather than into her natural surroundings. From Rome to Corinth to Ephesus and back to Rome again, Priscilla was a team player and a grace-filled enterpriser for the Lord.

We may not face physical dangers like Priscilla did, but other fears or circumstances can obstruct our willingness to be as enterprising as she. Let's pray that we may faithfully go the distance, be filled with God's grace, and work as a team to accomplish God's will in the earth.

GRACE FOR A THIEF

God so greatly loved and dearly prized the world that He
[even] gave up His only begotten (unique) Son, so that
whoever believes in (trusts in, clings to, relies on) Him shall
not perish . . . but have eternal (everlasting) life.
JOHN 3:16 AMP

"Jesus, remember me when you come into your kingdom."

Jesus answered him, "I tell you the truth, today you will be with me in paradise." This passage from Luke 23:42-43 NIV is a conversation between a thief and Jesus. The amazing thing about these two verses isn't just that Jesus is promising paradise to a criminal—it is that these words of grace are spoken while they are both dying slow and painful deaths, hanging from crosses. This thief would never have an opportunity to live for Christ—he was going to die that very day. Yet salvation came to him, even as he faced his final hours. Does something about this seem unfair to you?

GRACE FOR TODAY

GOD'S GRACE IS A FREE GIFT TO ANYONE WHO ASKS FOR IT.

Even on the cross, Jesus chose to forgive all the acts of thievery that this man had ever committed. All it took was for that criminal to believe that Jesus could save him. He had nothing to give Jesus in return but his faith. That may not seem fair to those of us who are trying to live our lives for Jesus—until we realize that nothing we do can earn His grace either.

Whether we have committed one sin or one million, we all need Jesus' forgiveness. And whether we accept His grace when we're 5 or 105, we all get the same infinite grace. That is what grace is—a free gift that we don't deserve. This is exactly what Jesus gave to the thief on the cross—just because the thief asked for it.

No matter the sin, no matter how early or late the hour, whoever asks for and receives God's grace will one day stand rejoicing in Heaven—along with that redeemed thief.

What's in Your Basket?

Someone may argue, "Some people have faith; others
have good deeds." I say, "I can't see your faith if you don't
have good deeds, but I will show you my faith through my
good deeds."
JAMES 2:18 NLT

GRACE FOR TODAY

GOD'S GRACE AT
WORK IN THE LIFE OF
THE BELIEVER
PRODUCES RICH,
ABUNDANT FRUIT
THAT IS APPARENT TO
ALL.

A successful television commercial for a credit card company asked the question, "What's in your wallet?" That campaign succeeded so well that the credit card vaulted into one of the most recognized in America, with a 95 percent national awareness among consumers, according to some surveys.

What percentage of time would you estimate you are recognized as a Christian? Is it at least 95 percent of the time?

If you've ever watched a basket weaver, he takes long wooden slats and weaves them together to make a beautiful work of art. Our Christian life can be compared to one of the baskets. Our witness is woven together with faith and works. We accept Jesus Christ as Savior by faith; and as a result, we have a desire to work for Him. When we delight in God, He produces the desire within us to live godly lives and do godly works. Jesus told the Pharisees and Sadducees to "produce fruit in keeping with repentance" (Matthew 3:8 NIV). The fruit of the Spirit will be a natural result of a person's identification with Christ.

According to the apostle Paul, the fruit of the Spirit is love, joy, peace, patience, kindness, goodness, faithfulness, gentleness, and self-control. Shall we compare salvation to an apple tree? In this analogy, the root of the tree is faith, and the works are the fruit. Is there fruit present in your life? Do you exhibit fruit as a witness and the result of faith and works woven together in your life? Others cannot see your faith. They do see your works. Let's be recognized as followers of Christ—too percent of the time.

STUDENT OF THE WORD

By John MacArthur Jr.

Let me share how I study the Bible, and how the Bible has come alive to me. I began in 1 John. One day I sat down and read all five chapters straight through. It took me 20 minutes. The next day, I sat down and read 1 John straight through again. I did this for 30 days. Do you know what happened at the end of 30 days? I knew what was in 1 John.

Next, I went to the Gospel of John. I read the first seven chapters for 30 days, the next seven for the next 30 days, and the last seven for 30 days. In 90 days, I had read the entire Gospel of John 30 times. Where does it talk about the Good Shepherd? Chapter 1, right-hand column, starts in the middle.

Where does it talk about the vine and the branches? Chapter 15. Where does it talk about Jesus' friends? Chapter 15, over in the next column and a little farther down. Where does it talk about Jesus' arrest in the garden? John (8. The restoration of Peter?

John 21. The woman at the well? John 4. The Bread of Life? John 6. Nicodemus? John 3. The wedding at Cana? John 2.

You might say, "My, are you smart!" No, J am not smart. I read it 30 times. Even I can get it then! Isaiah said to learn "precept upon precept, line upon line, . . . here a little, and there a little" (see Isaiah 28:10-13). Then you have hidden it in your heart. After a while you are no longer a concordance cripple! 36

FATHER,

You were so gracious to have given us Your written word. I want it to be a part of me. As I am faithful to hide it in my heart, I pray that it will transform me and make me a fruitful disciple.

AMEN

Study to shew thyself approved unto God, a workman that needeth not to be ashamed, rightly dividing the word of truth.
2 TIMOTHY 2:15 KJV

KISSING FISH

The mouths of the righteous utter wisdom, and their
tongues speak justice.
PSALM 37:30 NRSV

A small variety of Kissing Fish lives in the coral reefs of the Caribbean Sea. It's bright blue, fast in the water, and about two to three inches long. But the most fascinating thing about this fish is its "kiss." Often while snorkeling, a person can find two of these fish with their lips pressed against one another and their fins thrashing in the sea.

GRACE FOR TODAY

JESUS IS TO ME ALL
GRACE AND NO
WRATH, ALL TRUTH
AND NO FALSEHOOD;
AND OF TRUTH AND
GRACE HE IS FULL,
INFINITELY FULL.

CHARLES HADDON
SPURGEON

At first glance, they may appear to be having a serious underwater romance, but looks can be deceiving. These pint-sized bullies are actually participating in underwater martial arts—jaw to jaw. These fish are ferociously territorial, and they guard with their jaws what they perceive to be their own personal coral reef. This fish would probably not be a good candidate for your aquarium!

Unfortunately, Kissing Fish aren't the first to deceive with their mouths. Long before Jesus was sentenced to die on the cross, the Pharisees made secret plans to trap Him into saying something wrong so they could rid themselves of Him. Jesus had been preaching in the synagogue, but He hadn't been ordained by the Sanhedrin. He was not obeying their manmade rules but was infringing on what they considered their territory, and they hated Him.

Let's make sure we don't act like the Kissing Fish and stake out a claim to an idea or a way of doing things that causes us to battle over what we perceive to be our turf. Tunnel vision can block out our peripheral vision for what God wants us to see and do. Only through being open to God's wisdom can our opinions, words, and actions be filled with His grace.

PRAYER CHAIN

Fire goes out for lack of fuel, and quarrels disappear when
gossip stops.
PROVERBS 26:20 NLT

"I'm just telling you this because I know you'll pray . . ." Are they sincere words X of love and hope or a lead-in line that opens the door to full-blown gossip? "Pray for Ted and Sally. They're in marriage counseling. Sister James said she wasn't surprised one little bit with the way she treats him in public." "That Collins boy needs prayer—I've heard he's a troublemaker and a cheat. Whatever will his parents do?"

The compassion of God speaks for the people, not about the situation. The true character and nature of God seeks to offer mercy, grace, and comfort. Compassion is on the lips of those who carry the heart of the Father into the lives and homes of those who are hurting. It lifts the hurting to the throne of God's grace.

No matter how desperate someone is for conversation, we are to choose to honor God and people with positive conversation. Gossip dishonors others. You can turn the tide of any exchange, and well you should. One quick solution amidst such a conversation is to offer to pray for the person right then. Very few people will refuse your offer, and you can take that moment to join your faith with all of those in the "discussion group." Consider what compassion would say and how compassion would pray. Choose to be a part of the answer instead of compounding the person's problem. It's a way that you can step up and make a difference to those around you.

GRACE FOR TODAY

COMPASSION IS ON THE LIPS OF THOSE WHO LIFT THE HURTING BEFORE THE THRONE OF GOD'S GRACE.

GO WITH THE FLOW

When you go through deep waters and great trouble, I will be with you. When you go through rivers of difficulty, you will not drown!
ISAIAH 43:2 TLB

A recent movie made for the huge IMAX screen is called *Amazon*. The film shows the incredible resiliency of the rainforests of the Amazon River basin. The trees and wildlife flourish in conditions that look very difficult to the casual observer. During the rainy season, forty-seven feet of water can cover the basin floor! But this flooding serves a purpose, and the inhabitants of the Amazon make the most of it. The floodwaters benefit the native people by providing a habitat for specific fish. Only during this time of high waters can the natives find an abundance of this fish. The root systems of the trees grow more readily when deeply submersed, and in turn they feed and protect the tree dwellers that are vital to the ecosystem. "Going with the flow" seems to be the motto of the Amazon.

GRACE FOR TODAY

WHEN THE FLOODWATERS COME, GO WITH THE FLOW OF GOD'S GRACE.

Sometimes we feel the floodwaters rise around us. The stresses of work, finances, relationships, or health problems pour down. We feel like we might drown. But if we take hold of the rock of God's grace, we can begin to see the rainy season in our lives as a time of healing and growth. The rushing waters of difficulty can bring an abundance of strengthening prayers your way. Hard times increase your trust and help your roots grow deep into the soil of God's Word. In turn, the things you learn can help feed and protect others in the body of Christ.

Perhaps the strange and wonderful cycles of the Amazon hold a lesson for us in this journey of faith. When we look at the rain in our lives as part of the outpouring of God's grace, instead of a drowning flood, we will grow and find healing for ourselves and for others. Maybe our motto should also be "go with the flow" — the flow of God's grace.

WATER OF THE WORD

I thirst for God, the living God. When can I come and stand
before him?
PSALM 42:2 NLT

During the busy days of summer and vacations, have you ever let your garden go unattended? The plants droop, the leaves become brittle, and new growth withers on the vine. The taller plants buffeted by the wind do not have the strength to stand. Even a plant in rich soil will wither and die if water is withheld. It takes water to release nutrients into the soil to make them available to the plant. When you fill a container with refreshing water and pour it onto the plants, they begin to perk up. The flowers come to life.

We may complain about reading the Bible and wonder what relevance it has in our everyday lives, but then we find ourselves drooping. Sometimes we can be almost dead spiritually and not even notice how parched we've become, how thirsty we are for the water of God's Word.

GRACE FOR TODAY

A LIFE SOAKED IN THE WORD OF GOD IS VIBRANT AND FULL OF GRACE.

Our gardens are much better off if we periodically water them, instead of waiting until they are almost dead before getting out the watering can. We cannot mist only the tops of the plants. We need to soak the soil so the roots will receive the moisture needed. The real strength of a plant comes from its roots.

How many times do you read a few Scriptures to soothe your conscience, but rarely study the Word of God? Our souls need to soak in the Word of God. Without the Living Water, without personal fellowship with the Lord, our souls can get no nourishment. We are better off if we make it a habit to drink from the spiritual well on a periodic basis. Then when the strong winds of life blow, we will be able to stand. Are you thirsty?

MEDITATION

"Be still, and know that I am God."
PSALM 46:10 NIV

GRACE FOR TODAY

GOD LONGS TO COMMUNE WITH US AND FILL US COMPLETELY. MEDITATING ON HIM MAKES THAT POSSIBLE.

How often are we actually still . . . really quiet and contemplative? Author Madeleine L'Engle said, "Deepest communion with God is beyond words, on the other side of silence."

Jesus often went away to pray and be alone with God. In Gethsemane Jesus' soul was overwhelmed with sorrow, so He left His companions and talked to His heavenly Father in the quiet of the garden.

How often do we seek a place just to be with our heavenly Father? How often do we just think about Him? More importantly, how often do we care about His view on what we are thinking? "May my meditation be pleasing to him, for I rejoice in the Lord" (Psalm 104:34 NRSV).

In the psalms, meditation was a way to study your own soul, heart, and mind. A time to take stock of what's inside there and perhaps what shouldn't be in there. A personal review of your soul might not be a bad thing now and then. "I will meditate on all your works and consider all your mighty deeds" (Psalm 77:12 NIV). This type of pondering fosters a renewed awe in God's love. Meditation lets you really contemplate God's laws and gives insights into what pleases Him. It's not enough just to listen to a sermon every Sunday. God wants your mind to review, contemplate, and understand so that your heart knows Him. Meditation is not emptying your mind, but filling it completely about and with God. It is finding that quiet spot in life so that you can quiet every part of you to experience the grace of fellowship with your Heavenly Father.

GOD'S IN CONTROL

By John MacArthur Jr.

God's grace saves us, helps us cope with our anxieties, equips us for service, and enables us to grow spiritually and to be rich in God. Like God's peace, it is always available, and there is no limit to it. And again, like God's peace, the conditions for receiving it are trusting God, forsaking sin, enduring the refining process, doing good, and living by the Word. As we are what we ought to be, God infuses us with His peace and grace. And that has a wonderful way of crowding out anxiety.

A few days after presenting this very message to my congregation at Grace Church, I had an unprecedented opportunity to apply it to my life: I was notified that my wife and youngest daughter were in a serious auto accident, and that my wife, Patricia, would probably die. Everything seemed like a blur to me, the details frustratingly sketchy. I was afraid she was already dead.

During my hour-long drive to the hospital, I had a lot of time to reflect on the severity of the situation. Yet I experienced a deep and settled peace simply because I knew God had not failed me— His grace was at work in my family's lives, and He was in complete control. I am happy to report that God spared both their lives, and that Patricia has recovered beautifully. If you too rely on God's grace, He will see you through the most difficult trials.[37]

FATHER:

I thank You for the grace that is at work in my life no matter what happens. And I thank You for the peace that coaxes as a result. I know that You will never fail me.

AMEN

The grace of our Lord was poured out on me abundantly, along with the faith and love that are in Christ Jesus.
1 TIMOTHY 1:14 NIV

WHEN DARKNESS FAILS

When darkness overtakes the godly, light will come
bursting in.
PSALM 112:4 NLT

Power outages are no fun. They are especially frustrating when they last for long periods of time. We come to realize how much we need light when we have to go for days without it. The simplest tasks become difficult when you have to do them in the dark. Even recognizing your own family becomes hard in the darkness of the evening. What a relief it is when the lights spring to life again as power is restored!

GRACE FOR TODAY

GOD OFFERS THE CANDLE OF HIS GRACE WHILE YOU WAIT FOR THE LIGHT.

Times of darkness in our lives are even more troubling than power outages. When difficulties cast a shadow across our souls, it can feel like the light will never shine again. We find it hard to do anything—it takes effort to just get through each day. Even the faces of loved ones seem obscured by the gloom surrounding our hearts.

We cannot escape the dark times. Storms come into everyone's life. Sickness will lay you low. Money will get tight. Relationships will get rocky. What can we do when darkness falls and we feel lost?

When the power goes out, we light candles so we can see our way from room to room. The light may be small, but it cuts through some of the darkness and allows us to see enough to take one step at a time. The warmth of that little flame takes away some of the chill, while we wait for the light to return.

When darkness comes to your life, God promises never to leave you. You can hold on to the candle of His grace. Even when you only can see one step at a time, He holds your hand and bids you to trust Him to lead you through the night. Hold on to the warmth of hope until the dawn comes. Light will suddenly come shining through again, and your joy will return.

EXPLORE THE GIFT

God saw all that he had made, and it was very good.
GENESIS 1:51 NIV

Saint Augustine said, "The world is a book, and those who do not travel read only a page." How much of the book have you read and how much do you want to read? God created an amazing world, and that world is His gift to us. There's an explorer in all of us who wants to discover uncharted waters, whether that's globe trotting or city hopping. It doesn't really matter which because travel in any form expands our vision of God, the world, and ourselves.

GRACE FOR TODAY

THE WORLD IS A GIFT FROM GOD THAT HE INTENDED US TO EXPERIENCE TO THE FULL.

Watching the surf ride a tropical beach or the moon fill a desert horizon inspires awe in the Creator. In fact, viewing our fragile planet from space has had a profound impact on a lucky few. Astronaut Edgar Mitchell summed it up, "My view of our planet was a glimpse of divinity."

Travel has a way of broadening our viewpoint. World traveler and author Mark Twain commented, "Travel is fatal to prejudice, bigotry, and narrow-mindedness; and many of our people need it sorely on these accounts. Broad, wholesome, charitable views of men and things cannot be acquired by vegetating in one little corner of the earth all one's lifetime." Traveling instills in us both an esteem for others and an intimate compassion. Experience begs us to search for understanding and action because we can not ignore what we see, what we hear, what we touch, and what we feel. Experience touches our souls.

Jesus traveled among us, and our world will never be the same again. Go out and experience the world; read all the pages and write a new chapter in your life. Experience the world and let the world experience you.

New Year

To this end we always pray for you, asking that our God will
make you worthy of his call and will fulfill by his power
every good resolve and work of faith.
2 THESSALONIANS 1:11 NRSV

Grace for Today

GOD DOESN'T KEEP
SCORE OF YOUR
FAILURES. HE GIVES
YOU OPPORTUNITIES
TO BE SUCCESSFUL
AND HELPS YOU
CONQUER YOUR
MOUNTAINS, ONE AT
A TIME.

Anything that makes us stop and take stock of ourselves can't be a bad thing. With hope and a little skepticism, we plan our New Year's resolutions. Will this be the year we accomplish our resolves? John Chrysostom said, "When we once begin to form good resolutions, God gives us every opportunity of carrying them out."

So clearly, we are the weakest link in the resolution equation. Perhaps that weakness comes from our allowing things to become habits. And habits become so much a part of us that we forget how to live without them. Maybe habits are what really make the person and not his or her clothes. What are your habits making you?

Perhaps the problem is that we make a list and annually try to fix our entire being all at once. Any change should be made in manageable steps. We should set a goal and have faith that God will help us achieve that goal. Jesus said, "Truly I tell you, if you have faith the size of a mustard seed, you will say to this mountain, 'Move from here to there,' and it will move; and nothing will be impossible for you" (Matthew 17:20 NRSV).

Having faith doesn't mean we won't fail or stumble; it just means that we may not fall on our heads because God is there to catch us. So often we stop trying because we failed once or twice or more. God isn't keeping score of the failures. He's there to give us the opportunities to be successful.

Don't make a resolution list this year. Just pick one thing and allow God to help you conquer it.

THE THORNS OF SIN

In the paths of the wicked lie thorns and snares, but he
who guards his soul stays far from them.
PROVERBS 22:5 NIV

Have you ever tried to trim a rose bush? When pruning roses, it's best to wear long sleeves and a sturdy pair of leather gloves. No matter how careful you are, the thorns can painfully puncture or scratch your hands and arms. The branches seem to reach out on their own accord, scratching and leaving marks at every turn.

Just like an encounter with thorns wounds us physically, we are wounded spiritually after an encounter with sin. Solomon said in Proverbs that evil deeds ensnare. Sin becomes like a cord wrapped around the fallen one, holding the victim tight. We must stay away from sin, so as not to be ensnared. But when we fall, we can ask for forgiveness. God will forgive us, and the blood Jesus shed for us on the cross will cover our sin and set us free.

Have you become so entangled with thorns that you have had to wrench yourself free? Have you felt wounded after a bout with sin? Its tentacles can reach farther than the initial wrongdoing. Anyone who has suffered with an addiction will tell you that. But Jesus prevailed over sin and purchased our freedom from every sin and anything that binds. Praise the Lord, He not only provides forgiveness but also gives us the power to overcome! We depend on the Holy Spirit to help us set our minds on what God wants. As the apostle Paul exhorted, let us count ourselves dead to sin but alive to God.

By His power we can stay away from sin—and prickly rose bushes.

GRACE FOR TODAY

GOD'S GRACE PROVIDES THE STRENGTH WE NEED TO BOTH
AVOID SIN AND TO OVERCOME IT.

GRACIOUS WORDS

How sweet are your words to my taste, sweeter than honey
to my mouth!
PSALM 119:103 NIV

"I love you."
"Can I pray for you today?"
"Please let me know if I can help you."

Words like these make a difference. Just reading them gives you a feeling of worth and comfort. When we hear words of grace we are changed. Our hearts are softened. Our attitudes often change quite suddenly. We feel lifted up, and our problems don't seem quite so overwhelming. Gracious words are truly powerful.

GRACE FOR TODAY

GOD'S GRACIOUS WORDS ARE MEANT TO BE RECYCLED!

God has given us a whole book of gracious words that come straight from His heart. He uses words to teach us, guide us, and reveal himself to us. He uses words to tell us how much He loves us.

When you are sad and lonely, God says that He will never leave you, that He is close to you when you are brokenhearted. When you feel confused, He says that He will give you wisdom when you ask for it and that He will guide you when you listen for His direction. When you are happy, He says that His own heart is glad and that others should be glad with you. God's Word speaks what we need to hear in every situation.

God also wants us to take His words to heart and use them as an example of how to speak to others. All those gracious words that you have received from the Lord are also the right words to use when others need encouragement, guidance, or love. God's gracious words are a gift—a gift that keeps on giving whenever they are heard and whenever they are spoken.

TO BE NEAR HIM

By John MacArthur Jr.

Jesus was talking to His disciples and asked, "Who do men say that I am?" They answered, "Oh, some people think You are Jeremiah; some people think You are Elijah; some people think You are one of the prophets."

He said, "Who do you think I am?"

Peter responded, "Thou art the Christ, the Son of the living God" (Matthew 16:16). Then, I feel sure, he wondered, Where did that come from?

Jesus said, "Flesh and blood did not reveal this to you, Peter, but My Father in heaven did" (w. 13-17).

Peter probably said, "I thought so. I surely didn't know that." You see, when Peter was near Jesus, he not only did the miraculous, he said the miraculous. Is it any wonder he wanted to be near Him?

When he was near Christ, Peter had miraculous courage. He was in the Garden of Gethsemane when a whole band of soldiers—as many as five hundred—came to arrest Jesus. They came marching in with all their regalia. In front of them came the chief priests, and before the chief priests came the servants of the priests. Peter was standing with the Ford. Maybe his thoughts went something like this: They think they are going to take Jesus away. No, they won't.

Since Peter did not ever want to be removed from the presence of Jesus, he took out a sword. He started with the first guy in line, who happened to be Malchus, the servant of the high priest. The Bible says Peter cut off Malchus' ear, but if I know Peter, he was going for his head. Peter was ready to take on the whole Roman army. You see, when he was with Jesus, he had miraculous courage.[38]

FATHER GOD,

Without You, I can't do anything significant. But with You, through Your grace, I can be a part fo the miraculous. Work through me today.

AMEN

By you I can crush a troop, and by my God I can leap over a wall.
PSALM 18:29 NRSV

PURE AS GOLD

People are watching us as we stay at our post, alertly, unswervingly . . . in hard times, tough times, bad times; when we're beaten up, jailed, and mobbed; working hard, working late, working without eating; with pure heart, clear head, steady hand; in gentleness, holiness, and honest love.
2 CORINTHIANS 6:4-6 MSG

Gold is considered valuable because it is scarce and has many desirable properties. It is soft and malleable and can be shaped into most any item desired. Yet, as valuable as it is, it cannot be used for beautiful jewelry without going through a difficult refining process first.

GRACE FOR TODAY

GOD HELPS US THROUGH FIERY TRIALS IN SUCH A WAY THAT WE EMERGE AS PURE AS GOLD.

For gold to be hard enough to be made into jewelry, it must be combined with another metal such as copper or silver called an alloy. This requires separating the gold from the ore and other impurities as well as adding the alloy.

The process begins when a crusher breaks the ore into fragments and a rod mill grinds the ore into pulverized particles. A cyanide solution is then poured onto sand in a leaching tank to dissolve the gold. The unrefined gold material is heated in a smelter to a temperature of 1,830°F to 2,010°F, and chlorine gas is added. The metals are removed as chlorides, and the process is complete when the gold content has reached a purity of 99.6 to 99.7 percent.

Sometimes we go through a similar refining process. We may feel crushed and broken, wondering if we will survive the smelting fires. Yet, God promises never to give us more than we can handle and helps us through our trials, teaching us to depend on His grace. Then we become pliable in His hands and open to His desires for our lives. Just like the beautiful ring on your finger, you can withstand the fires of life and come out pure as gold and full of grace.

SUGAR AND SPICE

We also rejoice in our sufferings, because we know that
suffering produces perseverance; perseverance, character;
and character, hope.
ROMANS 5:3-4 NIV

Sadie Delany's friends claimed she was as sweet as molasses and full of grace. And for 109 years, she spread that sweetness around to the people who came into her life. Bessie said of her sister, "Sadie is sugar, and I'm the spice." The sisters had contrasting personalities, with Bessie being the sharp-tongued spitfire and Sadie the mild-mannered peaceful one.

GRACE FOR TODAY

GOD'S GRACE STRENGTHENS US AND GIVES US THE ABILITY TO PERSEVERE. HE ALWAYS CAUSES US TO COME OUT ON TOP.

Their father, born a slave, was freed when he was seven years old. He went on to become a vice principal of a school and America's first elected African-American Episcopal bishop. Their mother instilled self-discipline, compassion, and confidence in the girls; and through her they learned perseverance.

"Papa always taught us that with every dollar you earn, the first ten cents goes to the Lord," said Sadie. "The next ten cents goes to the bank for hard times, and the rest is yours to spend wisely."

"For over one hundred years, we have followed his advice," added Bessie.

In spite of living through decades of segregation and discrimination, these sisters' lives were blessed by the Lord. Sadie became the first African American to teach domestic science in New York City, where she taught for thirty years. Bessie became the second African-American woman licensed to practice dentistry in the state of New York. The Delaney sisters celebrated a century of achievements in their best-selling book, Having Our Say.

Perhaps your obstacles may not be as overwhelming as those the Delaney sisters faced, but still they are obstacles you must overcome. The Lord has promised to be there for us no matter what we are facing, if we will turn to Him and persevere.

MAKING A DIFFERENCE

She sets about her work vigorously; her arms are strong for
her tasks. She sees that her trading is profitable, and her
lamp does not go out at night.
PROVERBS 31:17-18 NIV

Lydia grew up in a world of business and commerce in the city of Thyatira, which is now part of Turkey. More trade guilds were located in Thyatira than in any other city of its day.

Lydia was called "a dealer in purple cloth" (Acts 16:14 NIV), and she probably belonged to the Guild of Purple-Sellers, famed throughout the Roman Empire for royal garments. Purple dye came from a rare kind of shellfish. When exposed to sunlight, the veins of the shellfish produce one tiny drop of purple dye per fish. Thus, the purple dye for clothing was extremely rare and costly.

GRACE FOR TODAY

ALL WRITING COMES
BY THE GRACE OF
GOD, AND ALL DOING
AND HAVING.

RALPH WALDO
EMERSON

Religion and business were linked in Thyatira. Coins carried the image of Tyrimnos, their protecting god, whom the people considered to be a divine ancestor of the town's leading families. Lydia was a Gentile who could have found a prominent position in Thyatiran religious life. Instead she chose to worship the Jewish God. This set her apart from her customers and probably caused her to risk losing business because of her faith.

When Paul came to town, she became filled with God's grace. She and her household were baptized. Identifying herself with Christ and His followers now put her at risk with her Jewish customers. Nevertheless, she didn't let her business enterprise limit her faith. The Philippian church grew out of her home, and the members consistently sent Paul money to support his work.

Lydia shows us how much a businesswoman can affect her world. If you follow Lydia's example of enterprising faith you, too, can make a difference in your world.

A Steady Focus

Let us fix our eyes on Jesus, the author and perfecter of
our faith.
HEBREWS 12:2 NIV

Each day is filled with choices from the seemingly trivial — what to wear, what gift to give to a friend for her birthday, what to fix for dinner — to the life-changing choices of whether or not to get married, buy a house, have a baby, or even retire.

You can perceive your choices as problems or opportunities. It's easy to become lost while searching for the answer and to lose sight of what prompted you to begin the search in the first place.

Jesus has the answer for every decision you face. But if all you talk about is the problem, that is a sure indication that you don't have your eyes on the answer. We identify with what we focus on. With your eyes on the problem, it will only loom larger and larger. With that frame of mind, it's easy to offer excuses, which will further convince you that there is no answer. It's impossible. It can't be done. I'm too tired, too sick, too late. What if I fail?

But there is hope! In reality, you already have the answer because the Great One who holds all the answers lives within you! Shift your focus from the problem to the answer — Jesus — the author and finisher of your faith. With your eyes on Him, the challenge you're facing will diminish in your own sight; and the answer will seem closer than it did before you refocused.

Keep your eyes on Jesus! He is the answer.

Grace for Today

GOD'S ANSWER TO OUR LIFE IS ALWAYS JESUS. AND HIS
ANSWER IS ENOUGH.

MISSION

[Jesus said,] "Blessed are the merciful, for they will be
shown mercy."
MATTHEW 5:7 NIV

GRACE FOR TODAY

JESUS STILL HEALS
AND TOUCHES THE
UNTOUCHABLES
TODAY THROUGH
OUR WILLING HEARTS.
HE IS A
COMPASSIONATE,
INVOLVED SAVIOR.

Actor and composer Oscar Levant joked, "I've given up reading books. I find it takes my mind off myself." That may be an extreme form of self-obsession, but we are a self-focused culture. Mission and charity work is a way for us to focus all our emotions and energies away from self and toward others. But true caring isn't a product of duty or guilt. True caring is an extension of our love for humanity. missionary doctor Wilfred Thomason Grenfell commented, have always believed that the Good Samaritan went across the road to the wounded man just because he wanted to."

Joy is an essential part of compassion and giving. The Bible tells us not to give reluctantly or because we feel we have to but because we want to. God loves a cheerful giver.

Missionary David Livingstone didn't believe in armchair compassion. He dedicated his life to love in action just like his Savior did. In a time when leaders shunned the poor and the sick, Jesus waded into their masses, healing and touching the untouchables. He was a compassionate, involved Savior.

We must not be content that our little corner is prosperous and happy because our God loves the entire world. Our attitudes and actions towards our global village reflect to the rest of the world what we value. We are judged by our actions both at home and abroad. Eric Liddell said, "We are all missionaries . . . Wherever we go, we either bring people nearer to Christ, or we repel them from Christ." When asked to serve others, we can say to God, "Here am I. Send me."

PLANNED NEGLECT

By John MacArthur Jr.

The more you study the Word of God, the more it saturates your mind and life. Someone is reported to have asked a concert violinist in New York's Carnegie Hall how she became so skilled. She said that it was by "planned neglect." She planned to neglect everything that was not related to her goal.

Some less important things in your life could stand some planned neglect so that you might give yourself to studying the Word of God. Do you know what would happen? The more you would study the Word of God, the more your mind would be saturated with it. It will be no problem then for you to think of Christ. You won't be able to stop thinking of Him.

To be Spirit-filled is to live a Christ-conscious life, and there is no shortcut to that. You can't go and get yourself super-dedicated to live a Christ-conscious life. The only way you can be saturated with the thoughts of Christ is to saturate yourself with the Book that is all about Him. And this is God's will, that you not only be saved but that you also be Spirit-filled.[39]

FATHER GOD,

I want to be saturated with Your Word and have the mind of Christ. I realize that the only way this can happen is if I give Your Word first place in my life and "neglect" the things that prevent me from giving myself wholly to Your precepts. I need Your grace to be disciplined in how I manage my time. Lead me as I study and meditate on Your Word, so I can think and act like Jesus today.

AMEN

In your lives you must think and act like Christ Jesus.
PHILIPPIANS 2:5 NCV

ANNA AND CHARLEY

The Lord will work out his plans for my life—for your
lovingkindness, Lord, continues forever.
PSALM 138:8 TLB

Writer Hannah Whitall Smith once told the story of a woman—let's call her Anna—who was fearful of what God would ask of her if she said, "Your will be done." She finally confided in a close friend about her struggle.

GRACE FOR TODAY

GOD WANTS THE BEST FOR YOU!

The friend told Anna to imagine that her beloved son, Charley, came to her and said that he wanted to obey her always. Charley was going to completely trust his mother to do the very best for him. She asked Anna, "If Charley gave himself over to you in complete trust, would you plan for him only the most difficult, tedious, and painful of tasks?" Anna immediately declared that she would want to plan only the most wonderfully fulfilling things for her darling boy.

Anna's friend smiled. "Do you think that God loves you any less? He loves you infinitely more! Don't you think that God, in His grace, would want to plan the best for you?" Anna felt that her friend's words had come straight from her heavenly Father. Her fear began to lift at that very moment.

Many of us can relate to Anna's fears. We know that we should be willing to follow God's will, but deep down we are terribly frightened of what the cost might be. When we find ourselves gripped by these worries, we need to remember the story of Anna and Charley. God is unfathomably more loving and gracious than the most adoring parent. He wants the very best for us. He delights in blessing us. When we come to Him and say, "I trust You to do the very best for me," He will not betray that trust. While His will might require something difficult, He will always provide the strength and grace. And in the end, we will find wonderful fulfillment in following the will of our loving Father.

LOVING CREATION

God gave them his blessing and said: Have a lot of children! Fill the earth with people and bring it under your control. Rule over the fish in the ocean, the birds in the sky, and every animal on the earth.
GENESIS 1:28 CEV

God created the earth and then blessed it to be prosperous and healthy. These are not the actions of an indifferent God. Jesus understood God's loving nature — time and time again He illustrated that love in His stories about God. But creation also responds to the Creator. "Then I heard every creature in heaven and on earth and under the earth and on the sea, and all that is in them, singing: 'To him who sits on the throne and to the Lamb be praise and honor and glory and power, for ever and ever!'" (Revelation 5:13 NIV).

God was the first ecologist, and He put mankind in charge of His world. How are we doing so far? Are we failing rapidly, or are we just learning our task too slowly? Martin Luther reflected on the relationship between Creator, creation, and humans, "God writes the gospel not in the Bible alone, but on trees and flowers and clouds and stars." Every aspect of nature was created for us. Maybe it's time we treasure this planet like God cherishes it. Scientist George Washington Carver said, "I love to think of nature as an unlimited broadcasting station, through which God speaks to us every hour, if we will only tune in."

GRACE FOR TODAY

GOD CREATED EVERY ASPECT OF NATURE AS A GIFT FOR US, AND HE CONTINUALLY SPEAKS TO US THROUGH IT.

Is this generation of humanity tuning out? Have we stopped listening and stopped trying to care for our planet? In our complexity, have we lost the simplicity of loving this gift? People of faith should be the most active in preserving the natural beauty of our world. We should be standing guard and protecting our inheritance because that was the first and most important job we were given to do. We are the planet's custodians. Let's be conscientious stewards.

THE GRACE

You have pain now; but I will see you again, and your
hearts will rejoice, and no one will take your joy from you.
JOHN 16:22 NRSV

Living every day with chronic pain and sickness is a battle spiritually, mentally, and physically Some days suffering rules your world and makes you feel helpless and hopeless. Without hope in God, how can we endure our suffering? We can't.

Jesus was familiar with suffering. "A woman who had been suffering from hemorrhages for twelve years came up behind him and touched the fringe of his cloak, for she said to herself, 'If I only touch his cloak, I will be made well.' Jesus turned, and seeing her he said, Take heart, daughter; your faith has made you well'" (Matthew 9:20-22 NRSV). We also sympathize with this woman's desperation because we still suffer today.

GRACE FOR TODAY

GOD WILL GIVE US
THE GRACE, WISDOM,
AND FAITH TO
ENDURE SUFFERING.

However, can we still love God even if He never heals us? John Henry Newman answered that question for himself, "I will trust Him. Whatever, wherever I am, I can never be thrown away. If I am in sickness, my sickness may serve Him; in perplexity, my perplexity may serve Him; if I am in sorrow, my sorrow may serve Him. My sickness, or perplexity, or sorrow may be necessary causes of some great end, which is quite beyond us. He does nothing in vain." His answer—love, trust, and serve God in health and sickness. With God's grace you can be an inspiration to others even in sickness.

Even the disciples and apostles suffered physical ailments, but this in no way dampened their faith. The apostle Paul was no stranger to suffering; and he encouraged us to rejoice, to pray constantly, to be thankful always because God was completely trustworthy. And He will give us the grace, wisdom, and faith to endure. Perhaps the most amazing lesson we learn through sickness is to love the healer not just the healing.

PERSEVERANCE

We also glory in tribulations, knowing that tribulation produces perseverance; and perseverance, character; and character, hope.
ROMANS 5:3-4 NKJV

Have you ever felt like giving up when it looked like all odds were against you and the challenges you faced were impossible? Has there ever been something you desired to accomplish—but then halfway through, you realized the task was harder than you'd first thought—too demanding and required too great a sacrifice?

GRACE FOR TODAY

GOD HAS GIVEN US ALL OF THE PERSEVERANCE WE NEED TO MEET THE CHALLENGES IN OUR LIVES.

Just quit, you said to yourself. But something deep within beckoned you onward. Sure, quitting seemed the easy way out, but you knew the anguish of defeat would be greater than the struggle to finish. So you kept going. Through tears, through doubts, through the fog of the unknown, you determined you wouldn't give in to fear, weakness, or intimidation.

And surprisingly, the further you went, the stronger you became! You stretched beyond your limitations—pursued your dream, your goal. You held on to the purpose of your quest. You were forever changed. And perseverance had its way, depositing determination and patience into your being.

Perseverance produces amazing results. The Bible is replete with examples. It was perseverance that motivated the woman with the issue of blood to press in and touch the hem of Jesus' garment. Perseverance is what initiated Paul and Silas' singing behind locked bars. Perseverance is what energized Noah to continue building the ark when others mocked him. And it's what propelled Esther to go before the king for her people.

Never give up! Remember, with Christ, you can do all things! Perseverance is the rocket fuel of your heart, and with God, there is an endless supply to help you meet every challenge in life.

THE GRACE OF GIVING

Just as you excel in everything—in faith, in speech, in
knowledge, in complete earnestness and in your love for
us—see that you also excel in this grace of giving.
2 CORINTHIANS 8:7 NIV

GRACE FOR TODAY

IT REALLY IS BETTER
TO GIVE THAN TO
RECEIVE!

We've all heard that "it is better to give than to receive." We've probably all said these words at least once. And sure, we believe it—it is always good to be generous. Giving is definitely the right thing to do. But is giving also the fun thing to do? We're not so sure about that one. Frankly, it is pretty fun to receive!

But take a moment to think of some of the times when you have given to others. Remember the look of surprise and delight on the face of your friend when she opened that birthday gift? Or the smile on the face of a child when you took time to play with him? While receiving gifts is great, most of the time we remember much longer the joy we felt upon giving than we do on the things we've been given.

Perhaps the reason for that joy we feel comes from the fact that "it is better to give than to receive" isn't just a nice saying. These words actually come from the Bible—they are God's Word. (See Acts 20:35.) He knows that when we obey Him by giving to others—through gifts, money, or our time—we actually do receive! Joy, fulfillment, and the pleasure of our Father are all gifts that we get when we give. God made the world to work this way because He loves a "cheerful giver." When you give, He makes sure that the blessing overflows back to you!

So have some fun today—give! Send a card to someone, just because. Help a neighbor rake leaves or pull weeds. Write a check and send it to a mission that could really use it. The opportunities for giving are endless—and the rewards you receive are too!

SAFE SEX

By John MacArthur Jr.

I think sex is a glorious thing. God invented it. If He invented it, it is good. But He designed it for the beauty of the marriage relationship and nowhere else. For a person to think that he or she can cheat God and get kicks out of sex apart from marriage is to believe the devil's lie.

It is absurd for a person who is living in sexual impurity to say, "God, show me your will." Such a person is not even doing what this text of Scripture says is His will. Why should God disclose some further will?

Stay away from immoral sex. That is a simply principle. Someone inevitably says, "How far away?" Far away enough to be pure. Sanctified. Set apart wholly unto God.

Am I saying that you can't hold hands with the one you love? That is not the issue. Do I mean that you can't kiss? I don't mean that, either. The Bible says, "All things are lawful unto me, but all things are not helpful. All things are lawful for me, but I will not be brought under the power of any" (1 Corinthians 6:12 NKJV). You can be blessed by God only so long as you are controlling what you do for His honor. When lust controls you, you have crossed the line. It's a simple principle.[40]

FATHER,

Your Word is very straightforward on the subject of sex. Clearly You intended it for our pleasure, but within the confines of marriage only. I am committed to respecting Your boundaries: I know they are for my good. Strengthen me by Your grace so that I can avoid temptation and not fall prey to the power of lust. Let me enjoy this gift nin the way you intended.

AMEN

This is the will of God, your sanctification: that you abstain from fornication; that each one of you know how to control your own body in holiness and honor, not with lustful passion, like the Gentiles who do not know God.
1 THESSALONIANS 4:3-5 NRSV

LISTENING FOR GRACE

I heard the voice of the Lord saying, "Whom shall I send?
And who will go for us?" And I said, "Here am I. Send me!"
ISAIAH 6:8 NIV

As Melanie made her way through the tunnel to the airplane, she noticed a woman with a small infant in line behind her. Melanie immediately thought, *Oh no – please don't let them sit next to me for this four-hour flight!*

As it usually happens, soon the young mother and child showed up to sit in the aisle seat next to Melanie. She must have given the woman a less than convincing smile because the woman immediately said, "She's a really good baby – I promise!"

Melanie felt very guilty – her face had betrayed her feelings. And deep down she heard a small whisper that said, Talk to her.

In spite of her earlier feelings, Melanie was soon chatting with her seat-mate, Veronica, like an old friend. They continued to talk throughout the long flight. When Melanie asked if the baby, Lily, was her first child, Veronica's eyes misted. She had adopted Lily only four months before. Veronica had given birth to twin baby girls less than a year ago, but both had died soon after birth.

> ## GRACE FOR TODAY
>
> WHEN WE LISTEN FOR IT, WE CAN HEAR GOD'S VOICE OF GRACE DIRECTING US TO HELP.

Melanie heard the whisper of the Lord in her heart once more, Veronica's seat assignment wasn't an accident.

As the plane flew on, Melanie listened to Veronica's story and offered some words of hope and encouragement about the grace of God. When they landed several hours later, a friendship had begun. Over the next few months, Melanie and Veronica wrote letters and chatted on the phone. Melanie was able to send some Christian books on grief that were a great comfort and help to Veronica.

God's grace shows up in the most interesting places. When we are willing to hear His still, small voice, we receive opportunities to be vessels of that grace, sometimes in spite of ourselves. When we open our eyes and our hearts, we can be a blessing – and we will be blessed as well.

DISCOVERING FAMILY

In you the orphan finds mercy.
HOSEA 14:5 NRSV

Adoptive mother Valerie Harper said, "However motherhood comes to you, it's a miracle." The miracle of motherhood is not in the process of birth but in a life full of caring. The joy of adoption often comes on the heels of great frustration and disappointment. But God understands all your mixed feelings and doubts and has compassion for your desire to be a mother. "He gives the barren woman a home, making her the joyous mother of children. Praise the Lord!" (Psalm 113:9 NRSV). An adopted child is God's gift to you because He sets the lonely into families. Adoption is about God finding a home for a child and discovering that home in you.

In the Bible, Moses was adopted by Pharaoh's daughter and raised as a prince. Esther was orphaned and lived with her caring cousin Mordecai. Even God selected a loving earthly father for His Son Jesus. But the most amazing aspect of adoption is that God has the capacity to love each of us as His adopted children. We can cry, "Abba Father" because God is our eternal parent.

Parenting in any situation is never without obstacles and challenges. It will be fraught with sacrifice, disappointment, worry, joy, pride, laughter, and most of all love.

Sharing your life with your spouse was the first beautiful thing you did for your family. The second is sharing your life and home with a child to create that family. Family is God's joy and His design for us.

GRACE FOR TODAY

FAMILY IS GOD'S JOY AND DESIGN FOR US.

STEP OUT

It is God who works in you to will and to act according to
his good purpose.
PHILIPPIANS 2:13 NIV

GRACE FOR TODAY

GRACE FUELS THE
ACTION THAT LEADS
TO YOUR DREAM.

Are you waiting on God? You may be surprised to find God is the one waiting on you to make a move. Each day is a new opportunity for God-given success. God really does want you to experience His blessings. When you look good, He looks good.

So many people are missing great opportunities to accomplish something phenomenal because they're waiting for the perfect time to step out. Those who are determined to wait to have children until everything in their life is in perfect order will very likely still be waiting years from now. They may think about it, pray about it, and dream about doing something that's been in their hearts and minds a long time. They're looking for the courage to launch that dream company or write that first book that has burned in their hearts for years.

It takes action fueled by grace to reach the destination of your God-given dream. It takes courage. But when you step out and put action behind your expectation, God meets you there and turns your hope into reality. Only when you put His plan into action can you experience receiving the strength that fuels your determination to see the end result.

Nothing is achieved without hard work and perseverance—and a lot of grace. Let grace work for you. Take a step of faith today that will move you closer to your dream. It doesn't have to be a leap—just one little step.

DATING

As an apple tree among the trees of the wood, so is my
beloved among young men.
SONG OF SONGS 2:3 NRSV

The guy is most definitely hot and most definitely putting out the signals. But is he the right kind of guy to date? Sometimes we rush into dating without much consideration about our present and future compatibility. But once your heart's stuck in your throat, it's hard to walk away.

If you can't picture him as the main attraction at your wedding, why date him in the first place? Recreational dating can bring a lot of heartache while you're just killing time, waiting until God sends Mr. Right.

GRACE FOR TODAY

GOD HAS THE PERFECT SOUL MATE FOR YOU; THERE'S NO RUSH.

One way of getting to know someone in a less intense environment is to go out together with a group of people for a period of time. It takes the pressure off of "dating" and gives you both an opportunity to observe each other.

Find out if you share common interests and future dreams. What if you want to live on a farm with a house full of kids, but he dreams of living on a sailboat just the two of you? Sure, love can conquer all, but it can also make for frustrated lives later on. Now is the time to talk because your future happiness is in the balance.

Do you see eye to eye on issues of faith? You need someone you can share every aspect of your life with. Someone to pray with you, go to church with you, and help teach your children about the importance of God. For this reason, the Bible warns you not to be unequally yoked.

These issues seem really far away when you're just checking a guy out—but far away has a funny way of becoming very near in a very short time. So date with caution and godly wisdom. Look for godly character in that special someone, and listen to what God is telling you. He knows who is Mr. Right and the right time for him to come into your life.

239

THE SECRET DRAWER

Take me by the hand; lead me down the path of truth. You
are my Savior, aren't you?
PSALM 25:5 MSG

Author Nathaniel Hawthorne grew up in Salem, Massachusetts, with his widowed mother and his books. As a child, he was injured in a ball game and spent several years, mostly indoors, reading. His maternal relatives recognized his literary talent and financed his education at Bowdoin College. He wrote his first novel in 1828 but was disappointed by its failure. As a result he began to question his ability to write.

GRACE FOR TODAY

GOD KNOWS THE DREAM YOU HOLD IN YOUR HEART, AND HE HAS ALREADY GONE BEFORE YOU AND PREPARED THE WAY.

Hawthorne married and accepted a position as "measurer of salt and coal" at the Boston Custom House, but eventually he lost his post for political reasons in 1849. When his wife, Sophia, suggested he write full-time, he asked, "What will we live on?"

She took his arm and led him to a secret drawer in the kitchen. She opened it, and he saw that it was filled with money. She said, "I've saved a little each week, so that when the time came for you to fulfill your dreams, we'd have enough money to live on for an entire year."

Hawthorne sat down and penned *The Scarlet Letter*. The first edition sold out in ten days. It contrasts Puritan morality with passion and individualism and continues to be read as a classic today.

Sophia believed in her husband and helped him realize his dreams. Our Father in heaven believes in you and wants you to fulfill your dreams as long as they are in His will. By delighting yourself in Him, you make way for Him to plant His desires within your heart. (See Psalm 37:4.) Let Him take you by the hand and lead you to the secret drawer He has hidden for you.

EXACTLY LIKE HIM

By John MacArthur Jr.

When Peter was filled with the Holy Spirit, he had the same power as when he was standing next to Jesus Christ! Now here's something exciting! Do you know what the Spirit-filled life is? It is living every moment as though you are standing in the presence of Jesus Christ! Not too complicated, is it? Someone might think I am confusing the issue because the Holy Spirit and Christ are different. But by what name does Paul call the Holy Spirit? "The Spirit of Christ" (Romans 8:9). Jesus said that when He went away, He would send *allos* "another" Comforter (John 14:16). There are two words in the Greek for another: *heteros* and *allos*. *Heteros* means another of a different kind, and *allos* means another of exactly the same kind!

Here is my Bible. If I said to you, "Give me *heteros biblos*," you could give me any book. If I said to you, "Give me *allos biblos*," you would have to give another Bible exactly like mine, with all my markings and cuts and cracks. This is *allos*. When Jesus said, "I am going to send you another Comforter," He said *allos*, another exactly like Me. The Spirit-filled life is nothing more than living in the conscious presence of the indwelling Christ.[41]

HEAVENLY FATHER,

There is no greater privilege than for me to be like Christ. Not only does that glorify You, it makes my life grand adventure, with You at the center. Fill me with Your Spirit so that I may be "exactly" as Jesus was when he walked the earth. Think through my mind, see through my eyes, speak through my lips, heal through my hands. When others see me, let them see you..

AMEN

Be filled with the Spirit. Speak to one another with psalms, hymns and spiritual songs. Sing and make music in your heart to the Lord.
EPHESIANS 5:18-19 NIV

A Symphony of Life

We are pressed on every side by troubles, but we are not crushed and broken. We are perplexed, but we don't give up and quit. We are hunted down, but God never abandons us. We get knocked down, but we get up again and keep going.
2 CORINTHIANS 4:8-9 NLT

GRACE FOR TODAY

THE GRACE OF GOD'S JOY LIFTS US ABOVE EVERY CIRCUMSTANCE.

Everything seemed to be going right for Cameron and Fiona. They were newly engaged, and their relationship was growing deeper every day. They were excited about planning their wedding and their future together.

One day, only a couple weeks after their engagement, Cameron found a strange lump on his neck. When the doctor sat him down and gently explained to him that he had cancer, Cameron was shocked. The bright future he had planned with Fiona was suddenly clouded with doubt.

Most of Cameron and Fiona's engagement was spent in hospitals as Cameron went through surgery, chemotherapy, and radiation. He was often very sick and weak. But through it all, Cameron was the picture of joy. He praised God to anyone who would listen. Fiona's heart ached as she watched him go through so much pain; but she, too, found great joy in God's grace to them both.

Cameron and Fiona's wedding was a time of great celebration as Cameron was now declared cancer-free. Many people publicly praised the Lord for Cameron's incredible example of grace under fire. But the celebration would be short-lived. A year later, Cameron's cancer returned.

No one would have blamed Cameron for expressing some bitterness. But bitterness did not seem to be a part of this young man's vocabulary. Once again he spoke boldly of God's grace to him. Everyone who heard his story was amazed at his joyful attitude.

Today Cameron is once again cancer-free. In addition to healing him, God has blessed the couple with two children—something they were told could not happen. The grace of God's joy fills Cameron and Fiona's lives—a joy that goes beyond circumstances because their God has proven faithful.

IS EVERYBODY HAPPY?

Take the helmet of salvation and the sword of the Spirit,
which is the word of God.
EPHESIANS 6:17 NIV

Have you ever thought of yourself as a warrior? The Bible says you are. And it isn't that high-tech, smart bomb, sissy type either. It's fierce, hand-to-hand combat-a battle for our very souls. The enemy we are fighting has one focus — to kill us, steal from us, and utterly destroy us. And he might do it too, if it were not for the One who fights alongside us.

God knows our mortal enemy. He is not surprised by his tactics or fooled by his deceptions. And He has provided every piece of protective armor needed to come through the battle unscathed. He has given us the belt of truth. Our enemy cannot defeat us when we know who we are in God and who God is in us. He has dressed us in the breastplate of righteousness. No longer are we subject to the wages of sin and the burden of shame. We are, instead, citizens of God's kingdom, living in right standing with our Creator. He has given us faith to shield us from our enemies fiery darts, salvation to ensure eternal life. He has even placed in our hands the ultimate weapon, more powerful than anything known on earth — the Word of God.

You may not be a strong woman or an aggressive one. But if you are God's woman, you are a warrior. So strap on your armor, take hold of your sword, and put the enemy of your soul to flight. It's what God has called you and equipped you to do.

GRACE FOR TODAY

GOD HAS PROVIDED YOU WITH EVERYTHING YOU NEED TO
FIGHT AND WIN THE BATTLE FOR YOUR SOUL.

SEARCH

You will eat the fruit of your labor; blessings and prosperity
will be yours.
PSALM 128:2 NIV

Unemployment affects you and your entire family, and that fact alone adds more pressure to an already stressful situation. The first thing to remember in a completely out-of-control situation is that God is in complete control. "The LORD is close to the brokenhearted; he rescues those who are crushed in spirit" (Psalm 34:18 NLT).

Unemployment raises all kinds of fears about your family's future. Author, teacher, and minister Mary Morrissey, states, "You block your dream when you allow your fear to grow bigger than your faith." Remember, unemployment is temporary, but God's provision and love are eternal. When God is for you, who can be against you?

GRACE FOR
TODAY

————————

GOD'S PROVISION
AND LOVE ARE
ETERNAL. HE IS IN
COMPLETE CONTROL
OF YOUR FUTURE.

Once the shock has dissipated, sit down and ask God to help you find inspiration, direction, and initiative in finding the right job for you and your family. Unemployment can be a chance for you to completely reassess what you need and want out of future employment. It actually gives you the freedom to explore new doors of opportunity.

You may only want a job, but God wants two important things from you first. Your faith and trust in Him is paramount. God is your business manager, and He will open doors of opportunity that will make you shine.

The second is to have confidence in who you are and how God created you. God will give you the resolve, resources, creativity, and confidence to find that new job. David said this of God during times of crisis; "When I called, you answered me; you made me bold and stouthearted" (Psalm 138:3 NIV). Have confidence that you will handle this crisis well and that God will put you in charge of many more things new and exciting.

EVERY STEP OF THE WAY

The jar of flour was not used up and the jug of oil did not
run dry, in keeping with the word of the LORD spoken by
Elijah.
1 KINGS 17:16 NIV

An inspiring story in the Bible is about the widow of Zarephath in the above passage. The only food she possessed was a handful of flour in a jar and a little oil. There was a severe drought in the land, and she honestly believed that she and her son were going to die of starvation. She didn't know where to find their next meal.

When Elijah instructed the widow to share her bread with him, she realized there was barely enough for her and her son. Elijah told her his instructions came from the Lord, so she obeyed; and her flour and oil were supplied throughout the drought. She believed in God's grace, confident that He would provide for her even though she didn't know how.

Betsy and Corrie ten Boom experienced a similar provision. When they entered Ravensbrook concentration camp, the girls hid a vitamin bottle and a Bible in Betsy's sweater. Betsy miraculously walked past the guards without being searched. Each morning Corrie placed a drop of the liquid vitamins on Betsy's black bread and also shared the precious drops with others who were ill. The bottle seemed to be filled with an endless supply of drops, just like the oil that the poor widow of Zarephath shared with Elijah.

God doesn't show us how our lives will unfold in the future. However, He does assure us of His continuing presence and His grace; and He promises to provide for us if we trust Him every step of the way.

GRACE FOR TODAY

GOD IS MY STRONG SALVATION. WHAT FOE HAVE I TO FEAR?
IN DARKNESS AND TEMPTATION, MY LIGHT, MY HELP IS NEAR.

JAMES MONTGOMERY

New Start

Bless the LORD, O my soul, and forget none of His
benefits; . . . Who redeems your life from the pit, who
crowns you with lovingkindness and compassion.
PSALM 103:2,4 NASB

Grace for Today

THE WORLD IS
ROUND AND THE
PLACE WHICH SEEMS
LIKE THE END MAY
ALSO BE ONLY THE
BEGINNING.

IVY BAKER PRIEST

Suicidal thoughts can be both alluring and incredibly deceptive, but they provide only one option when in reality we live in a world full of options and solutions. Phil Donahue said, "Suicide is a permanent solution to a temporary problem."

When you are profoundly depressed, you tend to isolate yourself when what you really need is to talk to someone who cares and has a clearer perspective on your life.

Time is your best friend. When you feel overwhelmed by suicidal thoughts, you must give yourself another day or week to think about things. Extend your deadlines. You need time to get your emotions under control and take time to really look at your life situation.

Suicide doesn't fix anything. Life is the remedy because without it you have no other choices left. God loves you and envisions a good life for you even when you can't. "Surely I know the plans I have for you, says the LORD, plans for your welfare and not for harm, to give you a future with hope" (Jeremiah 29:11 NRSV).

Jesus is waiting to help you with all your problems and burdens. Not just some. Your needs are all important to Him. He wants to help you deal with all of them. He is humble in heart, gentle; and He will give you rest from your despair and hardships.

Those are promises that you can trust and depend on, no matter the situation. Have faith in God and His Son Jesus: pray for their help. Talk to friends, family, and professionals, and give yourself time to heal your mind and spirit. There are better days ahead.

AN AWESOME WEAPON IN THE HANDS OF GOD

By John MacArthur Jr.

We ought to keep our bodies in subjection to insure that we are honoring God. That includes controlling the way we dress and the things we do with our bodies. This principle covers the whole area of the lust of the flesh, and not just sexual things. A person can dishonor God by overdressing to attract attention to oneself. Gluttony also puts one in the position of dishonoring God and committing sin because it is obvious to everyone that the glutton cannot control the desire to eat. Nothing that gratifies the body to the dishonoring of God can have a place in the will of God.

Robert Murray McCheyne spoke at the ordination of young Dan Edwards in the 1860s. He said something like this: "Mr. Edwards . . . do not forget the inner man, the heart. The cavalry officer knows that his life depends upon his saber, so he keeps it clean. Every stain he wipes off with the greatest care. Mr. Edwards, you are God's chosen instrument. According to your purity, so shall be your success. It is not great talent; it is not great ideas that God uses; it is great likeness to Jesus Christ. Mr. Edwards, a holy man is an awesome weapon in the hand of God." (See 2 Timothy 2:21.) McCheyne was right, and God's will is that you be holy — sanctified.[42]

GOD,

I want to be Your instrument of honor. By the power of Your grace, help me to live a holy life, one that is wholly given to You and Your ways, so I can be effective as Your disciple. Let my life shine as an example of the goodness that a holy life in you brings.

AMEN

God did not call us to be impure, but to live a holy life.
1 THESSALONIANS 4:7 NIV

LONG-DISTANCE GRACE

[God] will rescue us because you are helping by praying for us. As a result, many will give thanks to God because so many people's prayers for our safety have been answered.
2 CORINTHIANS 1:11 NET

Jane had always been fearful about going on an overseas missions trip. But when her church began planning a trip to Haiti, she felt God speaking to her heart. In spite of her apprehension, Jane took a step of faith and signed up to join the team.

GRACE FOR TODAY

GOD'S GRACE IS NOT LIMITED BY TIME OR DISTANCE.

Jane's fear didn't completely go away, but she felt a definite sense of God's presence as the team landed on the island nation. The joy in the smiling faces of the people there warmed her heart and gave her added assurance that she had done the right thing.

On the third day of the trip, Jane woke up with terrible stomach cramps. As she lay on her cot, she began to cry. She was frightened and disappointed that she was missing out on a day of ministry. She cried to God for help and soon drifted off to sleep. When she woke up an hour later, she realized that her pain was gone. To her joy and relief, she felt fine and was able to rejoin the rest of the team.

When she returned home, Jane talked about her experience in Haiti with her nephew, Mark. When she mentioned her bout with stomach cramps and her quick recovery, Mark's eyes grew brighter. "Aunt Jane, our school was having a campus-wide day of prayer that morning. My friends and I were praying for you at the exact time you were healed!"

God's grace isn't limited by space and time. When we need Him, no matter where we are, He is there. And His grace can connect the hearts and souls of His children across the miles. When we call to our Father, He answers in amazing ways with His amazing grace.

LITTLE AL

[Jesus said,] "The master was full of praise. 'Well done, my good and faithful servant. You have been faithful in handling this small amount, so now I will give you many more responsibilities. Let's celebrate together!'"
MATTHEW 25:21 NET

Little Al was frail at birth, and because of his unusually large head, some feared he was abnormal. But his mother, Nancy, who was a devout Christian, never gave up hope as she prayed for her seventh child.

Al grew into an inquisitive youngster. Once his mother became alarmed when she couldn't find him for several hours. She finally located him in the barn, sitting on a makeshift nest in a straw box. He was trying to hatch eggs! If the hens could do it, why couldn't he?

GRACE FOR TODAY

GOD IS OUR CREATOR. GOD MADE US IN HIS IMAGE AND LIKENESS. THEREFORE WE ARE CREATORS.

DOROTHY MAY DAY

Al was bored with classroom routine and doodled and daydreamed in school. After his teacher commented that staying in school would be a waste of time for Al, Nancy decided to homeschool her son; and he developed a passion for science.

Al's first significant inventions were an improved stock ticker machine, the phonograph, and a motion picture camera that paved the way for the movie industry. However, Thomas Alva Edison is best known as the creator of the incandescent light bulb, and there are more than one thousand patents issued in his name. Nancy nurtured her son's creativity and encouraged him to channel it into ways that ushered into the world a new wave of technology. When speaking of his mother, he said, "She cast over me an influence that has lasted all my life."

God has blessed each of us with our own gifts of creativity. He expects us to use them to glorify Him and expand His kingdom. What talents has God blessed you with? How are you using these precious gifts to glorify Him and help others?

JUST RIGHT

We know and rely on the love God has for us. God is love.
Whoever lives in love lives in God, and God in him.
1 JOHN 4:16 NIV

Think about those special times when everything in your world seemed just right. Was it when you and your husband held your newborn for the first time and you finally felt like a family? Perhaps it was a quiet moment on your porch swing, watching the sun come up — just you and God. Maybe it was during the party you gave your parents for their thirtieth wedding anniversary, and you felt like a little girl again.

As you reflect on those precious moments in your life, you will most likely discover a common thread of love — the love of life, family, friends, and your heavenly Father. It's no wonder that in those special times, the world seems exactly right. Absolute bliss. You are experiencing God's design and plan for you and all of humankind. His very essence is love.

Think about the first time you experienced the presence of God. You knew He was there. Although He was unseen, it was as if He were tangible. You knew He touched you with His love — a moment when your spinning world stopped.

Love will outlast everything else. In the midst of love, it seems the world stands still. We experience utter bliss. When everything seems just right, it is as though everyone is holding their breath for you to catch a preview of the perfection you were created for — God's amazing love.

GRACE FOR TODAY

IN THE MIDST OF LOVE, ETERNITY MAKES THE WORLD STAND STILL.

Follow the Shepherd

The LORD is my shepherd; I shall not want. He maketh me
to lie down in green pastures: he leadeth me beside the
still waters.
PSALM 23:1-2 KJV

Psalm 23 is a favorite passage for millions of people. When we read about still waters and green pastures, we are transported to a wide, open meadow of lush grasses beside a cool, clear lake. They are words that paint a picture of peace and tranquility.

When David wrote this Psalm, however, he was writing from his own experience as a shepherd in the arid and rocky hills of the Middle East. Green vegetation was scarce, and water was hard to find. As the shepherd, David's job was to guide the sheep to tiny morsels of vegetation that were sprouting among the dry rocks. They had to depend on him totally for each little bite. And the life-giving water they needed might only be a little puddle. If the sheep wandered and didn't stay close to their shepherd, they might not get what they needed to survive.

GRACE FOR TODAY

THE GOOD SHEPHERD GIVES US THE GRACE WE NEED FOR EACH STEP IN THE DESERT TIMES OF LIFE.

The words of this famous Psalm take on an even deeper meaning when you picture a dry, desert landscape instead of lush greenery. Our lives often seem more like hot, dry places than lush, emerald fields. Yet it is during those desert times that we learn what it means to need the grace of God for every step. With the words of Psalm 23, God is promising us that He will guide us to each new morsel of hope and each small pool of contentment, if we will only follow Him closely. Grace makes even the smallest piece of vegetation seem like lovely green pasture.

So the next time you read Psalm 23, try picturing a dry Palestinian hillside. And remember that no matter how rough the terrain of your life, with the Lord as your shepherd, you can look forward to His goodness and love all the days of your life.

A WAY WITH WORDS

The tongue that brings healing is a tree of life.
PROVERBS 15:4 NIV

Some people are said to have a way with words. They are able to phrase what they say in a way that is appealing to the listener or present concepts in a particularly persuasive manner. Their words sing with rhythm and tones; they incite colorful images. Such people are inspiring and often leaders. You may be one of these verbally gifted people, or you may know someone who is. Their words are powerful, but natural.

GRACE FOR TODAY

WHEN THE WORDS WE SPEAK ARE GOD'S, WE BRING LIFE AND HEALING TO THOSE WHO HEAR.

The Bible tells us that there is yet another type of gifted speaker. These people's words are more than powerful, more than persuasive; they are divine and eternal. These are people whose words are inspired by the Spirit of God. In 1 Corinthians 2:13 NCV, Paul says: "We speak about these things, not with words taught us by human wisdom but with words taught us by the Spirit. And so we explain spiritual truths to spiritual people."

As a woman, you will have many opportunities to speak words that are divine and eternal. They will come as you instruct your children in the ways of God, as you provide encouragement for friends and family. These marvelous healing words may be yours as you share the beautiful truth of God's love and grace with a neighbor or coworker. You may speak these words while in prayer, seeking God's will, invoking His blessings, lifting up your needs and the needs of others, or praising God for His great and mighty deeds. Even if in the natural, you stammer and lisp, you have been given a special gift—a divine way with words.

SALT AND LIGHT

By John MacArthur Jr.

If we Christians would live the kind of life the Bible describes, we would knock the world right off its pins. But sometimes the world can't distinguish us from itself. The apostle Paul calls us who are Christians working for non-Christian employers to give them an honest day's work for a day's pay and show them that is the norm for a Christian. (See Ephesians 6:5-8.)

If you are the citizen of a certain state, obey the laws of that state so that people might know that your faith is real, that it reaches and influences every area of your life. You may ask, "Am I supposed to obey every law in the land?" Yes, every law. If you do not agree with them, that doesn't change the matter. Obey them. If you know a way to work politically to change poor laws, fine; but until they are changed, obey them.

The only time a believer is ever to violate the law of the land is when the law either forbids him to do what he has been told to do by direct command from God or commands him to do what God forbids.

God wants us to be the kind of citizens in the world who will draw the attention of the world. We need to have the qualities of salt and light (Matthew 5:13-16). That involves submission, which is clearly commanded in the Scripture.[43]

HEAVENLY FATHER,

Please forgive me for the times I haven't obeyed the laws of the land. It is a privilege to live in our free country—a gift of grace—and I want to uphold the laws so that we can enjoy peace. Help me to set a good example and be the salt and light that this world needs.

AMEN.

Remind your people to submit to the government and its officers. They should be obedient, always ready to do what is good.
TITUS 3:1 NLT

GOOD INTENTIONS

Let us hold fast the confession of our hope without
wavering, for He who promised is faithful.
HEBREWS 10:23 NKJV

GRACE FOR TODAY

PERHAPS NO
PROMISE IN LIFE IS
MORE REASSURING
THAN THAT PROMISE
OF DIVINE
ASSISTANCE AND
SPIRITUAL GUIDANCE
IN TIMES OF NEED.

HOWARD W. HUNTER

Gail's friend Jennifer had been very ill. When Gail visited her in the hospital, she noticed that Jennifer had lost a lot of weight. This prompted her to promise her friend that she'd treat Jennifer to dinner at her favorite Italian restaurant upon her release from the hospital.

Jennifer spoke up and reminded Gail, "Well, I hope you come through this time. You know, you promised me a fish dinner a long time ago."

When Gail heard her friend's response, she felt the blood rush to her face. She vaguely remembered making that promise but had forgotten all about it.

How many times has that happened to you? You have good intentions but then don't follow through. Many busy moms are reminded that they've forgotten a promise when they hear a whiny, "But, Mom! You promised!"

On the other hand, many, if not all of us, have been on the receiving end of broken promises. Family and friends have made promises that they did not keep. When you make a promise, you are giving your word.

Aren't you thankful that you can count on God to keep His promises? At times we may blatantly break promises, but God cannot lie. He keeps every one, for they are grounded in His character. He has the absolute ability and the uncompromising integrity to fulfill them. God gave us a promise in the provision of His Son, Jesus Christ. Salvation is a promise of God to all who repent of their sins and believe on Jesus.

Let's promise ourselves to be like Him — to let Him teach us to make promises we can keep and to follow through on our intentions.

CELEBRATE

Male and female He created them.
GENESIS 1:27 NKJV

There has never been such an amazing time to be a woman. We have more freedom and more opportunities than any other women in history. We are free to celebrate the amazing and complicated creatures that we are. We are wives, mothers, daughters; but we are also scientists, healers, performers, leaders, soldiers, teachers, Olympians, explorers, and so much more. We can be what we want to be, but most importantly what God wants us to be.

How do you become the woman you want to become? You can learn from other women. Read about great women in the Bible like Miriam, Huldah, Rachel, Esther, Rahab, Mary, Martha, Ruth, and Naomi—women whose deeds live on in history. Read inspirational stories of women learning about themselves and their Creator. Look at the example of Deborah, who was a prophetess, a wife, the leader of Israel, and a legendary warrior.

The most encouraging thing you can do is to read stories about amazing women in the past and today. Their lives teach and motivate us to be more. Find women mentors and learn from them at school, work, and most importantly at church. Get their advice and really listen to them. But in that search, don't forget to include the women in your own life—grandmothers, aunts, and great aunts. They have wisdom that will astound you. Author Nancy Friday commented, "When I stopped seeing my mother with the eyes of a child, I saw the woman who helped me give birth to myself." Women will make you wise. Madeleine L'Engle said, "I can't wait to become a wise old woman." And that's exactly what she became.

GRACE FOR TODAY

GOD GIVES US FEMALE MENTORS TO HELP US BECOME THE WOMEN THAT HE CREATED US TO BE.

You have the power to do anything and be anything you want to be. God created you, and He does have plans for your life. So don't let anybody hold you back. Celebrate the woman in you.

The Complacent Frog

Let integrity and uprightness preserve me, for I wait for You.
PSALM 25:21 NASB

It's been said that if you place a frog in boiling water, he will jump out. Yet, if the water is only warm, he will remain in the pot because he feels comfortable. If the water temperature continues to rise slowly, he will not even be aware of the change. Thus, his contentment will obscure the lurking danger. The result is fresh frog legs for dinner!

> ## Grace for Today
>
> GOD'S GRACE ALWAYS MAKES A WAY FOR US TO WALK IN INTEGRITY. REGARDLESS OF THE REACTION OTHERS HAVE TO OUR STAND, HE WILL HONOR US AND MAKE SURE WE COME OUT ON TOP.

Most of us know we shouldn't steal, commit adultery, or kill someone. These are black areas that we wouldn't consider crossing the line on, but what about the gray areas? We may be tempted to tell a little lie to get out of an uncomfortable situation. For example: your boss asks you to give false information to a customer. Do you follow his orders, or do you tell the customer the truth and jeopardize your job? This situation would be compounded if you were a single mom or had some other difficult extenuating circumstance.

The first lie is hard to tell, but the subsequent ones become easier and easier as we begin to rationalize our actions. The water in the pot continues to heat up without our even being aware of it.

It is so important not to compromise your values. If you are being tempted to lie, pray about the situation. If a boss asks you to lie or to do something unethical, inform him that you are uncomfortable making false statements to customers or clients. Hopefully he will respect your boundaries, but either way, you will preserve your integrity.

God knows the situations that confront us, and He will give us the grace and make a way for us to be true to His will. (See 2 Corinthians 10:13.) Sometimes we just need a little nudge to jump out of the pot!

PRAYER PARTNERS

We give thanks to the God and Father of our Lord Jesus
Christ, praying always for you.
COLOSSIANS 1:5 NKJV

Have you ever marveled at how something worked out for you, even when you didn't think it would? Have you wondered why you are so blessed in a particular area of your life? There could be several reasons for this, but one certain reason is the many people who have prayed for you—friends, neighbors, your parents and grandparents, as well as people who may not even know you. They have left you a legacy of prayers. Perhaps they prayed for your success in life—a good marriage, healthy children, or a prosperous profession. Maybe your life was spared as a direct result of prayers said on your behalf for safety, healing, or restoration.

> ## GRACE FOR TODAY
>
> GOD REMEMBERS EVERY PRAYER EVER UTTERED ON YOUR BEHALF. HE INSPIRED THEM.

If you can't think of someone who has prayed for you, do not doubt that someone has! No doubt God has moved on the hearts of many people to pray for you. Some know your name and your face. Others don't, but God put you on their heart at the very time you needed a prayer partner.

Think about the answered prayers you prayed as a child—dreams you dreamed. His mercy and love brought those things into reality. God has promised His grace to supply everything you will ever need. And when you can't do it alone, He is there fulfilling the many prayers prayed for you.

God never forgets the inquiries of His people. Whether they are your prayers or those of others, you are always on His heart and mind.

BEAUTY AND THE BEAST

If anyone is in Christ, he is a new creation; old things have
passed away; behold, all things have become new.
2 CORINTHIANS 5:17 NKJV

In the popular Disney version of *Beauty and the Beast*, we learn that the beast was once a handsome prince with wealth and privilege. In spite of all that he had been given, however, when an elderly woman went to his door to ask for help, he refused her arrogantly. Only then does he realize that the old woman was actually an enchantress. She swiftly punishes the prince for his greed and ingratitude by changing him into a hideous beast. His only hope to break the spell is for someone to truly love him, even in his frighteningly ugly state.

After years of living in misery and solitude, the beast is visited by a beautiful young woman. Their relationship is tumultuous in the beginning, but as the beast learns to open his heart to the possibility of love, the young girl begins to the see the potential behind the beast's rough exterior. In the end, the beauty comes to truly love the beast, in spite of all outward appearances, and this love transforms him into the prince he was meant to be.

Can you relate to the beast's story? Perhaps you have been greedy or ungrateful, mean-spirited or arrogant. Your actions have caused you to become someone that you don't want to be. You feel ugly inside, and you begin to wonder if anyone could really love you.

Don't give up hope. Look up in expectation. If you are willing to open your heart, God will enter it. He looks past your "beastly" exterior to the beauty you are meant to be. He will bring people into your life who will love you as you are and help you along the way. God's grace, like the magic of the beauty's love, will transform you. Invite Him in today.

PAY NOW OR PAY LATER

By John C. Maxwell

The value of a vision is that it encourages you to give up at any moment all that you are in order to receive all that you can become. You will be willing to let go of whatever might keep you from actually realizing that vision. You can probably think of times in your life when this happened to you. Do you remember when you first fell in love with the person you married? All of a sudden other members of the opposite sex were not that interesting to you anymore. You were willing to trade in the pool for the one.

I have found that you do one of two things in life: You either pay the price now and enjoy later, or you enjoy now and pay the price later. But you will always pay the price. I'm constantly amazed at the short-sightedness of people who are not willing to pay the price now. Some people are short-sighted about their bodies. They're not willing to give up those pleasurable things that are destroying their bodies now in order to gain a few good years later. Some people are short-sighted about their finances. They can't give up any of today's luxuries in exchange for tomorrow's financial security. And some people are short-sighted spiritually.

They are so caught up in the pleasures of today that they can't see the pain of tomorrow: they're not willing to totally sell out for God. They're trying to avoid the price, but the price will always be there. You can either pay it today and enjoy life tomorrow, or you can enjoy life today and pay the price, plus interest, tomorrow. You cannot avoid the price.[44]

FATHER,

I want to be wise and pay the price now for the vision You have for me. At those times when I'm tempted to take the easy road, give me Your grace to help me make good choices.

AMEN

Don't be misled . . . You will always reap what you sow!
GALATIANS 6:7 NLT

CHANGE IN ACTION

Little children, let us love, not in word or speech, but in
truth and action.
1 JOHN 3:18 NRSV

GRACE FOR TODAY

GOD DESIGNED US TO
INTERACT AND TAKE
ACTION IN HIS
WORLD, TO BE HIS
AMBASSADORS.

Sometimes we act as if the world is one big suggestion box; and we're quick to slip in a few suggestions to church leaders, the school board, or civic leaders; but that's about as far as we get. Our version of problem solving — we leave it for someone else. Suggestions are good, but personal action is better. Things don't change on their own — we change them because events change us inside. They make us care and make us take action. God designed us to interact and take action in His world. We are His ambassadors.

Dorothy Brooke, the wife of a British Major General, arrived in Cairo, Egypt, in 1930. She was horrified to see the physical conditions of the working horses of Cairo. They had open wounds, crippling hoof problems, diseases, and were malnourished. But Dorothy was smart enough to realize that this wasn't the result of pure neglect. It was a result of poverty and lack of husbandry skills on the part of their owners. Ironically some these horses were ex-British cavalry horses.

In four short years, Dorothy Brooke established the Old War Memorial Hospital, which provided free veterinary care to working horses of the area. Today this charity continues to help both horses and their needy owners in other countries. They treat millions of animals yearly around the world. It was a practical way to help poor owners maintain healthy working animals. It helped the community and the animals. It just took one woman of action and change.

Are you that kind of godly woman? One that sees the world, assesses the situation, plans an action, and accomplishes great things? Edwin Hubbel Chapin wrote, "Every action of our lives touches on some chord that will vibrate in eternity." You are the change God wishes to see in the world. Because of His grace it can start with you.

Warrior Princess

Though we walk in the flesh, we do not war according to
the flesh, for the weapons of our warfare are not of the
flesh, hut divinely powerful for the destruction of
fortresses.
2 CORINTHIANS 10:3-4 NASB

In J.R.R. Tolkien's *Lord of the Rings* series, a brave young woman figures prominently in the battle for Middle Earth. Arwen is the beautiful princess of the Elves. Her gentle spirit equals her beauty; but when she is called upon to do battle with the forces of evil, Arwen proves to be a great warrior as well.

As women with jobs, kids, and minivans, plus all the other stuff of life, we don't feel that we have much in common with a warrior princess like Arwen. We enjoy watching her battle and win over evil; but when we leave the theater, we quickly dismiss her story as a nice fairy tale—nothing more.

However, the truth is that we, too, are living in the midst of a world at war. All around us, a battle is raging between good and evil, between those who love God and those who serve His enemy. As daughters of the King of Kings, we are a part of His army of righteousness; and we are called to be His warriors.

The good news is that God's Word promises us victory in the end. But right now, the war is still being waged. We must fight on with the otherworldly weapons that nothing can defeat. Through the grace we receive in Christ, we are "more than conquerors" over "tribulation, or distress, or persecution, or famine, or nakedness, or peril, or sword" (Romans 8:35,37 NKJV).

Grace for Today

WE ARE WARRIORS OF THE KING, AND THROUGH HIS GRACE, WE WILL PREVAIL!

So, even while you're running to the grocery store, fixing dinner, working in your office, or reading to your children, remember that you are a warrior. Keep alert and ready for the battle cry to sound. You are a brave soldier in the army of your loving King—and He will lead you to victory!

HIDE AND SEEK

Moses said, "I pray You, show me Your glory!"
EXODUS 33:18 NASB

Most children look for affirmation from those around them—praise from a teacher, words of love from a parent, and confidence from a friend. It is no different as we look to the heavenly Father for the love, confirmation, and acceptance that only He can give us.

GRACE FOR TODAY

IN GOD'S GRACE WE FIND EVERYTHING WE'RE LOOKING FOR.

Moses, an ordinary man, made a request of God. Today we might say it like this: "If I'm really special to You, let me see You." God granted Moses' desire by displaying His "goodness" and "mercy." Moses discovered that God the person and His grace were inseparable. God's actions of goodness and love were the result of His true nature—who He really is.

Sometimes we feel disappointed when God's response to our desire is not what we expected. We want Him to take action with a flame of fire or a miraculous display of signs and wonders. We are hungry to see Him, yet He is forever with us. His still small voice speaks all the time, but often we miss it because we are listening for a booming voice of thunder.

Sometimes what we really want is right in front of us. Evidence of God's presence is clear in even the simple things in life. We see glimpses of His character in the way everything in life grows. Consider how God nurtures and cultivates our lives, like He created the soil to work on everything planted in it. Notice the fence post in your backyard. It's a dead piece of wood, yet the ground works to decompose it. As it breaks down and becomes part of the soil, its nutrients will contribute to the life of something planted there in the future.

The best way to realize and understand the God we serve is to remember that He is always with us. As we look for Him in every part of life, we'll find everything we're looking for in Him.

SAND CASTLES

Unless the LORD builds the house, they labor in vain who
build it; unless the LORD guards the city, the watchman
stays awake in vain.
PSALM 127:1 NKJV

Children enjoy going to the beach and building sand castles. Often they work for hours at this task. First they search for sand still moist from the previous night's high tide. Then using buckets, shovels, plastic molds, and serving spoons, they begin building their creations in the sand.

GRACE FOR TODAY

WE CAN BUILD FOR
ETERNITY IF WE WILL
BE SENSITIVE TO
GOD'S PLANS.

By late afternoon, the sun's reflection shimmers on the water; and the tide rolls in closer and closer to the sand castles. Finally, a breaker crashes into one of the sand castles and sweeps it out to sea. The children laugh and turn their thoughts to beach games, a campfire, and hot dogs.

Adults are often less wise than children. We build our own "sand castles;" and when a wave crests nearby, we try to stop it. We lose sight of our priorities. Water soaks our clothing, and salt stings our eyes. Still we shout, "It's my castle. I built it with my own hands. Leave it alone!"

The ocean becomes silent, and so does God it seems. Where did we go wrong? We tried to build our castle in just the right way, but we forgot that God made the sand and the ocean. If we try to build a sand castle in our own strength, Fie will remind us that our foundation is nothing but shifting sand. If our priorities get out of proportion, He will bring in the evening tide to help reshape the way we see things.

God has things for us to build that He plans to last forever, so He doesn't want sand castles to become too important to us—more important than He is. He wants the kingdom of Heaven to be the number-one priority in our lives.

ARE YOU BEING BULLIED?

[Jesus said,] "I told you these things so that you can have peace in me. In this world you will have trouble, but be brave! I have defeated the world."
JOHN 16:33 NCV

GRACE FOR TODAY

I NEED THY PRESENCE EVERY PASSING HOUR: WHAT BUT THY GRACE CAN FOIL THE TEMPTER'S POWER.

HENRY FRANCIS LYTE

Have you ever been bullied? Bullying takes place most frequently in school, beginning in elementary school, coming to a peak in middle school, and falling off in high school. It does not, however, disappear altogether.

A bully discourages or frightens with threats or behaves in a domineering manner to intimidate. Who is the biggest bully in your life? If you are a Christian, the answer is Satan. In 1 Peter 5:8 CEV the Word of God cautions us. "Be on your guard and stay awake. Your enemy, the devil, is like a roaring lion, sneaking around to find someone to attack."

Bullies seek power. Satan attempts to overcome God's people. He tries to bully Christians by convincing us that he can bring devastation into our lives. Even God's people, who know the voice of God, often cower at the intimidating roar of Satan.

But there is another Lion. He is the Lion of the Tribe of Judah, the only begotten Son of God, Jesus Christ. With one last statement, as He hung on the cross, He overcame every roar from Satan: "It is finished" (John 19:30 KJV).

At that moment all the power of the adversary was broken, the power of sin forever crushed and placed under His feet. We have no reason to dissolve into tears or beg for mercy. Triumph over Satan begins when we understand that the victory has already been won through Jesus Christ!

Schoolchildren often find safety in numbers. Find strength by surrounding yourself with other Christians. Go to church. Pray with others. Get into a good Bible study. You can live a life of victory.

The Happiest People in the World

By John C. Maxwell

Who are the happiest people in the world? Those who are living out their dreams. In giving themselves to something bigger than they are, they're giving themselves the impetus to rise above their problems. If you want to know real happiness, dream a dream that is bigger than you are; find something you can lose your life in.

When I counsel people, I find that their number-one problem is that they've lost their dreams, their goals, their purpose. When you lose a dream or your purpose in your marriage, you lose your marriage. When you lose your purpose for your health, you die.

Think of the great people who continued to pursue their dream into old age. Think of Moses, who at 80 years of age led 3.5 million people out of captivity. Or Caleb, who at 85 years of age said, "Give me that mountain." Or Colonel Sanders, who at 70 years of age discovered "finger lickin' good" chicken. Or Ray Kroc, who after 70 introduced a Big Mac to the world. Then there's Casey Stengel, who at 75 became the manager of the Yankees baseball team. And George Washington Carver, who at 81 became head of the Agriculture Department. There's Thomas Edison, who at 85 invented the mimeograph machine; and John Wesley, who was still traveling on horseback and preaching at age 88.

It's the dream that keeps us young; it's the vision that keeps us going.[45]

FATHER,

I want to be one of those happy people living their dream. Forgive me for the times I've lost right of the goal and settled for less. I know You're not through with me yet. Rekindle the dream You put in my heart, and fill me with Your grace to do my part in bringing it to pass.

AMEN

Do not cast away your confidence, which has great reward. For you have need of endurance, so that after you have done the will of God, you may receive the promise.
HEBREWS 10:35-36

ANDREA

[Jesus said,] "Whoever receives and accepts and welcomes
one little child like this for My sake and in My name
receives and accepts and welcomes Me."
MATTHEW 18:5 AMP

Andrea was a fifth-grader at Woodside Elementary. Most of her clothes were hand-me-downs that didn't fit, and she often went to school without brushing her hair. No one ever played with her at recess.

Miss Wilcox was a first-year teacher at Woodside. During her very first recess duty, she noticed little Andrea's solitary figure. Not realizing that this was how Andrea usually spent recess, the young teacher made a beeline for her, worried that she was hurt or sick.

GRACE FOR TODAY

SMALL GIFTS OF GRACE CAN CHANGE LIVES.

Miss Wilcox quickly discovered that Andrea was not hurt physically, but was very hurt emotionally. So, from that day on, Miss Wilcox spent recess with Andrea. For the first few weeks, the conversation was completely one-sided—Andrea refused to speak. But one day, the little girl quietly answered one of Miss Wilcox's questions. Slowly a true friendship began to grow between them.

At the beginning of the summer, Miss Wilcox married and moved away. She was sad to leave Andrea and prayed that God would take care of the shy little girl.

Years later, Miss Wilcox, now Mrs. Bryant, moved back to town. On her first day at Woodside Elementary, Mrs. Bryant went with her own little girl to school. The teacher met them at the door of the classroom. As the two women shook hands, a flood of recognition came over them.

Andrea beamed as she told her former teacher that it was because of her friendship that she decided to become a teacher too. "My whole life changed when you came and talked to me at recess that first day."

Who, through the giving of grace, has changed your life? Who may need the gift of grace from you in the same way today? A small word of kindness or a gentle touch may seem insignificant—but it is these small graces that can turn sorrow to hope.

WELCOME

Dear friend, when you extend hospitality to Christian brothers and sisters, even when they are strangers, you make the faith visible.
3 JOHN 1:5 MSG

Someone once said, "Hospitality is making your guests feel at home, even though you wish they were home." In ancient times hospitality wasn't optional; it was mandatory. If you didn't show hospitality to friends and strangers, you were considered rude, uncultured, and ungodly. The Bible says, when we entertain strangers, we could in fact be entertaining more heavenly guests—angels. Further, Jesus said that when we show hospitality to a stranger, it is like we are showing it to Him.

GRACE FOR TODAY

HOSPITALITY IS A REFLECTION OF GOD. IT WELCOMES EVERYONE WITH OPEN ARMS.

Jesus enjoyed the hospitality of many people. And He didn't feel any qualms about inviting himself over, as in the case of His surprise stay with Zacchaeus. Jesus also instructed His disciples to seek out hospitality. "Whatever town or village you enter, find out who in it is worthy, and stay there until you leave. As you enter the house, greet it" (Matthew 10:11-12 NRSV).

You could say the early church was founded on hospitality. Families opened their homes as a place of rest and gathering. Sometimes the women of a household were the first converts to Christianity. The home of Mary, the mother of John Mark, was the first place the disciple Peter went after he was freed from prison. She clearly opened her home to Christians despite the dangers.

We've turned hospitality into a domestic diva extravaganza. Hospitality isn't about a designer home and gourmet food. When you make it that, you lose the heart and soul of it. Opening your home is the sincerest act of love and sacrifice. And for some, hospitality is a spiritual gift God gives to empower a special kind of sharing. Welcome people just as you are. It's not about what you serve for dinner, but rather the friendship you share. No need to make it more.

SET THE TONE OF YOUR HOME

Work hard at living in peace with others.
PSALM 34:14 NLT

GRACE FOR TODAY

GENTLE GRACE THAT COMES FROM GOD CULTIVATES AN ATMOSPHERE OF PEACE THAT WILL TAME THE MOST VICIOUS OF TIGERS.

Family life can be taxing on your mind and your marriage. Although children are a joy, they are also an added responsibility. In spite of this stress, you have the power to set the atmosphere in your home. God has equipped you with everything you need to define your home life.

More times than not, you may feel like your home life is out of control and that you can never tame the tiger in your children. But there is hope. Your children will model your example. It may take awhile to see the results, but God's promises are true. He said that a gentle answer turns away wrath. Try that one on your teenager. It may take multiple attempts to control your surprise, anger, or frustration, but consistency is the key and will pay rich dividends.

When you feel a shouting match with your husband coming on, count the cost. Is resistance to his desires worth an atmosphere of chaos and hostility? Choose your battles—there doesn't always have to be one. The gentle grace from within you can cultivate an atmosphere of hope and peace that will tame the most vicious of tigers living in your home.

Give your children a picture of life with God. How would He respond to their demands? Ask Him for His grace in daily challenges and disappointments within your home. The change will most likely not be immediate, but the long-term effects of your choice for peace will bring a lasting lifestyle, a legacy that your children can carry into their own families one day. Live your best life, and you'll find an example worthy of your children to follow.

COMING HOME

You were continually straying like sheep, hut now you have returned to the Shepherd and Guardian of your souls.
1 PETER 2:25 NASB

During Lisa's early morning walk, a stray puppy seemed determined to follow her home. He fell into step with her, never leaving her side. Because she had dogs of her own, she kept him in her garage. Her heart melted at the sight of this mass of quivering, wagging, excited puppy all wrapped up in short black fur. He belonged to someone as evidenced by his healthy state, his friendly demeanor, and the tags on his collar.

Jesus Christ likened people to stray sheep. As our Shepherd, He cares for our protection and well-being. When He looked on the people with compassion during His earthly ministry, the Gospel writers say He saw them "as sheep without a shepherd." Jesus proved His love for us when He died on the cross. He came into this world of darkness and evil to rescue people who are lost. Jesus said He is the Good Shepherd who lays down His life for the sheep. He has saved us from the wolves of sin and death.

GRACE FOR TODAY

THE KING OF LOVE MY SHEPHERD IS, WHOSE GOODNESS FAILETH NEVER; I NOTHING LACK IF I AM HIS AND HE IS MINE FOREVER.

SIR HENRY WILLIAM BAKER

Have you ever heard the song "Lord, I'm Coming Home" sung during an altar call? The first verse says, "I've wandered far away from God. Now I'm coming home." Jesus calls us back into His fold. Do you know the Shepherd's voice?

Lisa called the number on the puppy's tags and, thankfully, found the owners who were quite eager to have the puppy back. Lisa did not have room in her house for another dog. Aren't you grateful that the Lord always has room in His family for one more person and that Jesus seeks those who have gone astray?

TIME TO RECHARGE

On the seventh day God ended His work which He had
done; and He rested.
GENESIS 2:2 AMP

Are you living life at breakneck speed? There is a reason it is called breakneck speed. The term implies that if you keep going at top speed, you'll eventually fall so hard that you break your neck. Accident and injury force you to rest the part of you that has suffered the injury—if not your whole body. Sometimes this is referred to as a forced rest.

Rest is important to the health of your body as well as your soul. Have you ever noticed that when you're tired, you make more mistakes with the task at hand? Your mind takes longer to process even normally effortless tasks. When we press ourselves past our limit, we risk mistakes in all avenues of life. Grouchiness or a short temper can injure friends and cause them to draw back from us.

Humans require time to recharge. We are engineered by God's own hand for down time. Throughout the Bible, God led people to times of refreshing and rest. Jesus withdrew from the crowds to commune with the Father and rejuvenate His energy. Even God rested after His work was completed on the seventh day of creation.

As you feel the need to "recharge your batteries," take some time to get quiet, to be still, to do nothing. Take a power nap. Soak in some sunshine on a garden walk—just you and God. Do something you really enjoy, take time to relax, and let your soul experience a refreshing. When you're rested, you're at your best.

GRACE FOR TODAY

REST REFRESHES YOUR BODY AS WELL AS YOUR SOUL.

Dream Come True

By John C. Maxwell

When you receive a vision that could change your life or you're grabbed by a dream that could really help you become what you want to be, there's a natural sequence that happens. First there's the *"I thought it"* stage. That's when a dream just flashes by. Could it be? Maybe this is for me. Next is the *"I caught it"* stage. After we think about the visions that God gives us, we begin to talk about that dream and see ourselves in it.

I think everyone goes through these first two stages. But stage three makes the difference between the person who will be successful. It's what I call the *"I bought it"* stage. After we catch that dream, there's a time when we have to make an investment in it. We have to buy that dream.

But just as the successful person buys it, the unsuccessful person fights it. They begin to rationalize; they begin to think about why it wouldn't work, why it's not possible. People who are not going to reach their dreams stop at this third stage and never become what they could become for God.

The fourth stage is the *"I sought it"* stage. This is where desire comes in: we begin to want it so much that it possesses every part of us. Finally comes the *"I got it"* stage. This is where I say, "It's mine; I'm glad I paid the price; I'm glad I dreamed the dream."[46]

———————

GOD,

Thank You for the dream You've put in my heart. I do want it to be fulfilled, and I am committed to do what it takes. At those times when I begin to waver or doubt, fill me with Your grace to hold on 'til the end. Thank you in advance for the glorious things to come.

AMEN

Do you not know that those who run in a race all run, but one receives the prize? Run in such a way that you may obtain it.
1 CORINTHIANS 9:24 NKJV

LAUS DEO!

I will praise You, O LORD, with my whole heart; I will tell of all Your marvelous works.
PSALM 9:1 NKJV

Two words, *Laus Deo*, are displayed on top of the Washington Monument overlooking the 69 square miles that comprise our nation's capitol. Since these words are 555 feet in the air, they probably go unnoticed by most people. Yet, they are meaningfully placed at the highest point over what is the most powerful city in the most successful nation of the world.

GRACE FOR TODAY

PRAISE TO THE LORD, THE ALMIGHTY, WHO RULES ALL CREATION! O MY SOUL, WORSHIP THE SOURCE OF THY HEALTH AND SALVATION! ALL YE WHO HEAR, NOW TO GOD'S TEMPLE DRAW NEAR; JOIN ME IN GLAD ADORATION!

JOACHIM NEANDER

What do those two Latin words composed of just four syllables and seven letters mean? Very simply, they say, "Praise Be to God!" (*Laus* is translated "Praise be"; *Deo* means "God.")

Within the monument itself are 898 steps and 50 landings. As a person climbs the steps and pauses at the landings, the memorial stones share various messages. On the 12th landing is a prayer offered by the City of Baltimore; on the 20th is a memorial presented by some Chinese Christians; on the 24th a presentation made by Sunday school children from New York and Philadelphia quoting Proverbs 10:7, Luke 18:16, and Proverbs 22:6.

One of the items deposited in the cornerstone of the Washington Monument when it was laid on July 4, 1848, was a Bible presented by the Bible Society.

At a time when prayer is being taken out of our schools and other Christian messages are being removed from public buildings, let's remember that God's message and His grace cannot be removed by our opponents; God and His Word are eternal. Keep the words *Laus Deo!* in your heart, and let your actions and the words of your mouth give praise to God.

I BELIEVE!

With the heart one believes unto righteousness, and with
the mouth confession is made unto salvation.
ROMANS 10:10 NKJV

The movie *Polar Express*, based on the beloved children's book of the same name, invites people young and old to revisit their belief in the spirit of Christmas.

The main character is a little boy who is struggling with doubts about his childhood belief in the magic of the season. On Christmas Eve, his heart is aching to hear the sleigh bells ringing—he wants so much to believe. When the boy boards the Polar Express train, the story takes you along on his journey back to belief. In the end, it is with great joy that the doubting little boy exclaims, "I believe!"

> ## GRACE FOR TODAY
>
> IF YOU BELIEVE IN HIS GRACE, IT DOESN'T MATTER WHERE GOD TAKES YOU.

As the boy gets off the train at the end of the story, the conductor assures him, "It doesn't matter where the train is going. What matters is deciding to get on."

The story of the Polar Express reminds us of our journey of belief in our Savior, Jesus Christ. When we first believe and are young in our faith, our belief is strong; and we are full of excitement. But as the worries of the world crowd in, we can start to lose our confidence. We still crave the joy we had when we first believed. Like the little boy hoping for the sound of sleigh bells, we look for grace, listen for it, and anticipate it at every corner. But doubt can cloud our hearts as we struggle to stand firm.

And then, in moments of quiet, when we wait with an expectant and listening heart, the Lord comes to us; and we are drawn back to our original belief with renewed fervor. God imprints His grace anew on our hearts as we return to our first love and declare, "I believe!"

Seize the Day

The human mind plans the way, but the LORD directs the steps.
PROVERBS 16:9 NRSV

Do you feel stuck, unable to make choices about yourself or your future employment? People often struggle in the wrong jobs because they just don't know where to start to make changes. Educator Laurence J. Peterson said this, "A rut is a grave with the ends knocked out."

Grace for Today

GOD CAN USE OUR DISSATISFACTION TO NUDGE US IN A NEW DIRECTION. HE WILL DIRECT OUR STEPS.

So what can you do to change your career? First, think and pray about where you want to be in the future and what you want to be doing. Inventor Charles F. Kettering said, "My interest is in the future because I am going to spend the rest of my life there."

And so are you. Sometimes a little dissatisfaction can be God's nudge in a new direction. But taking that new direction takes a special kind of courage, confidence, and determination.

Solutions are made in small directed steps. Once you decide where you want to go, the next step is to find out how to make that happen. Want a new career or better position? What qualifications do you need to make that change? Find out how to get them. Is it by taking a night class, retraining, getting a sponsor in your field, or volunteering? You'll be surprised at how a little movement forward can energize you and give you a new perspective on life.

Getting out of ruts just takes some vision and lots of planning. Like an Olympic athlete, your goals should continually challenge you. You should set them and discover how to scale them. It just means getting proactive about your life and your future. It means challenging yourself to go beyond what you thought you could do in order to do what God knows you can do. Composer Bernice Johnson Reagon said, "Life's challenges are not supposed to paralyze you, they're supposed to help you discover who you are." So who do you want to be?

SEARED OR CLEAR CONSCIENCE

I will maintain my righteousness and never let go of it; my
conscience will not reproach me as long as I live.
JOB 27:6 NIV

A young couple pulled into the driveway of what they thought might be their ideal house. When they exited their car, they looked at each other with dismay. "Do you hear that?" Gail asked. The roar of a nearby interstate highway nearly drowned out their conversation.

When asked if the road noise bothered her, the homeowner looked puzzled. "What noise?" She had lived with the constant hum of tractor-trailers for so long that she had become immune to it.

Did you know that our consciences function in much the same way? The Holy Spirit uses them as a tool to convict us. If we continue in sin, our defiled consciences become insensitive. The Bible describes this state in 1 Timothy 4:2. Paul said it's as if our consciences have been seared with a hot iron, or have lost the capacity for truth. A person whose conscience is no longer pricked used to believe the truth found in the Word of God, but gradually they ignored and rejected it.

The Holy Spirit helps us develop a good conscience through Spirit-led self-discipline. Paul wrote, "I try with all my strength to always maintain a clear conscience before God and man" (Acts 24:16 TLB). Ask the Lord to help you follow the example of Paul's self-discipline in keeping your conscience pure toward God and people. We can always go to the Lord and have our hearts and minds cleansed by confessing sin honestly before God and demonstrating an attitude of true repentance.

We face spiritual challenges every day. Keeping our consciences clear means that we must have spiritual strength to say no to life's temptations. Let's not become immune to sin. What is the state of your conscience today?

GRACE FOR TODAY

CONSCIENCE TELLS US WHAT WE OUGHT TO DO RIGHT, BUT IT DOES NOT TELL US WHAT RIGHT IS—THAT WE ARE TAUGHT BY GOD'S WORD.

HENRY CLAY TRUMBULL

A Work in Progress

Create in me a clean heart, O God. Renew a right spirit
within me.
PSALM 51:10 NLT

GRACE FOR TODAY

YOU ARE A WORK IN PROGRESS, BECOMING CONFORMED TO GOD'S IMAGE BY HIS GRACE.

When you accepted Jesus as your Savior, you were born from the Spirit of God. Your spirit was filled with light and life that comes from Him. Your spirit changed instantly to reflect a mirror image of the character of God.

The transformation in your soul is not instantaneous, however. That's why you may have struggled to kick the habits you developed before you became a Christian. Your mind has to learn a new, more positive way to think. You try to find God's perspective on life and look to His way of doing things each day. Your will has to choose to bend and yield to His purposes and plans for your life.

As you grow in Christ, you'll see changes even in your emotions — the thoughts and intents of your heart. As you are transformed into the image of His goodness, mercy, and grace, you will discover that you no longer have to work so hard to do the right thing. As you put forth the effort to connect with Him, you realize how important your relationship with Him really is. Your life becomes an opportunity to share everything with Him.

You are a work in progress — developing, growing, and changing into God's image. The more time you spend with Him, the more you reflect who He is in your life. You begin to do as He would do, speak as He speaks, and live life as He lives it through you.

CHANGED BY GOD'S WORD

By Evelyn Christenson

Should I let God change me through devotional reading or Bible study? That is not a fair question, because both are essential for a well-rounded, transformed life. Devotional reading is never a substitute for deep, systematic Bible study — but it is a complement to it. And the Lord does change me when I study His Word.

Paul gave Timothy excellent advice when he said, "Study to show thyself approved unto God" (2 Timothy 2:15 KJV). He also counseled him to: "Remember that from early childhood you have been familiar with the sacred writings which have power to make you wise and lead you to salvation through faith in Christ Jesus. Every inspired Scripture has its use for teaching the truth and refuting error, or for *reformation of manners and discipline in right living,* so that the man who belongs to God may be efficient and equipped for good work of every kind" (2 Timothy 3:15-16, NEB, italics mine).

I'm so grateful that God did not ask me to give up teaching the Bible when I prayed that He would make me the kind of wife He wanted me to be, for this would have deprived me of great joy. Digging into the Bible always produces joy and an excitement that changes me into a different person. My spiritual barometer, 1 John 1:4, applies here, "These things [are written] . . . that your joy [might] be full." Even if I'm willing to be changed by what God is teaching me, the end result is always joy. Deep Bible study also produces spiritual maturity — Christlikeness — in me.[47]

HEAVENLY FATHER,

Thank You for giving me Your holy written Word. As I study and meditate on it, transform me by Your grace so that I can become more and more like Jesus.

AMEN

Do not be conformed to this world, but be transformed by the renewing of your mind, that you may prove what is that good and acceptable and perfect will of God.
ROMANS 12:2 NKJV

BREAKING THE RULES

[Jesus said,] "Whoever becomes simple and elemental
again, like this child, will rank high in God's kingdom."
MATTHEW 18:4 MSG

As children we are taught to always follow the rules. We should take turns, share, listen when others are speaking, keep our hands to ourselves, and remember to say "please" and "thank you." These are good rules. They teach us to show kindness and to be fair in how we interact with others.

As adults, though, the rules all seem to change. We are supposed to always look out for ourselves and try to be number one. We should speak our minds and make sure our opinions are heard. To be a success in life, we should think of ourselves first and not worry too much about anyone who gets in our way.

GRACE FOR TODAY

LIVING LIFE BY THE LAWS OF GRACE MAKES LIFE MORE PLEASANT ALONG THE WAY.

When Jesus came to Earth, He taught people to break the rules—at least the adult rules that had come to be accepted as the way to live. Jesus said that instead of hating those who hurt us, we should love our enemies. He said that the first would be last and last would be first. He said that it was good to be poor in spirit, humble, hungry, thirsty, and persecuted— because then you will be given Heaven and Earth, filled up, and blessed.

When we really look at the rules of God's grace, we have no doubt that these are rules that come from another world—from a heavenly kingdom. They are the polar opposite of every rule of this world. God's rules are better seen in those we are taught to follow in grade school. Perhaps that's why Jesus said that to enter His kingdom we had to become like little children.

Try an experiment today. Live your life by the rules you learned in kindergarten. Take turns, let others go first, be polite and kind. You will find a renewed joy when you break the rules—and follow the laws of grace.

GOODWILL TO ALL

[Jesus] said to them, "Go into all the world and proclaim
the good news to the whole creation."
MARK 16:15 NRSV

Global goodwill seems to be an ever-elusive dream. On every television channel are stories of hatred in one form or another. How does hatred grow to such bitter proportions? Martin Luther King Jr. said, "Darkness cannot drive out darkness; only light can do that. Hate cannot drive out hate; only love can do that." Despite the struggles of men like Martin Luther King Jr., the world is still so fragmented. But the solution to hatred has always been and always will be love.

GRACE FOR TODAY

THE LOVE OF JESUS IS MEANT FOR ALL PEOPLE EVERYWHERE.

Jesus wanted the message of the Gospel to be preached to the entire world, to all people. He was completely inclusive and united. And that's how we should be in our relationships with others.

The way to stop hatred is to love all your neighbors—the ones next door and those on the next continent. Jesus came not as the ruler of the world, but rather the servant of a diverse world. "Whoever desires to become great among you, let him be your servant. And whoever desires to be first among you, let him be your slave—just as the Son of Man did not come to be served, but to serve, and to give His life a ransom for many" (Matthew 20:26-28 NKJV). What an amazing world it would be if we could all serve each other.

Martin Luther King Jr. envisioned that kind of a world. Despite the many horror stories we hear on the news, every day around the world there are small moments of great humanity and kindness. They may not seem to tip the scales, but if enough people seize that moment of brotherhood, it can change the world. Remember, you are the light of the world, so grab that moment when it comes.

GOD'S PLEASURE

Be glad in the LORD and rejoice.
PSALM 32:11 NRSV

GRACE FOR
TODAY

————————

GOD TAKES
PLEASURE IN YOU.

The movie *Chariots of Fire* portrayed the runner Eric Liddell's struggles in the 1924 Olympics between his Christian faith and the demands of the world. In the film, the character Eric tells his sister, "When I run, I feel God's pleasure." There is a joy that connects our souls to God when we feel Elis delight in us. And God does feel pride and delight. "When Jesus had been baptized, just as he came up from the water, suddenly the heavens were opened to him and he saw the Spirit of God descending like a dove and alighting on him. And a voice from heaven said, 'This is my Son, the Beloved, with whom I am well pleased'" (Matthew 3:16-17 NRSV).

Feeling God's pleasure also fills our hearts with complete joy. King David experienced that profound sense of spiritual joy when he brought the Ark of the Covenant to Jerusalem. He danced in front of God and his people. His joy was so overwhelming and demonstrative that his wife thought him vulgar, but David wasn't ashamed. Thomas Watson said, "The more we enjoy of God, the more we are ravished with delight."

Even during profound times of persecution, Christians have been blessed with the feeling of complete unshakable bliss. When the apostle Stephen was brought to answer false charges, his manner surprised even his enemies. When they looked at him, they literally saw the face of an angel. Sensing God's joy clearly isn't always a reflection of our own feeling of well-being because it can come in times of intense strife, a peace that goes beyond all understanding.

Those moments when we so completely feel our heavenly Father's love and pride may seem fleeting and rare. It's not because God doesn't often feel that way about us— it's more that we forget to listen.

ETERNAL PERSPECTIVE

If then you were raised with Christ, seek those things which are above, where Christ is, sitting at the right hand of God. Set your mind on things above, not on things on the earth.
COLOSSIANS 3:1-2 NKJV

Do you remember how tall adults seemed when you were a child? You looked up to them, hoping one day to be as tall. How about your childhood home with its vast rooms and a back yard that stretched for miles? We grow up, only to realize that Mom and Dad are of average height and the house we grew up in had rooms of modest size and it had a small yard.

Our perspective changes. A positive outlook will cause you to see a glass as half-full as opposed to half empty. A Christian perspective views eternity instead of only life on Earth.

Is your mind fixed on things above or things below? Many people live only for job advancement and material possessions. It is not uncommon to find that we become so wrapped up in the details of this life that we lose sight of eternal life. What should we be focusing on in this life? Are we thinking only as far ahead as today or possibly a few months? Perhaps we are planning for retirement now, which means that we plan for years into the future. But what about a hundred years from now? Or a thousand?

Remember, this world is not your home. We are only visiting. We will be truly home only when we enter Heaven. The apostle Paul said, "For me to live is Christ and to die is gain" (Philippians 1:21 AMP). For Paul, Heaven meant that he'd be in Jesus' presence.

Paul had a heavenly mindset, but committed himself to earthly service, making each day count. The time is short and our days limited. Are you using every moment for service of Jesus Christ and living with eternity in mind?

GRACE FOR TODAY

OUR TIME ON EARTH IS ONLY TEMPORARY. OUR REAL HOME IS HEAVEN.

PARENTING

I asked the LORD to give me this child, and he has given
me my request.
1 SAMUEL 1:27 NLT

Some new parents are so frightened of parental failure that they become completely immobilized. This fear of somehow unintentionally damaging a child psychologically can become a huge burden and can actually block successful parenting.

GRACE FOR TODAY

JESUS IS THE PERFECT PARENTING MODEL. HE IS LOVING, FORGIVING, AUTHORITATIVE, WISE, AND AVAILABLE. HE WILL LIVE THROUGH YOU.

John Wilmot commented, "Before I got married I had six theories about bringing up children; now I have six children, and no theories." Parenting isn't about raising a theory or going by the latest book; it's about raising a child—your child. Thankfully, you're not parenting alone. God has given you the grace to combine wisdom, love, and discipline in a style that works differently for each unique child.

There is no such thing as the perfect parent or the perfect child. Parents and children meet somewhere in the middle ground, a state of grace where imperfections meet. God's mercy and understanding come when a family learns each others' failings and loves each other with unconditional love, just as God does.

Each day pray for God's guidance to make right, godly choices for your children, and then simply make them. God is amazingly creative in His responses to our behavior, and we should be as well. There is never just one way to teach or discipline a child. Be creative, be loving, firm, forgiving, and willing to admit when you're wrong. Our children learn by example, and if you use Jesus as your parenting role model, how can you go wrong? Jesus was loving, forgiving, authoritative, wise, and available. Jesus said, "Let the children alone, and do not hinder them from coming to Me; for the kingdom of heaven belongs to such as these" (Matthew 19:14 NASB).

Parenting is about making mistakes and sometimes doing exactly the right things. The bottom line is your child needs a parent—and that parent is you!

A DROP OF GRACE

By Johannes Tauler

All the works which people and animals could ever accomplish without the grace of God are an absolute nothing, as compared with the smallest thing which God has worked in people by His grace. Even the smallest drop of grace is better than all earthly riches that are beneath the sun, and it is given more richly by God to the soul than any earthly gift. It is given more richly than brooks of water, than the breath of the air, than the brightness of the sun; for spiritual things are far finer and nobler than earthly things. The whole Trinity, Father, Son, and Holy Ghost, gives grace to the soul, and flow immediately into it.

Grace looses us from the snares of many temptations. It relieves us from the heavy burden of worldly anxieties and carries our spirit up to heaven, the land of spirits. It kills the worm of conscience, which makes sins alive. It is a very powerful thing. The person who receives even a tiny drop of grace is ruined for all else.

Grace makes, contrary to nature, all sorrows sweet, and brings it about that a person no longer feels any enjoyment for things that formerly gave great pleasure and delight. On the other hand, what formerly was found to be disgusting, now delights and is the desire of the heart—for instance, weakness, sorrow, inwardness, humility, self-abandonment, and detachment from others. All of this is very dear to a person, when this visitation of the Holy Ghost—grace—has in truth come to them.

FATHER,

Your grace is so very precious to me, for it has the power to transform me and set me free. I lay my pains and inadequacies at Your feet and exchange them for the wholeness and joy that Your grace produces. Thank You, Father.

AMEN

[The message of God's grace] is able to give you strength, and it will give you the blessings God has for all his holy people.
ACTS 20:32 NCV

PERFECT GRACE FOR AN IMPERFECT WORLD

[Jesus] said to me, "My grace is sufficient for you, for power
is perfected in weakness."
2 CORINTHIANS 12:9 NASB

GRACE FOR TODAY

GOD'S GRACE ABOUNDS TO ALL OF US WHO STRUGGLE WITH THE EVERYDAY IMPERFECTIONS OF LIFE.

Do you find yourself feeling defeated by your own imperfections and those of the world you live in? You get blamed for a mistake at work. It isn't your fault, but it still gets you one of those "Can I speak to you in my office?" talks from your boss. Your best laid plans for a quiet family dinner at the table fall apart when your oven dies and leaves the roast cold and raw. You long to have one of those lovely, perfect homes like you see on TV, but all your attempts at organization end up making a bigger mess than you started with. It can all leave you feeling worthless and overwhelmed at the end of the day.

If you find yourself feeling this way, try this little exercise—read about Peter, Paul, and Mary—not the sixties folk singers, but Peter, Jesus' disciple; Mary, sister of Martha and Lazarus; and Paul the apostle. Their stories show us deep faith and trust in God. But, do you know what else they teach us? These stories show that God's grace abounds to all of us who struggle with the everyday imperfections of life.

- Peter took a literal step of faith onto a raging sea to walk with Jesus—and then he let fear take over and nearly drowned.
- Paul was an incredible witness for Christ, but he also struggled with a "thorn in the flesh" and heated disagreements with his fellow missionaries.
- Mary just wanted to be with Jesus, but she found herself criticized and misunderstood by her very own sister.

Through the unfathomable grace of God, these people are known as God's champions—His beloved and faithful followers! God pours out His grace on the fearful, the weak, and the misunderstood—on everyone. You can be assured that He will never fail to do the same for you.

BUILDING MEMORIES

I thank my God every time I remember you.
PHILIPPIANS 1:3 NRSV

You build an education, a home, a career, financial security, a future. But perhaps the greatest treasure you can build for your children and grandchildren is memories. Pierce Harris wrote, "Memory is a child walking along a seashore. You never can tell what small pebble it will pick up and store away among treasured things." Building memories is a carefully crafted talent. Mostly it takes time to design and orchestrate moments that touch the soul of a family. And sometimes those moments are spontaneous and unrehearsed art, but you must be present to paint the colors of the day. Author Hortense Calisher wrote, "A happy childhood can't be cured. Mine'll hang around my neck like a rainbow, that's all, instead of a noose."

The thing we forget as adults is that children don't remember if the carpet was always perfectly vacuumed or the grass mowed every Saturday without fail. But they will remember the day you went to catch tadpoles and got covered in mud. Or when you suddenly stopped the car to chase a hot air balloon across a farmer's fields to see if you could discover where it would land. Or a rainy day building birdhouses or crooked chocolate cakes.

GRACE FOR TODAY

GOOD MEMORIES ARE A GIFT FROM GOD TO US. THEY ARE THOSE MOMENTS IN TIME THAT YOU CARRY WITH YOU INTO ETERNITY.

Memories pass from one generation to another as your children become memory builders themselves. You can see it on their faces as a memory flashes past and brings with it a smile. Thomas Campell wrote, "To live in hearts we leave behind is not to die." Memories are fragile and fleeting creations; once gone they can never be built again. But the supply is endless and today can be the start of another project.

BEYOND THE BIRD

God says, "He who offers a sacrifice of thanksgiving honors Me."
PSALM 50:23 NASB

Thanksgiving Day invokes images of families sitting at tables bursting with food. And perhaps it's the one day of the year when families across the country actually say a prayer of thanksgiving to their Creator. But Robert Caspar Lintner wrote, "Thanksgiving was never meant to be shut up in a single day."

GRACE FOR TODAY

THE HEAVENLY FATHER'S GRACE IS ALWAYS RAINING DOWN ON US, GIVING US MUCH TO BE THANKFUL FOR EACH DAY.

Being thankful is an everyday privilege. Recounting our blessings in front of others seems to bring reality to them. It makes our blessings tangible. You acknowledge it, and so do witnesses. The Bible tells us, "O give thanks to the LORD, call on his name, make known his deeds among the peoples" (1 Chronicles 16:8 NRSV). A thankful heart humbles us, encourages our own faith, and inspires others. On Thanksgiving Day, our achievements take a backseat to God's generosity. The simple truth is, we can have no achievements without His blessings.

We are dependent on God for everything in all situations, not just on holidays. So we should be thankful in all circumstances. Jesus himself constantly gave thanks to His Father during the course of even everyday events. When He broke bread with strangers and friends, Jesus gave thanks every time. This was a Son in constant appreciation of His Father. Think about it. Don't we like a grateful child? Doesn't God?

Jesus thanked God before He raised His friend Lazarus from the dead. He looked up to Heaven and thanked God for hearing Him. How did He know that God heard Him? Because Jesus knew God always heard Him. Just as He always hears both our requests and our thanksgiving.

Jesus did all things to be the example for us to follow. So give thanks on Thanksgiving Day, but also the next day and the next. Show others your enduring love and respect for your Heavenly Father's enduring love for you.

THE NAME ABOVE EVERY NAME

God highly exalted [Christ Jesus,) and bestowed on Him
the name which is above every name.
PHILIPPIANS 2:9 NASB

Pills come in various shapes and sizes. Some of the smallest are the most powerful. One tiny nitroglycerin pill can prevent acute chest pain by relaxing the heart's blood vessels to increase blood flow and oxygen supply. As one pill can make a change in our physical body, one name—the simple five-letter name of Jesus—can change our spiritual lives forever.

The name Jesus means, "Jehovah saves." His very name proclaims that He is God's vessel for salvation. When we confess with our mouth the Lord Jesus and believe God raised Him from the dead, we have eternal life. (Romans 10:9.)

Nitroglycerin may control chest pain, but it does not cure it. When the apostle Peter prayed in the name of Jesus for a man who had been lame since birth, he took him by the right hand, helped him up, and instantly the man's feet and ankles became strong. The man jumped up and began to walk. When questioned about the healing, Peter said, "His name, through faith in His name, has made this man strong, whom you see and know" (Acts 3:16 NKJV).

Early disciples understood the power in the name of Jesus, and they knew how to use that power to receive His blessings and to bless others. If used for an extended period of time, nitroglycerin can lose its effectiveness, but the name of Jesus never loses power. His name endures forever. At the name of Jesus, eventually every knee will bow, and every tongue will confess that Jesus Christ is Lord, to the glory of God the Father.

God has given Jesus the highest name. And that name is one He has given you permission to call on. Call on Him with confidence today.

GRACE FOR TODAY

HOW SWEET THE NAME OF JESUS SOUNDS IN A BELIEVER'S EAR! IT SOOTHES HIS SORROWS, HEALS HIS WOUNDS, AND DRIVES AWAY HIS FEAR!

JOHN NEWTON

PENNIES FROM HEAVEN

Be careful how you walk, not as unwise men but as wise,
making the most of your time, because the days are evil.
EPHESIANS 5:15-16 NASB

What would you do if a benefactor called and said, "I've decided to deposit 86,400 pennies in your account each morning? This gift comes, however, with one stipulation: you must spend the entire amount every day. None of the pennies can be carried forward to the next day. At midnight, the balance will be cancelled, but each morning, you will receive a new deposit of pennies."

We would all like to have a benefactor like that, wouldn't we? Yet, we do. God has given each of us 86,400 seconds in each day. What we do with this deposit of time is very important because 86,400 seconds per day is all we will ever have. Any seconds wasted cannot be retrieved. We need to learn to use our time wisely.

GRACE FOR TODAY

GOD HAS GRACIOUSLY GIVEN US 86,400 SECONDS EACH DAY, AND HE HAS A PLAN FOR EACH ONE.

How we set up our priorities determines how we spend our time. Those of us who are mothers probably spend a lot of time taking care of our children, driving them around to various activities. Those of us who are married run errands and do things for our husbands. If we have full-time jobs, we juggle household chores and personal time with the hours spent at work. It can be difficult to carve out time with God for daily devotions and prayer. It is not uncommon to feel like we are running in circles.

Take a few minutes to write down an average of how many hours you spend daily on each of your activities. Are you pleased with how your time is allotted? If not, ask God to help you revise your schedule.

Remember: Time is God's gift to you. What you do with your time is your gift to God.

GRACE AND PEACE

By Martin Luther

The greeting of the apostle Paul when he says, "Grace and peace to you" is amazing to people of the world. Only those who belong to Christ comprehend the two words, grace and peace. Grace releases sin, and peace makes the conscience quiet.

The two fiends that torment us are sin and conscience. But Christ has defeated these two monsters and trodden them under His foot. Therefore these two words contain the whole sum of Christianity in their meaning. Grace contains the remission of sins, and peace contains a quiet and joyful conscience.

But peace of conscience can never be had, unless sin is first forgiven. But sin is not forgiven by the fulfilling of the law; for no one is able to satisfy the law. The law shows us sin, accuses and terrifies our conscience, declares the wrath of God, and drives one to desperation.

And one cannot take away sin through the works and creations of people, like strict rules, religious practices, vows, and pilgrimages. But there is no work that can take away sin; but instead works increase sin. For the perfectionists and merit-mongers, the more they labor and sweat to bring themselves out of sin, the deeper they are plunged into it. For there is no means to take away sin, but through grace alone.

Therefore Paul, in all the greetings of his letters, sets grace and peace against sin and evil conscience. The words themselves are easy. But, it is hard to be persuaded in our hearts, that by grace alone — not by any other means either in heaven or in earth — we have remission of sins and peace with God.

FATHER,

I am so thankful that when I miss the mark, I can rely on Your grace to release me from sin and restore me. Knowing that I don't have to be perfect to please You puts my soul at rest and gives me peace. I love You, Lord.

AMEN

Grace to you and peace from God our Father and the Lord Jesus Christ.
1 CORINTHIANS 1:3 NKJV

FAMILY

Don't refuse to help your own relatives.
ISAIAH 58:7 NCV

GRACE FOR TODAY

FAMILY IS A MASTERPIECE AND DESIGN OF GOD. YOURS IS GOD'S GIFT TO YOU, AND YOU ARE HIS GIFT TO THEM.

Bishop Desmond Tutu said, "You don't choose your family. They are God's gift to you, as you are to them." Ever feel like getting in the return line? No, you can't pick your family, and the fact that they're a gift makes it even more complicated. Family will know you, annoy you, embarrass you, disappoint you, amaze you, cheer you, surprise you, and love you.

No family is perfect. You'll be pleased to know that no family is really "normal," never neatly packaged. Family, for better or worse, is a part of you for life. Look at the story of Joseph: His brothers tried to kill him and sold him into slavery. But despite it all, Joseph loved them—with boundaries, of course.

Even Jesus' earthly family didn't fully understand His lifestyle. "Then Jesus entered a house, and again a crowd gathered, so that he and his disciples were not even able to eat. When his family heard about this, they went to take charge of him, for they said, 'He is out of His mind'" (Mark 3:20-21 NIV). Those verses are just so wonderfully and typically family. It makes Jesus' life so normal and so like ours, a masterpiece and design of God.

The Bible is a fascinating chronicle of family life at its noblest and most degenerate. God has made our family to be our responsibility, however. Biblically we must provide for our family, and not just the ones we like. Next time that phone rings with family matters, put the excuses aside. Make time to understand your family and to embrace it. It may shock the family members a little, but love them as Jesus loves you. Learning how to do that may be the reason your family with all its quirks is God's gift to you.

WALKING HIS WAY

Blessed is every one who fears the LORD, who walks in His
ways.
PSALM 128:1 NKJV

Can you imagine taking a walk with God? We read in Genesis that God walked with Adam and Eve in the Garden of Eden in the cool of the day. People walk for many reasons: for pleasure, to get rid of stress, to find solitude, or simply to get from one place to another. Today, nearly everyone who walks regularly does so because they think of the activity as good exercise.

The word *walk*, in the Bible doesn't refer to exercise, but symbolizes the way we live, the way we act, and the way we conduct ourselves. The Bible says Enoch and Noah walked with God.

Walking involves progress. When we look at our relationship with God, we should be able to see that we are moving toward a closer relationship with Him. Our attitudes and actions should be more and more like Christ's. Our knowledge about God should be increasing, and we should be seeking His will for our lives.

Just as walking for exercise improves our physical bodies, walking with God benefits us spiritually. Our souls grow healthy. Jesus said He is the way — the way to God and the way to eternal life. He can lead on the right path those who trust Him.

Some people exercise on weekdays, think of Saturday as an optional day, and skip Sundays. Unfortunately, some Christians view their Christian walk in a similar way, except they serve God on Sunday and skip the rest of the week. Let's be faithful to walk with God every day.

GRACE FOR TODAY

THE OPPORTUNITY TO WALK WITH GOD IS THE AWESOME
PRIVILEGE OF BELIEVERS.

MORE THAN ENOUGH

God's grace that can save everyone has come. It teaches us not
to live against God nor to do the evil things the world wants to
do. Instead, that grace teaches us to live now in a wise and right
way and in a way that shows we serve God.
TITUS 2:11-12 NCV

Weight loss is a billion-dollar industry that includes a diet for just about every lifestyle. The trouble is that those diets rarely work for the vast majority of women, leaving them feeling depressed and defeated. Erma Bombeck summed up her frustration with these words: "I've been on a constant diet for the last two decades. I've lost a total of 789 pounds. By all accounts, I should be hanging from a charm bracelet."

In recent times, most of us have learned that losing weight is less about dieting and more about making healthy lifestyle changes— eating better, exercising more. But for the woman who places her trust in God, it's also about understanding that she's not alone in wanting to feel better, look better, and be healthier.

God is the designer of the human body, and as with every other aspect of our lives, He has made a provision of grace to help us find a healthy balance in regard to our weight. In Galatians 5:23, nine virtues are listed. These are fruit of the Holy Spirit's work in our lives. Number nine, self-control, is the very thing we need to help us find and maintain a healthy weight.

Are you surprised to learn that God cares about your efforts to lose weight? He truly has covered all the bases, made every provision, anticipated every need. He is the God of "enough"; and His grace is more than you will ever need.

GRACE FOR TODAY

GOD'S GRACE IS MORE THAN ENOUGH TO MEET EVERY NEED
YOU WILL EVER HAVE.

The Road to Recovery

Your light shall break forth like the morning, your healing shall spring forth speedily, and your righteousness shall go before you; the glory of the LORD shall be your rear guard.
ISAIAH 58:8 NKJV

Substance addiction is a very personal and tragic affliction of choice. And addiction is most powerful when it is allowed to grow in secrecy and solitude. Daniel Goldman said, "That, of course, is the devil's bargain of addiction: a short-term good feeling in exchange for the steady meltdown of one's life."

William Griffith Wilson and Dr. Robert Holbrook Smith were both addicted to alcohol and both found recovery with God's help. In 1935 they were the cofounders of a program in Akron, Ohio called Alcoholics Anonymous. In 1939 they published the book Alcoholics Anonymous, and the Twelve Step Program was conceived, a spiritually based program that has helped millions of people around the world.

The twelve steps' hallmark is a realization that you are powerless against addictions and that only God can help you recover. That is a grace we often don't realize Jesus brings for us—God's help with the very weakness we thought would cause Him to walk away from us. But we have to be brave and admit we need that grace.

The apostle Peter said, "A man is a slave to whatever has mastered him" (2 Peter 2:19 NIV). Without question, substance addiction will focus your life energy on one all-consuming, destructive desire. But the Bible tells us that Jesus came to set captives free, even captives to addictions. And the Bible also tells us that no matter how many times we fall, Jesus is there to pick us up and love us.

There is no shame in getting help for addiction or taking that journey of recovery. Remember, God will walk that path of healing with you, no matter how many times you fall.

GRACE FOR TODAY

GOD WILL LEAD YOU AND WALK WITH YOU ON THE JOURNEY OF RECOVERY, ONE STEP AT A TIME.

GETTING IN SHAPE

Physical exercise has some value, but spiritual exercise is
much more important, for it promises a reward in both
this life and the next.
1 TIMOTHY 4:8 NLT

In his letter to Timothy, the apostle Paul referred to being in good
spiritual shape. "Train yourself to be godly" (4:7). The word Paul uses
here for training comes from the Greek *gymnasi*, from which we derive
the words for "gymnasium" and "gymnastics." This word conveys the
idea of rigorous, strenuous training.

GRACE FOR TODAY

GOD HAS PROVIDED
ALL THE TOOLS YOU
NEED TO BECOME A
SPIRITUAL
CHAMPION!

Many people have a physical training
plan, but most don't realize the importance
of having a spiritual training plan as well.
Not some pretentious program brimming
with rigid rules and guidelines, but a general
plan for making and noting spiritual progress.
That might mean a schedule for reading
through the Bible in a year or exercising our
prayer muscles by praying each day for
some specific need. This plan would also
include scheduling opportunities to serve
others. Unselfish service helps us grow strong in the virtues of kindness,
generosity, faithfulness, patience, and goodness.

Do you have a plan for getting in shape spiritually? If not, it may be
time to inventory your exercise equipment (Bible, study guides,
inspirational books, prayer partner or prayer group, church programs
where you can get involved, needs in your community). God's not
looking for perfection. His grace is there if you stumble or miss your
daily allotment of spiritual push-ups. He just wants you to be ready to
tackle the wonderful plan He has prepared for your life. He wants to
see you become a fit representative of the Kingdom of God in the
spiritual Olympics!

FAITH, HOPE, LOVE

By John Bunyan

Without faith there is no hope. To hope without faith is to see without eyes, or to expect without grounds; for "faith is the assurance of things hoped for" (Hebrews 11:1 NASB).

Faith will do what hope cannot do, hope can do what faith cannot do, and love can do things distinct from both of them. Faith goes in the front, hope in the middle, and love brings up the rear.

Faith is the mother — grace, for hope is born of her, but love flows from them both.

Faith comes by hearing, and hope by experience. Faith comes by hearing the word of God, hope by the trust that faith has given to it. Faith believes the truth of the word, hope waits for the fulfilling of it. Faith lays hold of that end of the promise that is next to us, but hope lays hold of that end of the promise that is fastened to the mercy-seat. For the promise is like a mighty cable that is fastened by one end to a ship, and by the other to the anchor. The soul is the ship where faith is, and to which the end of this cable is fastened; but hope is the anchor that is at the other end of this cable, and "which enters the Presence behind the veil" (Hebrews 6:19 NKJV).

———————

HEAVENLY FATHER,

Thank You for Your gifts of faith, hope, and love. There is nothing I could do within myself to deserve them, but I receive them because of Your grace. Give me wisdom and insight into each of these so that I can experience them in their fullness. Increase my faith as I hear Your Word. Keep me ever-mindful of Your faithfulness to me so that hope burns brightly in my heart. Envelope me in Your love. Finally I ask You to use me to minister these grace gifts to others.

AMEN

These three things continue forever: faith, hope, and love.
1 CORINTHIANS 13:13 NCV

THE CARROT

John told them, "If you have two coats, give one to someone who doesn't have any. If you have food, share it with someone else."
LUKE 3:11 CEV

Some of the most popular and fun animals to watch at the zoo are the orangutans. With their large size, long red hair, and expressive faces, they look almost human.

At feeding time, the trainer dumps oranges, carrots, and heads of lettuce onto the cement floor of the cage. On one occasion, a nimble female snatched the only carrot and secured it with her foot. Then she proceeded to grab her head of lettuce with one hand and her orange with the other. She scampered off to a corner of the cage and glared at the other two orangutans, daring them to touch her carrot.

She slowly ate her lettuce. Then she popped the orange in her mouth, eating first the fleshy pulp and then the entire peel! The other two orangutans ate their meals, all the while staring longingly at the carrot held tightly in the female's toes. Finally, when all else was devoured, she savored her favorite food—the plump, juicy carrot—not offering a bite to anyone else.

We laugh at the antics of the orangutans at the zoo, but sharing can sometimes be difficult for people too. Often children will fight over one particular toy when there are several other similar ones lying nearby. One of the first words they usually learn is "mine."

Hopefully, as adult women, we are beyond the antics of the orangutans and young children. We can share because God has promised to supply us with enough left over to share. When we see someone in need, let's respond with our actions, our checkbooks, and God's grace in our hearts.

PAST TENSE

Jesus said, "Go your way, and from now on do not sin again."
JOHN 8:11 NRSV

Past failures and wrongdoings are a heavy burden that many carry on their backs, and the strain is killing them. Dwelling on negative past events can be personal and relational quicksand.

Although we may have atoned for and tried to set things right regarding past wrongs, often we still can't seem to let go and release them into history. Dwelling on past regrets is counterproductive to the life God wants us to have. We must grasp one simple concept. When we ask God for forgiveness, those sins are washed away — as if they never existed. "Repent therefore, and turn to God so that your sins may be wiped out" (Acts 3:19 NSRV). With God's help, we're not the same person we were. We have changed and have learned from our mistakes. So if God isn't holding on to our past, why should we? We can't build a future by picking through the ruins of our past.

> ## GRACE FOR TODAY
>
> GOD PARDONS LIKE A MOTHER, WHO KISSES THE OFFENSE INTO EVERLASTING FORGIVENESS.
>
> HENRY WARD BEECHER

Jesus doesn't want us to harp on the past with crippling regret. He is forward-focused on our future conduct and isn't at all interested in dwelling on our past sins. This of course means that we in turn must give that same grace and forgiveness to ourselves and others.

Likewise, don't let family, friends, or associates drag you back to past, repented-for events. This isn't good for you or them—it just rekindles all kinds of negative emotions. Remind them that you're a different person and you'd like to talk about ways to improve your relationship now and in the future. "If anyone is in Christ, there is a new creation: everything old has passed away; see, everything has become new!" (2 Corinthians 5:17 NRSV).

Maybe it's time to take the past off your back and leave it behind where it belongs. Jesus makes all things new — including you.

ABIDING JOY

Rejoice always . . . for this is the will of God in Christ Jesus
for you.
1 THESSALONIANS 5:16,18 NKJV

The world often confuses happiness with joy. Happiness is that elusive feeling that comes and goes, depending on our outward circumstances. When our bills are paid and there's money in the bank, we are happy. But when the car breaks down and unexpected medical bills wreck our budget, we stop smiling.

We are all faced with trials that assail us and make us unhappy—things we have no control over. But trials cannot destroy anyone who possesses true joy. Like a natural spring that bubbles up from your innermost being, real joy is a deep and constant realization that nothing can ever rob you of God's assurance and peace.

Joy rests its head on God's chest and silently sings, "It is well with my soul." Abiding joy becomes an immovable force that motivates you when you feel like giving up. In John 16:33 NKJV, Jesus explains, "In the world you will have tribulation; but be of good cheer; I have overcome the world."

Joy is the fruit of our oneness with God. It is a constant companion that lives the words of Acts 2:28 NLT; "You have shown me the way of life, and you will give me wonderful joy in your presence."

In God's presence, you can experience the fullness of His joy. After every storm that visits your life, you can expect to see God's rainbow and the faithfulness of His promise.

It is your Heavenly Father's desire that you live life abundantly—with joy—always.

GRACE FOR TODAY

JOY IS THE FRUIT OF OUR ONENESS WITH GOD.

THE HEART OF FORGIVENESS

[Jesus said,] "Forgive, and you will be forgiven."
LUKE 6:37 NKJV

The newspapers are full of life's monstrosities — acts of crimes and violence that are unforgivable, at least on a human level. We can't imagine how sin could so grip someone that he or she would cause such harm to a fellow human being. We can't comprehend ever forgiving anyone who could inflict such pain.

In the history of mankind, there has been no greater suffering inflicted upon a human being than what Jesus experienced. He paid the ultimate price for our forgiveness when He hung on the cross. Yet, His directive was clear. As His blood spilled down upon His executioners, He spoke: "Father, forgive them; for they know not what they do" (Luke 23:34 KJV).

GRACE FOR TODAY

GOD'S GRACE CONFORMS OUR HEARTS TO MIRROR HIS HEART OF FORGIVENESS.

Despite the human suffering Jesus endured for us, He demonstrated a heart of forgiveness for all sin. Even ours.

Not only does His sacrifice set us free from a sentence of death; His words brand our hearts with the fire of His unconditional love. He says that with changed hearts, we, too, can forgive. Christ not only poured out His grace and love upon us; He poured it in us. Romans 5:5 NKJV proclaims, "The love of God has been poured out in our hearts by the Holy Spirit."

With Jesus' kind of love, through grace, we are given the mandate to forgive. God's Word clearly declares in Mark 11:26 NASB, "If you do not forgive, neither will your Father who is in heaven forgive your transgressions."

God, through His own Son, put a human face on suffering — and on forgiveness. He left us nothing to guess about. Because our hearts are united with His, we are able to step beyond what's humanly possible into divine forgiveness and unconditional love.

FAITH THAT MOVES GOD'S HEART

[Jesus said,] "If you have faith as a mustard seed, you will
say to this mountain, 'Move from here to there,' and it will
move; and nothing will he impossible for you."
MATTHEW 17:20 NKJV

We all have "Red Sea" moments in our lives when we're certain that unless God moves on our behalf, we'll drown.

It's easy to praise Him after we've reached the other side, but true faith praises Him in advance—before He parts the sea of our difficulties.

If faith has a voice, it is praise. It sings a song of victory in the face of impossibility before the battle is won, before the answer comes.

Children are great teachers in the faith department. They believe without reserve or hesitation. God longs to see the same kind of childlike faith in you and me—the kind of faith that believes anything is possible. The loaves and fishes parable paints a beautiful word picture of a little boy who innocently offered Christ the few loaves and fishes that were in his basket. In truth, that young lad actually handed Jesus much more than a small basket of fish and bread that day. He handed Jesus his faith. Loaves- and-fishes faith—it's the kind of faith that tells God, He is enough.

If you are facing a "Red Sea" moment today, or if you need God to move in your situation, trust Him and allow faith do its perfect work. Remember that one tiny grain of faith can move mountains. One offering of childlike faith into God's capable hands is mighty beyond belief.

GRACE FOR TODAY

GOD'S HEART IS MOVED WHEN HE SEES OUR FAITH AND
TRUST IN HIM.

The Blessing of God's Word

By George Muller

Through reading of the Bible, and especially through meditation of it, we become more and more acquainted with the nature and character of God. We then see more and more what a kind, loving, gracious, merciful, mighty, wise, and faithful being He is. When we recognize this, we know that in poverty, in suffering, in grief, in struggles with our service, and when we are without a job, we will rest on the ability of God to help us.

We have not only learned from His Word that He has almighty power and infinite wisdom, but we have also seen many examples in the Bible where His almighty power and infinite wisdom have been actually used in helping and delivering His people. We can rest on the willingness of God to help us. We haven't only learned from the Bible what a kind, good, merciful, gracious, and faithful being God is, but we have also read in the Bible, how in many different ways He has proved Himself to be so.

When we consider that God has become known to us through prayer and meditation on His own Word, it will lead us with a measure of confidence to rely on Him and therefore will be one way for God to strengthen our faith.

HEAVENLY FATHER,

Thank You so much for giving me the gift of Your written Word. As I meditate on it, flood my heart with light so that I can know You and experience Your grace in its fullness. I read of Your constant faithfulness in the pages pf my Bible, and it encourages my faith to know that You never change. I rely on You with my whole heart.

AMEN

In the beginning was the Word, and the Word was with God, and the Word was God.
JOHN 1:1 NASB

THE BLESSING OF COMMITMENT

He always stands by his covenant—the commitment he
made to a thousand generations.
PSALM 105:8 NLT

Life's greatest treasures and blessings come wrapped in one word—commitment. Commitment. The blessing of marriage, parenting, friendship, and the gift of God's infinite love would never be ours to experience if we were not willing to commit to those relationships.

GRACE FOR TODAY

EVEN OUR COMMITMENT IS A GRACE GIVEN TO US BY GOD'S UNFAILING COMMITMENT TO US.

When you first invited God into your heart, you knew it required commitment. But you were ready and willing to sign the promissory note, giving God sole ownership of your life. In return, He made you a promise—that if you would abide in Him, He would abide in you. He also promised that if you committed your life to Him, you would become His child and His heir.

The Bible depicts godly women who demonstrated wisdom and strength as committed servants of God. Today, teachers and doctors commit their training and life's work to helping others. Mothers commit their love to their children for a lifetime. Men and women commit to a marriage covenant.

Commitment brings steadfastness to our lives and keeps us focused on what we value most in this life. It is not only a privilege, but also a necessity. But in addition to that, commitment is a grace earned for us by Jesus' unfailing love for us. In Jeremiah 31:33 God says that He will write His law in our hearts. Our ability to commit ourselves to Him is a free gift of grace that comes from God's unfailing commitment to us.

Sink your roots down deep into God, our Vine, today. Abide in Him, and you will find all you need, even the loyalty to commit everything to Him.

CHONORING YOUR GIFT

A man's gift makes room for him, and brings him before great men.
PROVERBS 18:16 NKJV

Doesn't it feel good when you've used your gifting or talent to bless someone and make a difference? When you've honorably given the gifts and talents that are uniquely yours, there's a gentle and deep satisfaction that permeates your soul.

Everyone is born with gifts and talents. What we do with those gifts is up to us. We can keep them to ourselves or develop and use them to bless others and bring glory to God.

> ### GRACE FOR TODAY
>
> BY HIS GRACE, GOD HAS ENDOWED US WITH TALENTS AND GIFTS THAT WILL BRING HIM HONOR.

Do you ever wonder what your gift or talent may be? If it is not obvious and you're still searching to find out what it may be, ask yourself these questions: What motivates you? What do you feel passionate about? Do you love organizing? Are you good at teaching or speaking? Do you love to read or tell stories? Are you driven to find solutions when a need arises? Are you the first to make soup or care for someone who is sick? Do you love music and poetry?

Ask God to help you discover and develop your gifts and talents. God's Word promises that when your gift is in place, it will open doors and bring you before great men. When Christ was moved with compassion to use His gift of healing, His tender mercy brought Him attention and praise. But He was quick to point to the Father and give Him all the glory. Exercising your gift honorably is sacred — holy — a form of worship and a noble tribute to the Gift Giver.

You are God's handmaiden. What you are is God's gift to you. But what you become is your gift back to Him. Let your gift shine as a beacon of light for His glory!

INSIGHTFUL LIVING

The heavens are telling the glory of God; they are a
marvelous display of his craftsmanship.
PSALM 19:1 TLB

Taking time to "stop and smell the roses" is probably not on most of our to-do lists. The responsibilities and challenges of life can easily rob us of joyful awareness and insightful living.

God, the Master Artist, gave us nature to enjoy and savor. When was the last time you took some time to bask in God's wondrous bounty? Just as we look for the meaning in the artwork of the old art masters, your Master Artist wants you to step into the painting He has created just for you. Look and see. Observe. Think. And delight in the little things that often go unnoticed in the midst of your hurried schedule.

Have you ever stood and gazed at a sunset and truly allowed yourself to be caught up in the wonder of God's magnificent handiwork—marveled at His suspended curtain, brilliantly displayed with opalescent swirls of orange and purple hues against a sapphire blue sky? Have you ever captured the whispers of Heaven upon a gentle breeze or heard your heart harmonize with the song of a rippling brook?

Insight connects us to the splendor of our Creator. It unearths the treasure of bliss we knew as children when our eyes were keen with expectation. It gives our eyes a dimension of seeing with our hearts—takes us to a place of reflection, awe, and reverence for God's majesty in our lives.

God wants to rekindle your senses, refresh your spirit, and open your eyes to everyday delights and miracles He has painted upon the canvas of your life.

GRACE FOR TODAY

GOD CREATED THE BEAUTY OF THE EARTH FOR OUR
ENJOYMENT AND REFRESHMENT.

TRUSTING GOD'S WILL

"I know the plans I have for you," says the LORD. "They are plans for good and not for disaster, to give you a future and a hope."
JEREMIAH 29:11 NLT

Do you sometimes wonder where all the pieces of your life fit together in God's plan for you? You may get anxious or impatient in trying to see the whole picture. There will be times when a fragment of your life doesn't quite seem to fit what you'd envisioned or hoped it could be.

Learning to trust God's will for your life is a little like finding a plain brown box filled with pieces of a jigsaw puzzle. As you sort through countless pieces, you find yourself asking just what God's picture and will for you is. The answer doesn't always come immediately. It's only when you pick up each piece, hold it up to God, and ask Him to show you where it fits that you finally catch a partial glimpse of His plan and will.

> ## GRACE FOR TODAY
>
> WE CAN TRUST GOD'S PERSPECTIVE AND WILL FOR OUR LIVES, EVEN WHEN WHAT WE SEE MAKES NO SENSE.

Don't lose heart if you don't see the whole picture. God is always working and conforming your will to His. His direction and confirmations will assure you He is carefully placing each piece of your life's puzzle into place. He already knows the end result. Your job is to simply trust Him to complete the puzzle. He knows exactly where every piece of the puzzle fits.

There is no greater peace than being in the center of God's will. Give Him your dreams and goals and let Him sort out all the pieces. Seeking Him and His direction places you in the very center of His perfect will. You can trust the mountainous view of God's perspective and plan for your life—a view of completeness and eternal glory that far surpasses the jagged pieces of your life's puzzle.

THE ART OF SIMPLICITY

I fear, lest somehow, as the serpent deceived Eve by his craftiness, so your minds may be corrupted from the simplicity that is in Christ.
2 CORINTHIANS 11:3 NKJV

Do you find yourself longing for a less complicated, less frantic way of living? If so, you're not alone. For the past few years, there's been a sort of simplicity renaissance. Bookstore shelves are filled with books and magazines about simplifying our lives.

Since the beginning of time, when Satan first tricked Adam and Eve out of their pure and simple belief in God, he's continued trying to bring chaos into the lives of good people.

GRACE FOR TODAY

JESUS HELPS US TO LIVE SIMPLE LIVES BY SIMPLE TRUTHS.

Finding the path to simplicity is more than simply tossing the clutter out of our closets. It's a matter of rearranging our way of thinking. Sometimes it requires taking a giant leap off the fast track of the world's concept of progressive living before we can simplify our everyday lives and even our relationship to Christ.

Jesus warned about the trappings of this world. He came with a simple message. Life. He had one single motive. Love. The Pharisees didn't understand His simplicity and His disregard for what they deemed religious. They declared their building of temples, their rules, and their rituals as true religion. But 2 Peter 4 announces that we are the living stones of Christ's temple. It is people, not buildings, who are most important.

If we are not focused on simplicity, we miss what really counts—Christ's personal heart-to-heart relationship with us. Simplicity implores us to be more about "being" than doing.

There's a higher ground of rest where you can take refuge from the clutter and clanging noise of this world. It's a place where you hear the gentle voice of simplicity calling you to come and sit at Jesus' feet, listen to a story, share some laughter, or maybe even a few tears.

Sounds so simple, doesn't it?

THE PRECIOUS GIFT OF HOPE

By John Bunyan

Hope is the grace that relieves the soul when it is dark and weary. True hope has no problem with weakness or darkness; but rather strengthens the soul to stay in spite of and because of them. Paul said, "I am well content with weaknesses, with insults, with distresses, with persecutions, with difficulties, for Christ's sake; for when I am weak, then I am strong" (2 Corinthians 12:10 NASB). But this cannot be done where there is no hope, nor by anything but hope. For it is hope, and the use of it, that can say, "Now I expect that God should bring good out of all this."

"Hope that is seen is not hope" (Romans 8:24 NKJV). But we must hope for what we don't see. David said, "Why are you cast down, O my soul? . . . Hope in God" (Psalm 42:5 NKJV). Christians have no reason to mistrust the goodness of God, because of their weakness. The Psalmist said, "I would have despaired unless I had believed that I would see" (Psalm 27:13 NASB). By believing, they mean hoping to see.

There are several temptations that if hope is not in use, cannot be mastered, especially if the soul is in great and sore trials. There is irritation and impatience, fear and despair; and there is doubting and misunderstanding God's present work. All of these will take control if hope is not stirring; nor can any other grace put a stop to their tumultuous raging in the soul.

Hope in God makes all turmoil hush, and lays the soul at the foot of God.

DEAR GOD,

Your gift of hope is what keeps me going during the "dark nights" of life. Fill me with hope so that I may stand firm in my expectation that You are bringing good out of every situation I confront.

AMEN

May the God of hope fill you with all joy and peace in believing, that you may abound in hope by the power of the Holy Spirit.
ROMANS 15:13 NKJV

GIVING FROM A PURPOSED HEART

[Jesus said.]] "Freely you have received, freely give."
MATTHEW 10:8 NKJV

You've heard the saying, "It's the thought that counts." How true! Perhaps "thought" is the name of the seed that God first plants in our giving garden. Our thought initiates the giving process. The thought occurs to us, and we are motivated to carry it out, accomplishing God's purpose.

Your heart is a garden in which God plants many seeds into fertile ground to give you an abundant harvest of thoughtful impulse so that you might bless others. When God's love first takes root in your heart, a fervent desire to give begins to grow. Flowers and fruit, carefully designed by the Master Gardner, reproduce again and again in the proper seasons. From one harvest of giving to the next, what you give to others plants seeds into their lives that keep on giving.

GRACE FOR TODAY

THE DESIRE TO GIVE TO AND BLESS OTHERS IS A RESULT OF GOD PLANTING SEEDS OF LOVE AND GRACE INTO OUR HEARTS.

Giving is more than material gifts. Giving may involve seeds of hope in someone's heart or joy in a life waiting for God's truth.

The New Testament tells us to give what we have purposed in our heart. Has compassion for a sick friend been planted in your heart's garden today? Then you might offer from compassion's harvest a pot of soup or encouraging visit. Every time you've sent a card, a handwritten note, or a care package just to let someone know he or she is special, you have given with purpose. When you give money, time, and talents, you give eternal gifts from the heart. And these gifts keep on giving.

Aren't you glad that when God had a thought of you, He also sent a gift, Heaven's most treasured gift—Jesus? He loved you enough to send His very best.

COME ALL YE FAITHFUL

The angel said to them, "Do not be afraid; for see—I am bringing you good news of great joy for all the people: to you is born this day in the city of David a Savior, who is the Messiah, the Lord."
LUKE 2:10-11 NRSV

How can the celebration of something as beautiful and wonderful as Jesus' birth turn into something so hectic? The stress and strain of feeling like you have to have everything "just so" can snuff out the joy of the season and obscure its true meaning. If we aren't careful, our Christmas list can become just another to-do list, making the so-called "happy holidays" overwhelming and unbearable.

Often, as women, we demand too much of ourselves and tend to make things more complicated than they need to be. Christmas is really very simple—celebrating God's love for us in giving us His Son, Jesus. And celebrating our love for one another.

Instead of running around trying to create the perfect setting, why not go Christmas caroling with the kids? Do something, anything, with your family that causes you to focus on the real reason for the season.

Maybe you can serve Christmas dinner at a shelter or visit shut-ins. The main thing is to enjoy God's love this Christmas season and share it with others. So what if the cookies don't look like the ones you see on the cooking channel or that you bought holiday preserves this year instead of canning them yourself. Frank McKibben said it well: "This is Christmas; not the tinsel, not the giving and receiving, not even the carols, but the humble heart that receives anew the wondrous gift, the Christ." Spread the word.

GRACE FOR TODAY

JESUS IS THE TRUE GIFT OF CHRISTMAS THAT FREES US FROM HECTIC HOLIDAYS!

TRUE GIFTS

The wages of sin is death, hut the free gift of God is eternal
life in Christ Jesus our Lord.
ROMANS 6:23 NRSV

Most likely you've heard someone say, "Christmas is too commercialized today." Most often, the focus of the season from a business and marketing standpoint is that it is the biggest opportunity for financial gain. How many times have you purchased a toy with all the bells and whistles only to find that it never could have delivered what was promised. The focus is on profit — sometimes at the expense of omitting the true reason for the season.

GRACE FOR TODAY

GOD'S GRACE IS THE GIFT THAT KEEPS ON GIVING TO YOU AND THROUGH YOU.

Others might say the focus is more on the gift instead of the giver. We try to teach our children that it's the thought that counts, but more times than not, the focus is the gift. One common question asked of children at Christmas dinner: "What'd you get for Christmas?" instead of "Let's take a moment to thank God for the reason we celebrate Christmas — because He gave us the ultimate gift of eternal life through His Son. Let's thank Him for all of the gifts received today, but even more, let's thank Him for giving us each other."

In truth, Christmas is really all about grace — the opportunity to receive something undeserved. God, the giver, gave His greatest gift for us. Although we celebrate Jesus Christ's birth on Christmas Day, the gift of salvation and all that comes with it is available every day.

We have the opportunity to give gifts every moment of every day. God intended for His gift to become an endless supply of grace to give and receive from each other all the time. When you show someone favor, mercy, love, benevolence, or leniency, you tap into the grace God has given you. When you offer a smile, comfort, a kind word, or affection, you are giving God's grace to the world.

GOOD KING WENCESLAS

The generous prosper and are satisfied; those who refresh
others will themselves be refreshed.
PROVERBS 11:25 NLT

While it may not be one of the most popular Christmas carols, we've all heard it; and we probably all know at least some of the words. "Good King Wenceslas" has a jaunty tune, but a tongue twister of a title character. Maybe that's why it isn't on many top-ten lists of favorite Christmas songs.

GRACE FOR TODAY

BLESS OTHERS WITH THE GRACE YOU'VE RECEIVED, AND YOU WILL RECEIVE GRACE'S BLESSINGS.

The true story behind "Good King Wenceslas," though, is one worth telling, for it is all about grace. Wenceslas was actually a young duke who lived in Europe during the Dark Ages. He was a kind and just ruler who believed in Christ and wanted to order his kingdom in a way that would please God. Because of this, all his subjects—nobility and peasants alike—loved him.

And just like the song says, Wenceslas was known for his special kindnesses during Christmastime. On Christmas Eve, he would travel around his kingdom, taking gifts of new clothes, firewood, and food to the poorest of his people. As royalty he was under no obligation to visit these people personally; but compelled by his sincere love for Jesus, he found great joy in taking Christmas wishes and gifts to those in need.

So when Christmas rolls around again and you hear the happy tune of "Good King Wenceslas," remember the model of Jesus' grace that this young duke showed so long ago. And think of these final words of the song that bears his name as you celebrate the birth of our Lord: "Therefore Christian men, be sure/Wealth or rank possessing/Ye who now will bless the poor/Shall yourselves find blessing."

JUST LIKE MARY

[Mary said,] "Behold, henceforth all generations will call me blessed. For He who is mighty has done great things for me, and holy is His name."
LUKE 1:48-49 NKJV

GRACE FOR TODAY

THE GOD OF MARY—THE GOD OF GRACE—IS OUR GOD TOO.

When the angel Gabriel appeared to Mary to announce the coming of the Savior, he called her "highly favored" and "endued with grace." While we think most often about the grace Mary received when she was chosen to carry the Messiah, her whole life is a testament to the power of God's grace. Mary readily accepted the declaration of the angel. Immediately she faced the prospect of divorce when Joseph wouldn't believe the truth. In His grace, God intervened.

As any woman who has been through pregnancy and childbirth knows, Mary had to have a huge portion of grace to endure a donkey ride in her ninth month—and to then give birth in a barn! After this harrowing adventure, Mary and Joseph had to flee to Egypt. They stayed there, far from family and friends, until God told them it was safe to return home. And then, after being His mother for thirty years, Mary had to say goodbye to her son as He went to fulfill His mission.

Mary faced the greatest test of her faith as she stood at the foot of a cross and watched her beloved Son die. But her trust in the God who had pronounced her "highly favored" was not misplaced. While the disciples rejoiced at the resurrection of their Lord, Mary must have been more elated than any other. Not only was her Lord risen—her child had returned from the dead. God's grace had come through again.

Today we women aren't that different from Mary. We face fear, ridicule, hardships, and loss. And just like Mary, we have a God who is full of grace. He will be with us, just as He was with her. With Jesus as the Lord of our hearts, we, too, are "highly favored" and "endued with grace."

FIX YOUR MIND ON THIS

By Charles Spurgeon

Some people say, "I do not seem to have strength to collect my thoughts, and keep them fixed upon the important subjects which concern my salvation." If you are without strength in this area, there are many like you. You need not despair. Continuous thought is not necessary for salvation, but instead a simple reliance upon Jesus. Hold on to this one fact—"In due time Christ died for the ungodly" (Romans 5:6 NKJV). Fix your mind on that, and rest there.

Let this one great, gracious, glorious fact lie in your spirit till it perfumes all your thoughts, and makes you rejoice even though you are without strength, seeing the Lord Jesus has become your strength and your song. He has become your salvation. In the Scriptures it is a revealed fact that in due time Christ died for the ungodly when they were without strength.

Jesus did not die for our righteousness, but He died for our sins. He did not come to save us because we were worth the saving, but because we were utterly worthless, ruined, and undone.

He didn't come to earth for any reason that was in us, but solely out of the depths of His own divine love. In due time He died for those whom He describes, not as godly, but as ungodly, applying to them as hopeless an adjective as He could. Fasten to this truth, which is able to cheer the heaviest heart.

Let this text lie under your tongue like a sweet candy, until it dissolves in your heart and flavors all your thoughts; and then it will matter little when your thoughts are as scattered as autumn leaves.

FATHER,

I can't thank You enough for loving me while I was still yet a sinner. Help me to focus my thoughts on this great truth so that I can walk like the triumphant child of God You've made me.

AMEN

God demonstrates His own love toward us, in that while we were still sinners, Christ died for us.
ROMANS 5:8 NKJV

ENDNOTES

1. *The Comparison Trap.* Copyright 2003 by *Just Between Us* magazine. Published by Cook Communications Ministries. All rights reserved. Pages 25-26.

2. Ibid. Pages 31-32.

3. *A Journey into Spiritual Growth.* Copyright 1999 by Evelyn Christenson. Published by Chariot Victor Publishing, a division of Cook Communications. All rights reserved. Page 41.

4. *The Comparison Trap.* Pages 52-53.

5. *A Journey into Spiritual Growth.* Pages 135-136.

6. Ibid. Pages 157-158.

7. Ibid. Pages 193-194.

8. *Women in the Life of Jesus* by Jill Briscoe. Copyright 1986, 1999 by Briscoe Ministries, Inc. Published by Chariot Victor Publishing, a division of Cook Communications. All rights reserved. Pages 4-5.

9. Ibid. Pages 24-25.

10. *Lord, Change Me* by Evelyn Christenson. Copyright 2002, 1993, by SP Publications, Inc. Published by Cook Communications Ministries. All rights reserved. Pages 71-72.

11. Ibid. Page 152.

12. *Encouraging One Another* by Gene Getz. Copyright 1981,1997, 2002 by Gene Getz. Published by Cook Communications Ministries. AH rights reserved. Pages 120-121.

13. *Be Encouraged* by Warren W. Wiersbe. Copyright 2004 by Cook Communications Ministries. Published by Cook Communications Ministries. All rights reserved. Pages 38-39.

14. *What Happens When God Answers Prayer* by Evelyn Christenson. Copyright 1994,1996 by Victor Books/SP Publications. Published by Cook Communications Ministries. All rights reserved. Pages 19-20.

15. Ibid. Pages 188-189.

16. *Princess to Princess* by Kathy Collard Miller. Copyright 2003 by Kathy Collard Miller. Published by Cook Communications Ministries. All rights reserved. Page 46.

17. Ibid. Pages 64-65.

18. Ibid. Pages 102-103.

19. Ibid. Pages 129-130.

20. Ibid. Page 152.

21. *A Journey into Spiritual Growth.* Page 165.

22. *Encouraging One Another.* Pages

129-130.

23.*Be Free* by Warren W. Wiersbe. Copyright 1975 by SP Publications, Inc. Published by Cook Communications Ministries. All rights reserved. Pages 113-114.

24.Taken from a 1740 sermon by John Wesley.

25.*Stop Pretending* by Luis Palau. Copyright 1985, 2003 by Luis Palau. Published by Cook Communications Ministries. All rights reserved. Pages 18-20.

26.*Anxiety Attacked* by John MacArthur Jr. Copyright 1995 by John MacArthur Jr. Published by Cook Communications Ministries. All rights reserved. Pages 86-87.

27.*Be Encouraged.* Pages 36-37.

28.*Be Free.* Pages 16-18, 22.

29.*Anxiety Attacked.* Pages 15-16.

30.*Be Encouraged.* Page 64.

31.*Found: God's Will* by John MacArthur Jr. Copyright 1973 SP Publications, Inc. Published by Cook Communications Company. Published by Longmeadow Ministries. All rights reserved. Pages 12-13.

32.Ibid. Pages 14-15.

33.*Webster's II New Riverside Desk Dictionary.* Copyright 1988 by Houghton Mifflin Press; Stamford, CT. Page 121.

34.Ibid. Page 29.

35.Found: God's Will. Pages 20-21.

36.Ibid. Pages 28-29.

37.*Anxiety Attacked.* Pages 92-93.

38.*Found: God's Will.* Pages 23-24.

39.Ibid. Page 30.

40.Ibid. Pages 32-33.

41.Ibid. Page 26.

42.Ibid. Pages 33, 35-36.

43.Ibid. Pages 40-41.

44.*Be All You Can Be* by John C. Maxwell. Copyright © 2002 Published by Cook Communications Ministries. All rights reserved. Pages 54-55.

45.Ibid. Pages 60-62.

46.Ibid. Pages 50-51.

47.*Lord, Change Me.* Pages 52-53.

Additional copies of this and other
Honor Books titles are available
online or at your local bookseller.

The following titles are also available
in this series:

Daily Grace
Daily Grace for Teens
Daily Grace for Teachers

www.ingramcontent.com/pod-product-compliance
Lightning Source LLC
Chambersburg PA
CBHW071140130626
46553CB00004B/1458